Culturally
Responsive
Interventions

Culturally Responsive Interventions

Innovative Approaches
to Working with
Diverse Populations

Julie R. Ancis, Ph.D.
Editor

Brunner-Routledge

New York and Hove

Published in 2004 by
Brunner-Routledge
29 West 35th Street
New York, NY 10001
www.brunner-routledge.com

Published in Great Britain by
Brunner-Routledge
27 Church Road
Hove, East Sussex
BN3 2FA
www.brunner-routledge.co.uk

10 9 8 7 6 5 4 3 2 1

Cataloging-in-Publication Data is available from the Library of Congress
Hardback ISBN 0-415-93332-3
Paperback ISBN 0-415-93333-1

Dedication

To my first teachers, Helen and Joseph Ancis. My love and appreciation.

And to the memory of my beloved father who taught me
the beauty of diversity in all of its forms. I am forever grateful.

Contents

PART III: DIAGNOSIS AND PRACTICE

PART IV: CONCLUSION

Preface

It has become increasingly recognized that culturally responsive counseling services are imperative given the diverse client population worldwide. Articles and texts focusing on multicultural issues have burgeoned in the last few decades. In fact, multicultural counseling has been described as the fourth force in the profession (Pedersen, 1991; Ponterotto & Casas, 1991). More recently, the relevance and effectiveness of contemporary theories of counseling and psychotherapy for culturally diverse populations has been questioned (e.g., Ivey, Ivey, & Simek-Morgan, 1993; Sue, Ivey, & Pedersen, 1996). Several authors have described the culture-bound nature of contemporary counseling theories (Atkinson, Morten, & Sue, 1993; Katz, 1985; Pedersen, 1994). These authors argue that understanding the client's cultural and sociopolitical context is essential to accurate assessment, interpretation, and treatment (Sue, Ivey, & Pedersen, 1996). In fact, several studies suggest that culturally sensitive interventions may increase service utilization, length of treatment, client satisfaction, and therapy outcomes (Flaskerud & Soldevilla, 1986; Rogler, Malgady, & Rodriguez, 1989; S. Sue, Zane, & Young, 1994; Szapocznik et al., 1989).

Despite recognition that culturally responsive and relevant skills and interventions are integral to multicultural competence (e.g., Sue, Arredondo, & McDavis, 1992), the majority of multicultural counseling texts tend to focus on the knowledge component of competence. General cultural values, customs, and characteristics of racial and ethnic minority groups are often presented. Specific counseling approaches or interventions are rarely addressed (Zhang & Dixon, 2001). If approaches or interventions are discussed, they tend to be presented broadly. Moreover, contemporary counseling approaches are often applied to diverse populations without consideration to the interplay between the client's cultural context and his or her presenting problem or the intersections of multiple identity dimensions such as gender, race, ethnicity, and social class (Ancis & Sanchez-Hucles, 2000).

Although the multicultural counseling literature has served an important purpose in terms of increasing practitioners' awareness of the relevance of cultural competence, the literature on specific culturally consistent counseling interventions remains limited and fragmented. In fact, examination of the applicability of specific treatment procedures to culturally diverse populations has received limited attention (Rogler, Malgady, Costantino, & Blumenthal, 1987;

Sue, Fujino, Hu, & Takeuchi, 1991). Parham (1996) argues that critics of contemporary counseling and psychotherapy present compelling arguments regarding the limitations of traditional therapy but tend not to present alternatives. Similarly, few training programs actually provide training that prepares practitioners to be multiculturally proficient; that is, possess broad skills in working with multicultural populations (Quintana & Bernal, 1995).

Employing appropriate, relevant, and sensitive intervention strategies and skills is considered an essential component of cultural competence (Sue, Arredondo, & McDavis, 1992). However, the multicultural counseling literature and concomitant training fall short of promoting actual skill acquisition (Lee, 1997). The inadequacy of most counseling and psychotherapy approaches to explain and assist culturally diverse populations and the fragmented literature on culturally responsive interventions has significant implications. Mental health professionals lack the training and skills necessary to work with a culturally diverse population. Moreover, many individuals are not receiving needed assistance and support.

The purpose of this book is to fill the void in the multicultural counseling field by providing an organized compilation of culturally responsive counseling interventions with diverse populations and presenting problems. This text introduces the reader to a new body of innovative counseling interventions for working with diverse populations. This text is not meant to be an exhaustive compendium of interventions. Rather, it is an attempt to move the field toward purposeful, directional, and culturally responsive approaches to working with diverse individuals, families, and communities who present with particular presenting problems.

The approaches presented in this text do not merely represent the application of a contemporary counseling theory to a particular group. Rather, the interventions described are developed with consideration of culture as primary to assessment, diagnosis, and treatment. One objective of this text is to move beyond stereotyping of ethnocultural groups by demonstrating how culture relates to personal, familial, and societal histories in complex ways. Moreover, attention is paid to both cultural context and presenting problem versus the exclusive focus on one or the other, common to multicultural counseling texts, and traditional texts, respectively. The chapters are authored by individuals who serve as both academicians and clinicians or coauthored by academicians and clinicians in order to ensure the connection between theory and practice that is often missing in the literature. Each chapter includes a case study in which the particular intervention is described in detail. These case studies may be the source of class discussion and analysis. Such analysis is intended to facilitate students' critical thinking regarding counseling interventions as well as their understanding of how each approach may be specifically applied in clinical settings. The chapters and accompanying case studies are intended also to benefit more advanced practitioners as they interact with a heterogeneous clientele.

The text has four sections. Part I highlights culturally responsive interventions developed in the United States. The first chapter serves as an introduction to the text by reviewing research on clinical practice, including work with racial and ethnic minorities; the clinical significance of culture in terms of distress experience, expression, attribution, and treatment; cultural and contextual factors relevant to counseling such as acculturation; and aspects of culturally responsive practice. The approaches described in subsequent chapters emphasize the client's cultural values as primary to conceptualization and treatment rather than simply dimensions that need to be considered. The chapters describe treatment approaches developed from a cultural frame of reference with attention to the intersections of client's race, ethnicity, gender, class, acculturation level, and presenting problem. Interventions with American Indian, African American, and Hispanic populations presenting with specific concerns are highlighted.

Part II presents international applications of culturally responsive interventions. The section begins with an Indian psychiatrist's perspective on culturally sensitive practice. The challenges of using Western diagnostic categories in understanding emotional suffering in other cultures and an approach to culturally sensitive mental health care based on cultural epidemiology are described. Subsequent chapters describe interventions and approaches developed to address specific concerns in Japan, Israel, and South Africa.

Part III focuses on diagnosis. This section includes a chapter on diagnostic challenges and culture-bound syndromes. This topic has significant implications for culturally valid classification systems, assessment, and practice. Part IV includes a final chapter that presents a thematic analysis of the chapters in Parts I and II, and clinical implications.

Julie R. Ancis

References

Ancis, J. R., & Sanchez-Hucles, J. V. (2000). A preliminary analysis of counseling students' attitudes toward counseling women and women of color: Implications for cultural competency training. *Journal of Multicultural Counseling and Development, 28,* 16-31.

Atkinson, D. R., Morten, G., & Sue, D. W. (1993). *Counseling American minorities* (4th ed.). Dubuque, IA: Brown.

Flaskerud, J. H., & Soldevilla, E. Q. (1986). Pilipino and Vietnamese clients: Utilizing an Asian mental health center. *Journal of Psychosocial Nursing, 24*(8), 32-36.

Ivey, A. E., Ivey, M. B., & Simek-Morgan, L. (1993). *Counseling and psychotherapy: A multicultural perspective.* Boston: Allyn & Bacon.

Katz, J. (1985). The sociopolitical nature of counseling. *The Counseling Psychologist, 13,* 615-624.

Lee, C. C. (1997). The promise and pitfalls of multicultural counseling. In C. C. Lee

(Ed.), *Multicultural issues in counseling: New approaches to diversity* (2nd ed., pp. 3–13). Alexandria, VA: ACA.

Parham, T. A. (1996). MCT theory and African-American populations. In D. W. Sue, A. E. Ivey, & P. B. Pedersen (Eds.), *A theory of multicultural counseling and therapy* (pp. 177–191). Pacific Grove, CA: Brooks/Cole.

Pedersen, P. B. (1991). Multiculturalism as a generic approach to counseling. *Journal of Counseling and Development, 70,* 6–12.

Pedersen, P. B. (1994). *Culture-centered counseling: A search for accuracy.* Newbury Park, CA: Sage.

Ponterotto, J. G., & Casas, J. M. (1991). *Handbook of racial/ethnic minority counseling research.* Springfield, IL: Charles C Thomas.

Quintana, S. M., & Bernal, M. E. (1995). Ethnic minority training in counseling psychology: Comparisons with clinical psychology and proposed standards. *The Counseling Psychologist, 23,* 102–121.

Rogler, L. H., Malgady, R. G., Costantino, G., & Blumenthal, R. (1987). What do culturally sensitive mental health services mean? The case of Hispanics. *American Psychologist, 42,* 565–570.

Rogler, L. H., Malgady, R. G., & Rodriguez, O. (1989). *Hispanics and mental health: A framework for research.* Malabar, FL: Krieger.

Sue, D. W., Arredondo, P., & McDavis, R. J. (1992). Multicultural counseling competencies and standards: A call to the profession. *Journal of Counseling and Development, 70,* 477–486.

Sue, D. W., Ivey, A. E., & Pedersen, P. B. (Eds.). (1996). *A theory of multicultural counseling and therapy.* Pacific Grove, CA: Brooks/Cole.

Sue, S., Fujino, D. C., Hu, L., & Takeuchi, D. T. (1991). Community mental health services for ethnic minority groups: A test of the cultural responsiveness hypothesis. *Journal of Consulting and Clinical Psychology, 59,* 533–540.

Sue, S., Zane, N., & Young, K. (1994). Research on psychotherapy and behavior change. In S. Garfield et al. (Eds.), *Handbook of psychotherapy and behavior change* (4th ed., pp. 783–817). New York: Wiley.

Szapocznik, J., Santisteban, D., Rio, A., Perez-Vidal, A., Santisteban, D., & Kurtines, W. M. (1989). Family effectiveness training: An intervention to prevent drug abuse and problem behaviors in Hispanic adolescents. *Hispanic Journal of Behavioral Sciences, 11,* 4–27.

Zhang, N., & Dixon, D. N. (2001). Multiculturally responsive counseling: Effects on Asian students' ratings of counselors. *Journal of Multicultural Counseling and Development, 29,* 253–262.

Part I

Culturally Responsive Interventions

Chapter 1

Culturally Responsive Practice

Julie R. Ancis

This chapter presents a rationale for culturally responsive practice and interventions. Research on clinical approaches with diverse clients is reviewed. The author discusses the clinical significance of social and cultural factors in terms of distress expression, attribution, and treatment approaches. The influence of contextual factors such as acculturation, discrimination, and culture-related stressors on psychosocial functioning and therapy are examined. The author defines culturally responsive approaches and discusses their clinical significance in meeting the needs of an increasingly diverse population.

Demographic Diversity

The demographic composition of the United States has become increasingly racially and ethnically diverse (United States Census Bureau, 2001). This demographic shift has been attributed to both high immigration rates and differential birth rates (Sue & Sue, 1999). Population shifts include new immigrants, younger individuals of Latino descent (Judy & D'Amico, 1997), and a greater portion of Americans speaking a language other than English at home (U.S. Census Bureau, 2001). Conservative projections estimate that ethnic minorities will comprise over 50% of U.S. society by the year 2050 (U.S. Census Bureau, 2001). As a result, clinicians will interface regularly with culturally pluralistic populations (D'Andrea & Daniels, 2001; Lewis, Lewis, Daniels, & D'Andrea, 1998).

Relatedly, the mental health profession in the United States has increasingly recognized that psychological practice and interventions must be responsive to the needs of a diverse clientele. This recognition is evident in the development of several key documents. The American Psychological Association (APA) *Guidelines for Providers of Psychological Services to Ethnic, Linguistic, and Culturally Diverse Populations* (1990) outlines the importance of psychological services that are sensitive to factors such as gender, age, culture, and ethnicity. More recently, the *Guidelines on Multicultural Education, Training, Research, Practice, and Organizational Change for Psychologists approved by the American Psychological Association* (2002) outline a rationale and need for addressing multiculturalism and diversity in each domain. Documents such as the *Guidelines for Psychological Practice with Girls and Women* (American Psychological Association, 2003) attend to the interactions of such dimensions as gender, race, ethnicity, sexual orientation, socioeconomic status, and social context in psychological practice.

Attention to the importance of culture in psychological practice within the United States parallels ongoing developments worldwide. There has been a rapid growth of international population migration and relatedly population heterogeneity within nations of the world (Chiu, 1996). Moreover, there has been an increased focus on approaches and interventions designed to meet the needs of individuals and communities globally. The international counseling movement has focused on the training of clinicians and the development of professional counseling associations in locations such as Western Europe, Central and Eastern Europe, New Zealand, Africa, Asia, North America, and South America (Harper & Deen, 2003).

Clinical Practice with Diverse Clientele

Many racial and ethnic minorities, particularly American Indians, Asian Americans, African Americans, and Hispanics tend to underutilize traditional outpatient mental health services (Cheung & Snowden, 1990), despite the fact that prevalence rates for psychiatric disorders are analogous across ethnic groups (Hough et al., 1987; U.S. Department of Health and Human Services, 2000, 2001; Weissman, Livingston, Leaf, Florio, & Holzer, 1991). Among ethnic minorities who do use mental health services (Rogler, Malgady, Costantino, & Blumenthal, 1987; Sue, 1977), there are often high dropout rates after one session (Wierzbicki & Pekarik, 1993), infrequent use of therapy sessions (Krebs, 1971; O'Sullivan & Lasso, 1992; Solomon, 1988), and poor levels of functioning at the end of treatment (Jerrell & Wilson, 1997; Rosenheck, Leda, Frisman, & Gallup, 1997; Zane, Enomoto, & Chun, 1994).

Several hypotheses may explain the preceding findings, including barriers such as societal stigma and the use of alternative helping networks among individuals such as the extended family, clergy, or traditional healers; lack of bilingual or multilingual staff; culturally inconsistent treatment modalities; and prejudicial attitudes among mental health professionals (Ancis & Szymanski, 2001; Rogler et al., 1987; Sue, Fujino, Hu, & Takeuchi, 1991; U.S. Department of Health and Human Services, 2001). Sue, Ivey, and Pedersen (1996) asserted that contemporary counseling approaches do not adequately explain or predict the behavior of many racial and ethnic groups. Similarly, the relevance and effectiveness of contemporary theories of counseling and psychotherapy for culturally diverse populations has been questioned (e.g., Atkinson, Morten, & Sue, 1998; Ivey, Ivey, & Simek-Morgan, 1993; Katz, 1985; Sue, Ivey, & Pedersen, 1996). Culture-bound values of counseling such as a focus on individualism versus a more collectivistic notion of identity found in many non-Western cultures, are often inconsistent with the world views of many diverse clients (D. W. Sue, 1995). The Surgeon General's Report on culture and mental health (USDHHS, 2000, 2001) suggests that "cultural misunderstanding or communication problems between clients and therapists may prevent minority group members from using services and receiving appropriate care" (p. 42).

The Clinical Significance of Culture and Context

Culture has been defined in various ways in the behavioral sciences literature. Alarcón, Foulks, and Vakkur (1998) define culture "as a set of meanings, behavioral norms, and values used by members of a particular society, as they construct their unique view of the world" (p. 6). Reference points include habits, customs, political beliefs, social relationships, and language. Culture is both changing and permanent. Individual-culture interactions are viewed as contributors to the molding of styles and strategies. Cultural institutions, ideologies, and practices provide the context for and shape affect, behavior, and personality (Alarcón et al., 1998; Kirmayer, 2001). Because cultural norms prescribe and proscribe certain behaviors and norms for men and women, young and old, "ill" and "healthy," these dimensions and associated socio-identities may also be considered cultural constructs.

As such, culture has been found to have a significant influence on multiple dimensions of the therapeutic process. Culture influences the source of distress, the form and quality of illness experience, symptomatology, the interpretation of symptoms, modes of coping with distress, help seeking and response to treatment, and social responses to distress (Kirmayer, 2001; Kirmayer & Young, 1999; U.S. Department of Health and Human Services, 2001). The ways in which culture specifically influences illness expression, attribution, and treatment are reviewed in the following.

Expression, Attribution, and Treatment

The phenomenology of disorders and symptomatic expression seems to vary across cultures (Good & Kleinman, 1985; Kirmayer, 1989; Westermeyer, 1987). Culture influences internal ideation and external behavior. Kleinman (1988) describes how the experience of illness (or distress) is always a culturally shaped phenomena. Complaints of distress are often expressed through culture-specific idioms; a situation that often results in diagnostic challenges. For example, several studies have demonstrated that Asians demonstrate a greater number of somatic complaints compared to non-Asians (Kleinman, 1977; S. Sue & Sue, 1974). A number of explanations may account for this finding. Chinese traditional medicine's emphasis on the correspondence between human emotions and body organs may explain this tendency (Tseng, 1975). Asian patients complaints of suffering due to weakness of the kidney are often associated with psychosexual problems, elevated fire in the body or liver to anger or anxiety, and loss of soul to depression or disassociation (Tseng, 1997). Thus, somatization may be a way of expressing distress. An additional explanation may be that in societies influenced by Confucian notions, such as China, disorders such as depression can be perceived as self-centered and asocial. The expression of physical suffering and bodily pain, which are amenable to treatment and do not threaten social relationships, may be more acceptable (Kirmayer & Groleau, 2001; Yen, Robins, & Lin, 2000).

An association between somatic expression and anxiety and depression also has been recorded in countries such as Saudi Arabia, Iraq, Peru, and India (see Kleinman, 1988). Among South Indians, a significant relationship has been demonstrated among psychiatric stigma, somatization, and depression (Raguram, Weiss, Channabasavanna, & Devins, 1996; Raguram, Weiss, Keval, & Channabasavanna, 2001). Again, somatic complaints may be perceived as more socially acceptable expressions of distress. Interestingly, some research has shown that although depressed Chinese patients express complaints somatically, they admit to affective symptoms when asked about them directly (Cheung, Lau, & Waldmann, 1980–1981), thereby challenging the notion of experience versus expression.

Alarcón and Foulks (1995) describe how culture shapes many personality styles. One's sociocultural background often influences one's reactions to stimuli, coping style, problem-solving approaches, and social interactions. Some individuals may experience the formative influence of their culture in ways that emphasize the most salient features of their culture, and consequently develop the maladaptive and rigid traits of a Personality Disorder. Self-concept and self-image are influenced by cultural factors; such as child-rearing practices, intrafamily roles, and social expectations (Alarcón & Foulks, 1995). In some cases, culture may serve as a pathogenic/pathoplastic factor in the occurrence of clinical situations. For example, the "overcontrolled" problems such as fearfulness and sleep difficulties seen in Jamaican children compared to their U.S. counterparts may be attributed to Jamaican child-rearing practices in which subservience and submissiveness are reinforced. Conversely, the higher rate of "undercontrolled" problems such as fighting and disobedience among U.S. youngsters may be attributed to the expectation of nonconformity and brashness among this population (Lambert, Weisz, & Knight, 1989). Similarly, women's social roles, status, and life circumstances including limited access to power outside of the home may explain gender differences in rates of depression and symptom expression in Puerto Rican women (Koss-Chioino, 1999).

In addition to variations in symptom expression, individuals in various cultures hold different beliefs about the causes of illness (Torrey, 1972). For example, although primary care patients of diverse cultural backgrounds complain of somatic symptoms, they differ in their preferred attributions for these symptoms (Kirmayer & Groleau, 2001). Some attribute disruptive symptoms to metaphysical causes such as loss of the soul, spirit possession, sorcery, and angering a deity (Koss-Chioino, 1992). In some cultures, mental illness is often attributed to shameful causes, such as being unfair in social dealings, failure to respect nature, misdeeds in past lives, past family transgressions, immoral excesses, or personal weakness (Flaskerud & Soldevilla, 1986; Gong-Guy, Cravens, & Patterson, 1991; Lee, 2001). It is important to consider that some experiences, such as possession, may be considered a sign of "unnatural illness" or an experience against nature as determined by God. As such, the stigma of mental illness is often not associated with it (Koss-Chioino & Canive, 1993).

In addition, varying explanations of distress influence whether treatment is pursued. People in most of the world do not view health care services as an appropriate venue for emotional concerns. Rather, emotional difficulties are viewed as sociomoral problems and it is considered more appropriate to discuss these problems with a family member, elder, or spiritual or community leader (Kirmayer, 2001). Lay, cultural interpretations of distress may relate to interpersonal, intrafamilial struggles over power within a social group, such as the case of embrujado in Hispanic patients, rather than intrapersonal conflicts (Koss-Chioino & Canive, 1993). Moreover, among some clients, such as refugees from South East Asia, all conditions requiring mental health treatment are highly stigmatized, often resulting in the underutilization of such services (Gong-Guy, Cravens, & Patterson, 1991). Rather, mental health services are sought as a last resort, after family resources, traditional healers, and general medical approaches have proven ineffective.

Attributions also influence beliefs about cures for psychological problems and appropriate treatment (Shimoji & Miyakawa, 2000). Many cultural groups seek help from an indigenous leader or shaman (Das, 1987) and value experiences such as trances, dissociative states, communicating with spirits and gods, vision quests, and herbal remedies as therapeutic elements of healing (Koss-Chioino, 1992; Lebra, 1972). For example, Spiritist healers in Puerto Rico seek to eliminate pain and upset by bringing to the session spirits held responsible for the client's distress (Koss-Chioino, 1992). Remedies such as candle lighting, herbs, and aromatic baths may be prescribed (Koss-Chioino, 1995). Moreover, the medium-healer is not viewed as the agent of intervention in Spritism, but only a vehicle. Some Asian ethnic groups have been reported to believe that mental health can be attained through willpower and focusing on pleasant thoughts (Sue & Morishima, 1982).

Symptom attributional style has been found to affect the recognition rate of certain disorders. For example, patients who attribute their depression-related somatic symptoms to physical illness or environmental causes are less likely to have their depression recognized and treated by clinicians (Kirmayer & Groleau, 2001).

Culturally Based and Contextual Factors Relevant to Counseling

Historically, psychology has focused on biological determinants of behavior at the exclusion of historical and sociopolitical dynamics (Bronstein & Quina, 1988). The influence of individual's social, political, and economic context on one's behavior is often not considered or misinterpreted, often resulting in faulty diagnosis and inappropriate interventions. Sue, Ivey, and Pedersen (1996) argue that understanding the client's cultural and sociopolitical context is essential to accurate assessment, interpretation, and treatment.

Contextually based risk factors often influence an individual's world view and behavior and may make those with limited resources or protection more susceptible to mental disorders. Moreover, contextual factors linked to race or ethnicity, such as socioeconomic status or country of origin can increase the likelihood of exposure to these types of stressors (U.S. Department of Health and Human Services, 2000, 2001). Racial and ethnic minorities are often overrepresented among the vulnerable, high-need groups, such as homeless and incarcerated persons. The similar prevalence rate of mental disorders, combined with lower utilization and poorer quality of care, means that minority communities have a higher proportion of individuals with unmet mental health needs. Social and contextual factors relevant to individual's psychosocial functioning and to the therapeutic process are reviewed in the following.

Acculturation

Acculturation refers to the process of adapting to the rules and behavioral characteristics of another group of people (Smart & Smart, 1995). Typically, this refers to the process by which immigrants adapt to the host society. Acculturation is multidimensional as acculturation occurs across emotions, cognitions, and behaviors (Barón & Constantine, 1997). Language difficulties, cultural differences, changing socioeconomic status, underemployment, prolonged phases of social isolation, and disrupted social ties often accompany the process of acculturation (Vargas-Willis & Cervantes, 1987). Many immigrants experience acculturative stress, defined as a set of emotions and behaviors that include depression, anxiety, feelings of marginality and alienation, and identity confusion (Smart & Smart, 1995).

Forced acculturation to urban living and the dominant culture and unsatisfactory adjustment to a discriminatory social environment have been linked to the high rate of unemployment, alcohol and drug abuse, delinquency, and de-pression and adjustment reactions among American Indians (Choney, Berryhill-Paapke, & Robbins, 1995; LaFromboise, 1988). Similarly, research with Hispanic populations has demonstrated a relationship between acculturation levels, self-esteem, alcohol and drug abuse, delinquency, and depression (Rogler, Cortes, & Malgady, 1991). In addition, parent–child discrepancies in acculturation level combined with normative parent–adolescent intergenerational differences of-ten result in intrafamilial conflicts (Szapocznik, Kurtines, & Fernandez, 1980).

Research has demonstrated a relationship between acculturation and help-seeking attitudes. Studies have demonstrated that more highly acculturated Asian Americans had more positive attitudes toward seeking professional psychologi-cal help than those with lower levels of acculturation (Atkinson & Gim, 1989; Tata & Leong, 1994).

It is important to consider that attributes developed during the accultura-tion process can function as coping skills given the demands of the environment and social context (Choney, Berryhill-Paapke, & Robbins, 1995). Understand-ing and successfully negotiating customs, institutions, and policies associated with the dominant culture allows for a range of opportunities and flexibility in cognitive, behavioral, affective, and interpersonal domains.

Violence and Trauma

The number of refugees in the world today is estimated to be between 16 and 22 million (Kinzie, 2001). Many refugee and immigrant populations have experi-enced the trauma of war, indiscriminate killings, starvation, state-sponsored tor-ture, rapes, forcible detainment in refugee camps, and witnessed the death of family members and friends (Kinzie, 2001; Vernez, 1991). Repeated exposure to such catastrophic environmental stressors has been linked to the elevated preva-lence of psychopathology in Southeast Asian refugees (Kinzie, Sack, Angell, Clarke, & Ben, 1989; Mollica, Wyshak, & Lavelle, 1987). Posttraumatic stress disorder, often comorbid with depression, is prevalent among those refugees exposed to massive trauma (Boehnlein & Kinzie, 1995; Gafner & Benson, 2001). Moreover, postemigration experiences of cultural, language, and value differ-ences coupled with bereavement from multiple losses serve as further stressors that often hinder the adaptation and acculturation process (Nicholson, 1997). The severity and duration of stressors preemigration and postemigration often contributes to mental health difficulties, such as posttraumatic stress disorder, depression, and anxiety (Chung & Kagawa-Singer, 1993; Nicholson, 1997).

Clinicians' understanding of the experiences and needs of individuals ex-posed to trauma is imperative. Such needs include feeling physically and emo-tionally safe and experiencing predictability of relationships to establish basic trust (Kinzie, 2001).

Discriminatory Practices

Prejudice, racism, and discrimination have been viewed as stressors that affect psychological functioning, adjustment, social adaptation, and physical health. Racial discrimination in housing rentals and sales (Yinger, 1995), in hiring practices (Kirschenman & Neckerman, 1991), and administration of medical care (Shiefer, Escarce, & Shulman, 2000) continues to be documented. In many cases, prejudicial attitudes underlie discriminatory practices. National surveys have found that a significant percentage of Whites held disparaging stereotypes of African Americans, Hispanics, and Asians (Davis & Smith, 1990). Perceived racism has been cited as a contributor to impaired self-esteem among Asian Americans and African Americans (Asamen & Berry, 1987; Hughes & Demo, 1989); symptoms of depression in Asian, Latin American, and Caribbean immigrants (Rumbaut, 1994), Mexican adults (Finch, Kolody, & Vega, 2000), and Asians (Noh, Beiser, Kaspar, Hou, & Rummens, 1999); and psychological distress, lower well-being, and self-reported ill health among African Americans (Ren, Amick, & Williams, 1999; Williams, Yu, Jackson, & Anderson, 1997).

Some have argued that idioms of distress are often reflective of limited power and disrupted social relations (Littlewood, 1990). Cultural discontinuity and oppression have been linked to high rates of depression, alcoholism, suicide, and violence among aboriginal groups in the United States and Canada (Kirmayer, Boothroyd, Tanner, Adelson, & Robinson, 2000). Choney and co-authors (1995) describe the intergenerational posttraumatic stress experienced by American Indians as a function of racism and discrimination. Similarly, stereotypes of racial and ethnic minorities developed to rationalize discrimination and violence continue to be perpetuated (Ancis & Burke, 1997; Ancis, Sedlacek, & Mohr, 2000). For example, Jackson (2000) describes how the stereotype of African American women as sexually permissive was developed to rationalize the sexual exploitation of African American female slaves by their White masters. This stereotype is internalized by society and some African Americans. Jackson (2000) describes how the traumatization owing to the historical legacy of slavery, racism, sexual assault, and stereotyping has resulted in maladaptive defense reactions in African-American women.

Limited access to health care services and racism in clinical and institutional settings impede effective care for many refugees and racial and ethnic minorities (Kirmayer, 2001). Some immigrants may perceive systematic neglect from the majority and approach social service agencies with suspicion and mistrust (Acosta, 1979). The host culture may misjudge or condemn behaviors that reflect responses to an inequitable or oppressive context. Similarly, "guarded" behaviors as a result of discriminatory and difficult experiences may be erroneously labeled paranoid (Alarcón & Foulks, 1995).

Culture-Related Stressors

Cultural stressors may include economic and political conditions that contribute to the onset of psychological disorders. An example of such a condition unique to postreform China is traveling psychosis (lutu jingshen bing), an acute psychotic condition that occurred among people traveling over long distances in extremely crowded trains (Lee, 2001). This condition was first reported in the late 1980s, at a time when China's economic reforms involved vast regional economic disparities and massive domestic migration from rural to urban areas. Multiple causes are likely, such as fatigue, sleep deprivation, dehydration, anxiety, and homesickness (Lee, 2001).

Other stressors are associated with fulfilling the cultural demands of a particular society. For example, Arredondo (2002) discusses Latino culture and the institutional politics embedded in religious and social norms that suppress feminine energy and achievement. In dysfunctional families where traditional roles are carried out in an oppressive manner, depression, anxiety, and psychosomatic symptoms may result (Vasquez, 1994). In other societies, such as Japan, school systems have been characterized as focusing almost exclusively on academic success and promoting an excessive demand for conformity. In addition, children's failure to achieve high academic success is often associated with significant shame for families, particularly mothers, who are viewed as responsible for children's educational and occupational success (see Chapter 6). Individuals and families often experience much stress associated with meeting that ideal.

Cultural stressors, such as psychiatric stigma, are associated with both depression and somatization (Raguram et al., 1996, 2001). To the extent that psychiatric illnesses are associated with stigma in a given culture, minimization and denial may result; thereby reducing the likelihood of recognition and treatment (Chowdhury et al., 2001). International mental health organizations, such as the World Psychiatric Association and the World Federation for Mental Heath, have focused on reducing this stigma (Tseng, 1997).

Clinical Implications of Inattention to Culturally Based and Contextual Factors

Inattention to culture and other contextual factors within the mental health profession has significant implications for clients. Lack of services adapted to the linguistic and cultural backgrounds of patients may account for lower utilization rates of primary care mental health services among immigrants and ethnocultural minorities (Kirmayer & Minas, 2000; Lopez, 1988). Reported perceived barriers to using mental health services among respondents in a multicultural innercity neighborhood in Montreal included a feeling that their culture and ethnic background would not be understood (Kirmayer, Young,

Galbaud, Weinfeld, & Lasry, 1996; as cited in Kirmayer & Minas, 2000). Similar results have been found in other studies. For example, American Indians have been found to underutilize services owing to fear, mistrust, and perceptions that existing services are unresponsive and insensitive to their needs (Barter & Barter, 1974; Dukepoo, 1980). Similarly, fear of treatment itself has been found to be a significant barrier to treatment seeking among depressed African Americans (Sussman, Robins, & Earls, 1987). Among refugee populations, lack of service utilization is linked to a lack of trust in American health providers, as well as the fact that mental health treatment centers do not adequately address the cultural needs of populations other than middle-class Americans (Kinzie, Sack, Angell, & Manson, 1986). The most frequently reported barrier to accessing health care services among Cambodians was a belief that American health care providers did not understand Cambodian people (Blair, 2001).

Whereas cultural value conflicts may be the main cause of lack of initial contact with the system, ineffective or inappropriate services may account for the high dropout rate among clients (Atkinson & Gim, 1989). American Indians who engage in individual therapy often express concern about how conventional Western psychology superimposes biases onto their problems and shapes the behavior of the client in a direction that conflicts with Indian cultural lifestyle orientation (LaFramboise, 1988).

Client mistrust, apprehension about seeking professional services, and high dropout rate may be linked to realistic concerns as clients from culturally diverse groups are often subject to overdiagnosis, underdiagnosis, or misdiagnoses (Paniagua, 2001; Westermeyer, 1987). Race bias has been revealed in the differential diagnosis of schizophrenia and psychotic affective disorders in African-American, White, and Hispanic patients (Mukherjee, Shukla, Woodle, Rosen, & Olarte, 1983; Simon, Fleiss, Gurland, Stiller, & Sharpe, 1973). Research has demonstrated that African Americans are more likely to be diagnosed as schizophrenic or psychotic (Bulhan, 1985; Solomon, 1988). Moreover, African Americans are disproportionately hospitalized (Snowden & Cheung, 1990).

Culturally Responsive Interventions

As presented, culture plays an important role in the assessment, etiology, symptoms, and treatment of mental health problems (Doyle, 1998). However, contemporary counseling approaches are often applied to diverse populations without consideration to the interplay between the client's cultural context and his or her presenting problem or the intersections of multiple identity dimensions such as, gender, race, ethnicity, and social class. In fact, mainstream theories usually do not include cultural variables, and principles are assumed to be universally valid (Betancourt & López, 1993). Several studies suggest that culturally sensitive interventions may increase service utilization, length of treatment, client's satisfaction, and therapy outcomes (Flaskerud & Soldevilla, 1986; Rogler, Malgady, & Rodriguez, 1989; S. Sue, Zane, & Young, 1994; Szapocznik et al., 1989).

Many clinicians' inability to understand and incorporate culturally responsive approaches often prevents them from establishing a strong therapeutic alliance, demonstrated as significant to psychotherapy outcome (Wampold, 2001). For example, therapeutic alliance accounts for a significant portion of the variability in treatment outcomes (Martin, Garske, & Davis, 2000). Similarly, Wampold (1997) has demonstrated that outcome variances are often owing to therapist differences; that is, the therapist can effect therapy process and outcome and the relationship between the counselor and client. A strong therapeutic alliance can not be established if the counselor is unresponsive or dismissive of a client's beliefs, perceptions, and needs. Research also has supported the positive effects of clinician cultural sensitivity and client perception of clinician credibility, an important aspect of the therapeutic relationship (Strong, 1968). For example, in a study conducted by Gim, Atkinson, & Kim (1991), culture-sensitive counselors, who acknowledged the importance of ethnicity and cultural values in the client's experience, were rated as more credible than the culture-blind counselor. Similarly, Zhang and Dixon (2001) demonstrated a significant relationship between culturally responsive counselors, who conveyed an interest in and respect for other cultures and an appreciation for the cultural heritage of the interviewee, and Asian international student's ratings of counselor expertness, attractiveness, and trustworthiness. In addition, culturally responsive counselors were rated as more capable of being helpful in resolving academic, school, personal, or social problems than culturally neutral counselors.

Employing appropriate, relevant, and sensitive intervention strategies and skills is considered an essential component of cultural competence (Sue, Arredondo, & McDavis, 1992). It may be argued that approaches that are culturally consistent are more readily understood and accepted by clients, which may in turn contribute to ease of application and effectiveness. Clinicians employing culturally responsive approaches either integrate culture-specific theories and interventions with contemporary Western approaches, reconfigure traditional Western approaches, or implement novel strategies in assisting clients. Culturally responsive approaches incorporate the individual client or clients' biography, style, social network, and specific techniques and strategies appropriate to the client's culture, customs, and life habits (Witztum & Goodman, 1999). Intracultural variation is considered as individuals within cultures differ along a number of dimensions, including socio-identities such as gender, age, religion, and sexual orientation; experiences; personal perceptions; and interpretations of events. Fundamentally, approaches are responsive to the cultural influences on symptomatic expression and meanings of distress. This understanding informs culturally relevant goals and interventions that are consistent with the client(s)' life experiences, cultural values, and frame of reference. Moreover, culturally relevant approaches involve the entire therapeutic process and context, including the establishment of a therapeutic relationship, a healing environment, client expectations regarding the clinician's ability to help, and the implementation of a ritual (Wampold, 2001). Culturally responsive approaches are thus not limited to a specific procedure, such as relaxation training or cognitive restructuring, but encompass the entire interrelationship between the clinician and client(s).

It is important to acknowledge that aspects of one's social and cultural context, such as societal demands and cultural expectations, may be oppressive for certain of its members. The issue is whether the context presents difficulties for the individual(s). Of course there is a certain level of subjectivity in determining whether or not a context, situation, or issue is "problematic" and must ultimately be decided upon by the individual or group presenting for assistance. Such judgments are particularly challenging when dominant systems perpetuate inequity in oftentimes subversive ways. As such, difficulties may not be blatantly traceable to systemic inequities. Exploring options with clients and examining the potential consequences of those options can provide opportunities for growth. At the same time it is important for the clinician to realize that concepts such as power and oppression, as well as health and illness, often are culturally defined. Thus, flexibility and a willingness to entertain multiple perspectives are essential attributes of the clinician.

The implications of culturally responsive approaches for meeting the needs of an increasingly diverse population are manifold. It appears that the mental health profession has much to learn in terms of how culture and context influence clients, clinicians, and the helping process. This text represents a movement toward developing and implementing culturally sensitive, relevant, and effective therapeutic approaches that aim to relieve and minimize distress and create satisfying lives.

Discussion Questions

1. What types of research should be employed to identify the effectiveness of culturally responsive approaches with individuals, groups, and families? How should effectiveness be measured?
2. How may clinicians best improve their range of skills given client differences in distress expression, symptom attribution and preferred mode of treatment? What are the training implications of teaching clinicians to be more culturally responsive?
3. What other contextual factors besides the ones described in the chapter may impact clients' psychosocial functioning?
4. What steps can clinicians take to minimize cultural value conflicts and develop strong therapeutic alliances with clients?

5. How can contemporary counseling approaches be adapted to meet the needs of a diverse clientele? Alternatively, should contemporary counseling approaches be discarded for exclusively culture-specific approaches?

References

Acosta, F. X. (1979). Barriers between mental health services and Mexican Americans: An examination of a paradox. *American Journal of Community Psychology, 7*(5), 503–520.

Alarcón, R. D., & Foulks, E. F. (1995). Personality disorders and culture: Contemporary clinical views (Part A). *Cultural Diversity and Mental Health, 1,* 3–17.

Alarcón, R. D., Foulks, E. F., & Vakkur, M. (1998). *Personality disorders and culture: Clinical and conceptual interactions.* New York: Wiley.

American Psychological Association. (2002). *Guidelines for psychological practice with girls and women.* Manuscript in preparation.

American Psychological Association. (2002). *Guidelines on multicultural education, training, research, practice, and organizational change for psychologists.* Washington, DC: APA.

American Psychological Association. (1990). Guidelines for providers of psychological services to ethnic, linguistic, and culturally diverse populations. *American Psychologist, 48,* 45–48.

Ancis, J. R., & Burke, M. C. (1997). Human service students' attitudes toward working with an inner-city gang member: The case of Alphonse. *Human Services Education, 17,* 19–27.

Ancis, J. R., Sedlacek, W. E., & Mohr, J. J. (2000). Student perceptions of campus cultural climate by race. *Journal of Counseling and Development, 78,* 180–185.

Ancis, J. R., & Szymanski, D. M. (2001). Awareness of White privilege among White counseling trainees. *The Counseling Psychologist, 29,* 548–569.

Arredondo, P. (2002). Mujeres Latinas-Santas y Marquesas. *Cultural Diversity and Ethnic Minority Psychology, 8,* 308–319.

Asamen, J. K., & Berry, G. L. (1987). Self-concept, alienation, and perceived prejudice: Implications for counseling Asian Americans. *Journal of Multicultural Counseling and Development, 15,* 146–160.

Atkinson, D. R., & Gim, R. H. (1989). Asian-American cultural identity and attitudes toward mental-health services. *Journal of Counseling Psychology, 36,* 209–212.

Atkinson, D. R., Morten, G., & Sue, D. W. (1998). *Counseling American minorities* (5th ed.). Boston: McGraw-Hill.

Barón, A., & Constantine, M. G. (1997). A conceptual framework for conducting psychotherapy with Mexican-American college students. In J. G. García & M. C. Zea (Eds.), *Psychological interventions and research with Latino populations* (pp. 108–124). Boston: Allyn & Bacon.

Barter, E. R., & Barter, J. T. (1974). Urban Indians and mental health problems. *Psychiatric Annals, 4,* 37–43.

Betancourt, H., & López, S. R. (1993). The study of culture, ethnicity, and race in American psychology. *American Psychologist, 48,* 629–637.

Blair, R. G. (2001). Mental health needs among Cambodian refugees in Utah. *International Social Work, 44*(2), 179–196.

Boehnlein, J. K., & Kinzie, J. D. (1995). Refugee trauma. *Transcultural Psychiatric Research Review, 32,* 223–252.

Bronstein, P. A., & Quina, K. (1988). *Teaching a psychology of people.* Washington, DC: American Psychological Association.

Bulhan, H. A. (1985). Black Americans and psychopathology: An overview of research and theory. *Psychotherapy, 22,* 370–378.

Cheung, F. K., & Snowden, L. R. (1990). Community mental health and ethnic minority populations. *Community Mental Health Journal, 26,* 277–291.

Cheung, F. M., Lau, B. W. K., & Waldmann, E. (1980–1981). Somatization among Chinese depressives in general practice. *International Journal of Psychiatry in Medicine, 10,* 361–374.

Chiu, T. L. (1996). Problems caused for mental health professionals worldwide by increasing multicultural populations and proposed solutions. *Journal of Multicultural Counseling and Development, 24,* 129–140.

Choney, S. K., Berryhill-Paapke, E., & Robbins, R. R. (1995). The acculturation of American Indians: Developing frameworks for research and practice. In J. G. Ponterotto, J. M. Casas, L. A. Suzuki, & C. M. Alexander (Eds.), *Handbook of Multicultural Counseling* (pp. 78–92). Thousand Oaks, CA: Sage.

Chowdhury, A. N., Sanyal, D., Bhattacharya, A., Dutta, S. K., De, R., Banerjee, K., et al. (2001). Prominence of symptoms and level of stigma among depressed patients in Kolkata. *Journal of the Indian Medical Association, 99*(1), 20–23.

Chung, R. C., & Kagawa-Singer, M. (1993). Predictors of psychological distress among Southeast Asian refugees. *Social Science Medicine, 36,* 631–639.

D'Andrea, M., & Daniels, J. (2001). *Respectful counseling.* Pacific Grove, CA: Brooks/Cole.

Das, A. K. (1987). Indigenous models of therapy in traditional Asian societies. *Journal of Multicultural Counseling and Development, 15,* 25–37.

Davis, J. A., & Smith, T. W. (1990). *General social surveys, 1972–1990.* Chicago: National Opinion Research Center.

Doyle, A. B. (1998). Are empirically validated treatments valid for culturally diverse populations. In K. S. Dobson & K. D. Craig (Eds.), *Empirically supported therapies: Best practice in professional psychology* (pp. 93–103). Thousand Oaks, CA: Sage.

Dukepoo, P. C. (1980). *The elder American Indian.* San Diego, CA: Campanile.

Finch, B. K., Kolody, B., & Vega, W. A. (2000). Perceived discrimination and depression among Mexican origin adults in California. *Journal of Health and Social Behavior, 41,* 295–313.

Flaskerud, J. H., & Soldevilla, E. Q. (1986). Pilipino and Vietnamese clients: Utilizing an Asian mental health center. *Journal of Psychosocial Nursing, 24*(8), 32-36.

Gafner, G., & Benson, S. (2001). Indirect ego-strengthening in treating PTSD in immigrants from Central America. *Contemporary Hypnosis, 18,* 135–144.

Gong-Guy, E., Cravens, R. B., & Patterson, T. E. (1991). Clinical issues of mental health service delivery to refugees. *American Psychologist, 46,* 642–648.

Good, B. J., & Kleinman, A. M. (1985). Culture and anxiety: Cross-cultural evidence for the patterning of anxiety disorders. In A. H. Tuma & J. Maser (Eds.), *Anxiety and the anxiety disorders* (pp. 297–324). Hillsdale, NJ: Erlbaum.

Harper, F. D., & Deen, N. (2003). The international counseling movement. In F. D.

Harper & J. McFadden (Eds.), *Culture and counseling: New approaches* (pp. 147–163). Boston: Allyn & Bacon.

Hough, R. L., Landsverk, J. A., Karno, M., Burnam, M. A., Timbers, D. M., Escobar, J. I., et al. (1987). Utilization of health and mental health services by Los Angeles Mexican Americans and non-Hispanic Whites. *Archives of General Psychiatry, 44,* 702–709.

Hughes, M., & Demo, D. H. (1989). Self-perceptions of Black Americans: Self-esteem and personal efficacy. *American Journal of Sociology, 95,* 132–159.

Ivey, A. E., Ivey, M. B., & Simek-Morgan, L. (1993). *Counseling and psychotherapy: A multicultural perspective.* Boston: Allyn & Bacon.

Jackson, L. C. (2000). The new multiculturalism and psychodynamic theory: Psychodynamic psychotherapy and African American women. In L. C. Jackson & B. Greene (Eds.), *Psychotherapy with African American women: Innovations in psychodynamic perspectives and practice* (pp. 1–14). New York: Guilford.

Jerrell, J. M., & Wilson, J. L. (1997). Ethnic differences in the treatment of dual mental and substance disorders: A preliminary analysis. *Journal of Substance Abuse Treatment, 14,* 133–140.

Judy, R. W., & D'Amico, C. (1997). *Workforce 2020.* Indianapolis, IN: Hudson Institute.

Katz, J. (1985). The sociopolitical nature of counseling. *The Counseling Psychologist, 13,* 615–624.

Kinzie, J. D. (2001). Psychotherapy for massively traumatized refugees: The therapist variable. *American Journal of Psychotherapy, 55,* 475–490.

Kinzie, J. D., Sack, W., Angell, R., Clarke, G., & Ben, R. (1989). A three-year follow-up of Cambodian young people traumatized as children. *Journal of the American Academy of Child and Adolescent Psychiatry, 28,* 501–504.

Kinzie, J. D., Sack, W. H., Angell, R. H., & Manson, S. M. (1986). The psychiatric effects of massive trauma on Cambodian children: I. The children. *Journal of American Academy of Child Psychiatry, 25*(3), 370–376.

Kirmayer, L. J. (1989). Cultural variations in the response to psychiatric disorders and emotional distress. *Social Science and Medicine, 29,* 327–339.

Kirmayer, L. J. (2001). Cultural variations in the clinical presentation of depression and anxiety: Implications for diagnosis and treatment. *Journal of Clinical Psychiatry, 62,* 22–28.

Kirmayer, L. J., Boothroyd, L. J., Tanner, A., Adelson, N., & Robinson, E. (2000). Psychological distress among the Cree of James Bay. *Transcultural Psychiatry, 37,* 35–56.

Kirmayer, L. J., Brass, G. M., & Tait, C. (2000). The mental health of aboriginal peoples: Transformation of identity and community. *Canadian Journal of Psychiatry, 45,* 607–616.

Kirmayer, L. J., & Groleau, D. (2001). Affective disorders in cultural context. *Cultural psychiatry: International Perspectives, 24,* 465–478.

Kirmayer, L. J., & Minas, H. (2000). The future of cultural psychiatry: An international perspective. *Canadian Journal of Psychiatry, 45*(5), 438–446.

Kirmayer, L. J., & Young, A. (1999). Culture and context in the evolutionary concept of mental disorder. *Journal of Abnormal Psychology, 108,* 446–452.

Kirschenman, J., & Neckerman, K. M. (1991). "We'd love to hire them, but . . .": The meaning of race for employers. In C. Jencks & P. E. Peterson (Eds.), *The urban underclass* (pp. 203–234). Washington, DC: Brookings Institution.

Kleinman, A. (1988). *Rethinking psychiatry: From cultural category to personal experience.* New York: Free Press.

Kleinman, A. (1977). Depression, somatization, and the new cross-cultural psychiatry. *Social Science and Medicine, 11,* 3–10.

Koss-Chioino, J. (1992). *Women as healers, women as patients: Mental health care and traditional healing in Puerto Rico.* Boulder, CO: Westview Press.

Koss-Chioino, J. D. (1995). Traditional and folk approaches among ethnic minorities. In J. F. Aponte, R. Y. Rivers, & J. Wohl (Eds.), *Psychological interventions and cultural diversity* (pp. 145–163). Needham Heights, MA: Longwood.

Koss-Chioino, J. D. (1999). Depression among Puerto-Rican women: Culture, etiology and diagnosis. *Hispanic Journal of Behavioral Sciences, 21,* 330–350.

Koss-Chioino, J. D., & Canive, J. M. (1993). The interaction of popular and clinical diagnostic labeling: The case of embrujado. *Medical Anthropology, 15,* 171–188.

Krebs, R. L. (1971). Some effects of a White institution on Black psychiatric outpatients. *American Journal of Orthopsychiatry, 41,* 589–596.

LaFromboise, T. D. (1988). American Indian mental health policy. *American Psychologist, 43,* 388–397.

Lambert, M. C., Weisz, J. R., & Knight, F. (1989). Over and undercontrolled clinic referral problems of Jamaican and American children and adolescents: The culture general and the culture specific. *Journal of Clinical and Consulting Psychology, 57,* 467–472.

Lebra, W. P. (1972). (Ed.). *Culture-bound syndromes, ethnopsychiatry, and alternate therapies.* Volume IV of Mental Health Research in Asia and the Pacific. Honolulu: University Press of Hawaii.

Lee, S. (2001). From diversity to unity: The classification of mental disorders in 21st-century China. *The Psychiatric Clinics of North America, 24,* 421–431.

Lewis, J. A., Lewis, M. D., Daniels, J. A., & D'Andrea, M. J. (1998). *Community counseling: Empowerment strategies for a diverse society.* San Francisco: Brooks/Cole.

Littlewood, R. (1990). From categories to contexts: A decade of the "new cross-cultural psychiatry." *British Journal of Psychiatry, 156,* 308–327.

Lopez, S. (1988). The empirical basis of ethnocultural and linguistic bias in mental health evaluation of Hispanics. *American Psychologist, 43,* 1095–1097.

Martin, D. J., Garske, J. P., & Davis, M. K. (2000). Relation of the therapeutic alliance with outcome and other variables: A meta-analytic review. *Journal of Consulting and Clinical Psychology, 68,* 438–450.

Mollica, R. F., Wyshak, G., & Lavelle, J. (1987). The psychosocial impact of war trauma and torture on Southeast Asian refugees. *American Journal of Psychiatry, 144,* 1567–1572.

Mukherjee, S., Shukla, S., Woodle, J., Rosen, A. M., & Olarte, S. (1983). Misdiagnosis of schizophrenia in bipolar patients: A multiethnic comparison. *American Journal of Psychiatry, 140,* 1571–1574.

Nicholson, B. L. (1997). The influence of pre-emigration and postmigration stressors on mental health: A study of Southeast Asian refugees. *Social Work Research, 21,* 19–31.

Noh, S., Beiser, M., Kaspar, V., Hou, F., & Rummens, J. (1999). Perceived racial discrimination, depression and coping: A study of Southeast Asian refugees in Canada. *Journal of Health and Social Behavior, 40,* 193–207.

O'Sullivan, M. J., & Lasso, B. (1992). Community mental health for Hispanics: A test of the culture compatibility hypothesis. *Hispanic Journal of Behavioral Sciences, 14,* 455–468.

Paniagua, F. A. (2001). *Diagnosis in a multicultural context: A casebook* for mental health professionals. Thousand Oaks, CA: Sage.

Raguram, R., Weiss, M. G., Channabasavanna, S. M., & Devins, G. M. (1996). Stigma, depression and somatisation: A report from South India. *American Journal of Psychiatry, 153,* 1043–1049.

Raguram, R., Weiss, M. G., Keval, H., & Channabasavanna, S. M. (2001). Cultural dimensions of clinical depression in Bangalore, India. *Anthropology and Medicine, 8,* 31–46.

Ren, X. S., Amick, B., & Williams, D. R. (1999). Racial/ethnic disparities in health: The interplay between discrimination and socioeconomic status. *Ethnicity & Disease, 9,* 151–165.

Rogler, L. H., Cortes, D. E., & Malgady, R. G. (1991). Acculturation and mental health status among Hispanics: Convergence and new directions for research. *American Psychologist, 46,* 585–597.

Rogler, L. H., Malgady, R. G., Costantino, G., & Blumenthal, R. (1987). What do culturally sensitive mental health services mean? The case of Hispanics. *American Psychologist, 42,* 565–570.

Rogler, L. H., Malgady, R. G., & Rodriguez, O. (1989). *Hispanics and mental health: A framework for research.* Malabar, FL: Krieger.

Rosenheck, R., Leda, C., Frisman, L., & Gallup, P. (1997). Homeless mentally ill veterans: Race, service use, and treatment outcomes. *American Journal of Orthopsychiatry, 67,* 632–638.

Rumbaut, R. G. (1994). The crucible within: Ethnic identity, self-esteem, and segmented assimilation among children of immigrants. *International Migration Review, 28,* 748–794.

Shiefer, S. E., Escarce, J. J., & Schulman, K. A. (2000). Race and sex differences in the management of coronary artery disease. *American Heart Journal, 139,* 848–857.

Shimoji, A., & Miyakawa, T. (2000). Culture-bound syndrome and a culturally sensitive approach; from a viewpoint of medical anthropology. *Psychiatry and Clinical Neurosciences, 54,* 461–466.

Simon, R. J., Fleiss, J. L., Gurland, B. J., Stiller, P. R., & Sharpe, L. (1973). Depression and schizophrenia in hospitalized Black and White mental patients. *Archives of General Psychiatry, 28,* 509–512.

Smart, J. F., & Smart, D. F. (1995). Acculturative stress: The experience of the Hispanic immigrant. *The Counseling Psychologist, 23,* 25–42.

Snowden, L. R., & Cheung, F. K. (1990). Use of inpatient mental health services by members of ethnic minority groups. *American Psychologist, 45,* 347–355.

Solomon, P. (1988). Racial factors in mental health service utilization. *Psychosocial Rehabilitation Journal, 11,* 3–12.

Strong, S. R. (1968). Counseling: An interpersonal influence process. *Journal of Counseling Psychology, 15,* 215–224.

Sue, D. W. (1995). Toward a theory of multicultural counseling and therapy. In J. A. Banks & C. A. McGee Banks (Eds.), *Handbook of research on multicultural education* (pp. 647–659). New York: Macmillan.

Sue, D. W., Arredondo, P., & McDavis, R. J. (1992). Multicultural counseling competencies and standards: A call to the profession. *Journal of Counseling and Development, 70,* 477–486.

Sue, D. W., Ivey, A. E., & Pedersen, P. B. (Eds.). (1996). *A theory of multicultural counseling and therapy.* Pacific Grove, CA: Brooks/Cole.

Sue, D. W., & Sue, D. (1999). *Counseling the culturally different: Theory and practice* (3rd ed.). New York: Wiley.

Sue, S. (1977). Community mental health services to minority groups: Some optimism, some pessimism. *American Psychologist, 32,* 616–624.

Sue, S., Fujino, D. C., Hu, L., & Takeuchi, D. T. (1991). Community mental health services for ethnic minority groups: A test of the cultural responsiveness hypothesis. *Journal of Consulting and Clinical Psychology, 59,* 533–540.

Sue, S., & Morishima, J. K. (1982). *The mental health of Asian Americans.* San Francisco: Jossey-Bass.

Sue, S., & Sue, D. W. (1974). MMPI comparisons between Asian-American and non-Asian students utilizing a student health psychiatric clinic. *Journal of Counseling Psychology, 21,* 423–427.

Sue, S., Zane, N., & Young, K. (1994). Research on psychotherapy and behavior change. In A. Bergin & S. Garfield (Eds.), *Handbook of psychotherapy and behavior change* (4th ed., pp. 783–817). New York: Wiley.

Sussman, L. K., Robins, L. N., & Earls, F. (1987). Treatment-seeking for depression by Black and White Americans. *Social Science and Medicine, 24,* 187–196.

Szapocznik, J., Kurtines, W., & Fernandez, T. (1980). Biculturalism and adjustment among Hispanic youths. *International Journal of Intercultural Relations, 4,* 353–375.

Szapocznik, J., Santisteban, D., Rio, A., Perez-Vidal, A., Santisteban, D., & Kurtines, W. M. (1989). Family effectiveness training: An intervention to prevent drug abuse and problem behaviors in Hispanic adolescents. *Hispanic Journal of Behavioral Sciences, 11,* 4–27.

Tata, S. P., & Leong, F. T. L. (1994). Individualism-collectivism, network orientation, and acculturation as predictors of attitudes towards seeking professional psychological help among Chinese Americans. *Journal of Counseling Psychology, 41,* 280–287.

Torrey, E. F. (1972). *The mind game: Witchdoctors and psychiatrists.* New York: Emerson Hall.

Tseng, W. S. (1975). The nature of somatic complaints among psychiatric patients: The Chinese case. *Comprehensive Psychiatry, 16,* 237–245.

Tseng, W. S. (1997). Overview: Culture and psychopathology. In W.S. Tseng & J. Streltzer (Eds.), *Culture and psychopathology: A guide to clinical assessment* (pp. 1–27). New York: Brunner/Mazel.

U.S. Census Bureau (2001a). U. S. Census 2000, Summary Files 1 and 2. Retrieved from http://www.census.gov

U.S. Department of Health and Human Services. (2000, 2001). *Mental health: Culture, race and ethnicity–A supplement to Mental Health: A report of the Surgeon General.* Rockville, MD: U.S. Department of Health and Human Services, Public Health Office, Office of the Surgeon General.

Vargas-Willis, G., & Cervantes, R. C. (1987). Considerations of psychosocial stress in the treatment of the Latina immigrant. *Hispanic Journal of Behavioral Sciences, 9,* 315–329.

Vasquez, M. J. T. (1994). Latinas. In L. Comas-Díaz & B. Greene (Eds.), *Women of color: Integrating ethnic and gender identities in psychotherapy* (pp. 114–138). New York: Guilford.

Vernez, G. (1991). Current global refugee situation and international public policy. *American Psychologist, 46,* 627–631.

Wampold, B. E. (1997). Methodological problems in identifying efficacious psychotherapies. *Psychotherapy Research, 7,* 21–43.

Wampold, B. E. (2001). *The great psychotherapy debate: Models, methods, and findings.* Mahwah, NJ: Erlbaum.

Weissman, M. M., Livingston, B. M., Leaf, P. J., Florio, L. P., & Holzer, C. (1991). Affective disorders. In L. Robins & D. Regier (Eds.), *Psychiatric Disorders in America* (pp. 33–52). Toronto: Collier-Macmillan.

Westermeyer, J. (1987). Cultural factors in clinical assessment. *Journal of Consulting and Clinical Psychology, 55,* 471–478.

Wierzbicki, M., & Pekarik, G. (1993). A meta-analysis of psychotherapy dropout. *Professional Psychology: Research and Practice, 24*(2), 190–195.

Williams, D. R., Yu, Y., Jackson, J. S., & Anderson, N. B. (1997). Racial differences in physical and mental health: Socio-economic status, stress and discrimination. *Journal of Health Psychology, 2,* 335–351.

Witztum, E., & Goodman, Y. (1999). Narrative construction of distress and therapy: A model based on work with Ultra-Orthodox Jews. *Transcultural Psychiatry, 36,* 403–436.

Yen, S., Robins, C. J., & Lin, N. (2000). A cross-cultural comparison of depressive symptom manifestation: China and the United States. *Journal of Consulting and Clinical Psychology, 68,* 993–999.

Yinger, J. (1995). *Closed doors, opportunities lost: The continuing costs of housing discrimination.* New York: Russell Sage Foundation.

Zane, N., Enomoto, K., & Chun, C. (1994). Treatment outcomes of Asian- and White-American clients in outpatient therapy. *Journal of Community Psychology, 22*(2), 177–191.

Chapter 2

American Indian Constructionalist Family Therapy for Acculturative Stress

Rockey Robbins
Steve Harrist

This chapter describes the American Indian Constructionalist Family Therapy Model, a synthesis and application of American Indian and postmodern concepts. This approach is intended to benefit American Indian families who suffer from acculturative stress linked to multigenerational oppression, racism, and discrimination. The American Indian Constructionalist Family Therapy Model emphasizes strengths and possibilities, in contrast to the deficit model upon which many psychological theories are based. Clients are encouraged to examine multiple perspectives in combating oppressive discourses and beliefs and accept life's ongoing developments. The case study demonstrates the approach with an American Indian family presenting with acculturation stress.

Integration of American Indian and Postmodern Concepts

The use of many conventional therapeutic approaches with American Indians may reenact colonization. Duran and Duran (1995) contend, "Most approaches (psychological treatments) implemented on Native peoples are ongoing attempts at further colonization of their life-world" (p. 87). It has been proposed that exposure to orthodox Western psychotherapy is harmful to ethnic minorities (LaFromboise & Rowe, 1983; Lefley, 1986). American Indians may be adversely affected by tacit assumptions and values from dominant mainstream psychotherapy theories and practices that recapitulate colonial oppression intrapsychically. There is a particular need for relevant and helpful therapeutic methods when working with American Indian families. Duran and Duran argue for an American Indian therapy model that utilizes traditional American Indian thinking in conjunction with Western practice. They specifically allude to the investigations of oppression and domination by French poststructuralists and German critical theorists, whose concepts are discussed in this chapter (Duran & Duran, 1995, p. 87).

This chapter attempts to supplement traditional American Indian ideas concerning family healing, many of which exist in a fairly inchoate form, with postmodern ideas. Postmodern theory has become a potent force in psychology today and has potential for use with minorities, yet until its orientations are evaluated through the lenses of minority perspectives and applied in particular contexts, it will remain primarily a White and Western theory. In this chapter, we concretize American Indian and postmodern concepts into therapeutic strategies and describe how they were employed in a particular counseling context with an American Indian family experiencing acculturative stress. We call this synthesis and application of American Indian and postmodern concepts, the American Indian Constructionalist Family Therapy Model. We are vigilant in our attempt to avoid reinscribing colonial discourse. We are especially interested in offering an approach that will benefit American Indian families who suffer from stress linked with multigenerational oppression (historical ideological/cultural/and economic domination) and current feelings of alienation because of blatant and covert racism and discrimination, sometimes referred to as acculturative stress.

Culture and Context

The following description of the American Indian Constructionalist Family Therapeutic Approach is complex. It evolves from traditional American Indian beliefs, ceremony, and postcolonial and postmodernist thought.

Interconnectedness and Social Constructionist Theory

Although one cannot make sweeping generalizations about the teachings of American Indians, most elders teach a reverence for the earth, a spiritual kinship between all living things, and a tolerance for different beliefs and attitudes. European invaders used the Bible to prescribe truth, and their highly restricted interpretations led to destroying the earth, dominating other races, and persecuting groups and persons with alternative viewpoints. Helen Attaquin (1987), a Wampanoag, writes, "Indians don't believe there is one fixed and eternal truth; they think there are many different and equally valid truths. The Western mind allows only one truth, one political belief, one religion, and one chosen people—theirs" (p. 20). She later explains that traditional Indian people teach "that there is more than one way to view this earth and more than one way to share it. The cultural package that each of us is born into differs from other cultural packages.

For Indians everything that is perceived by the senses, thought about, or felt, dreamed about, or imagined, exists as an inclusive aspect of the real world" (p. 21).

Social constructionism, one of the foundations of postmodern thought, espouses ideas similar to the American Indian notion of reality being made up of relative truths in "cultural packages" that can be "shared." Gergen (1994) writes, "Social constructionism is a revolution that replaces the dualist epistemology of knowing mind confronting a material world with a social epistemology. Locus of knowledge is no longer taken to be individual mind, but rather patterns of social relatedness" (p. 129). Throughout history different communities have constructed unique cultural realities according to which members communicate and interact. Laclau and Mouffe (1985) note, "the fact that every object is constituted as an object of discourse has nothing to do with whether there is a world external to thought" (p. 108). The point is that meaning constantly emerges and changes through on going experience and discourse. Reality is not simply a mental construction of the observer. There is no simple or singular way of describing reality. We have internal images of reality that take on coherent meaning as part of a discursive system.

Although American Indian ideas about interconnectedness and social constructionism are similar in many ways, they are not a perfect simulacrum. Social constructionist theory might be characterized as humanist and intellectual, whereas American Indian thought includes more feelings related to our interconnectedness with nature. Postmodernists talk and write ad infinitum, emphasizing questioning, answering, questioning the answering, and answering the questioning. Traditional American Indians visit each other a lot and may go into the woods, fast, and shudder in silence as they experience meaning in their realization of their kinship to all people, trees, and mountains. The water's gurgle may modify a seeker's meaning structure, and he or she may come to realize that all things and all people should be respected on their own account. In a sense, an American Indian's encounter with nature is social because nature is viewed not as a dead object but as an interpenetrable subject. Both perspectives encourage openness to modification, tolerance, and mutuality.

Identity as Relational

Traditional American Indians are a communal rather than individualistic people. One's individuality is connected with one's participation in the clan and tribe. Leslie Silko (1977) writes, "people shared a single clan name and they told each other who they were . . . the people shared the same consciousness. . . . Christianity separated the people from themselves; it tried to crush the single clan name . . . because Jesus Christ would save only the individual soul" (p. 68).

Family therapists would do well to know something about the social constructions of Indian persons with whom they work or else they are bound to contribute to the further demise of American Indian cultures. For instance, specific persons within clans and extended families are often expected to assume leadership roles and offer advice in different situations. There are often specific protocol regarding the handling of important family matters. Certain persons are designated by birth to be called upon when specific circumstances emerge. It would be inappropriate for counselors to circumvent certain family members in some circumstances. To do so might upset the cohesiveness of family and tribe.

Postmodern thought emphasizes identity as relational. Philosophers in the West have typically "viewed man as a separate individual . . . an exclusive consciousness . . . a restricted island of consciousness" (Watts, 1958, p. 158). Descartes wrote, "I think, therefore I am" (1641/1960, p. 82). He could doubt all things but not doubt "I." Derrida (1973), the postmodernist theorist, deconstructs the famous remark. He contends that it is an affirmation of presence. Yet, he argues, presence cannot exist without absence. Consequently, "I" is deprived of its original authority. Presence must be supported by absence. They need each other to be or not to be. "I" exists only in relation. Identity does not exist in seclusion but is relational. Derrida argues that the concept of the individual agent does not disappear but exists in relation to others. Postmodernists do not deny the concept of individuality but emphasize its hybridity and multiplicity. Individuality emerges out of diverse influences and expresses itself through many roles. Both American Indian and postmodernist thought view individual being as existing only in a community.

Experience and Stories

In spite of attempts by their oppressors to divest American Indians of their tribal stories, many traditional American Indian families have tenaciously guarded them and passed them down with each succeeding generation. Many American Indian stories can not be written down and are told only at certain times of the year or only during ceremonies. Further, storytelling in general is a basic way for many American Indians to organize and understand the meaning of individual and tribal experience as well as the meaning of the natural world. Recently, one of the authors of this chapter was told by one of his Commanche friends that his grandmother filled up several cassette tapes of stories about her ancestors that had been passed down over the course of eight generations. In her novel, *Ceremony*, Leslie Silko (1977) further supports the importance of stories for American Indians when she writes, "You don't have anything if you do not have the stories" (p. 2). Traditional American Indians assume that stories yield coherence to experience, connect individuals to history, provoke being, and affect lives.

Stories are also basic building blocks of Narrative therapy. Narrative therapy evolved out of the social constructionism revolution. The Narrative approach is distinguished from more "mechanistic" approaches, which look at causal mechanisms operating beneath the surface. Linear problem solving shaves off part of the wholeness of experience and dramatically reduces meaning potential.

Narrativizing involves an element of construction that goes beyond problem solving. "Stories grow out of and reflect the flow of our lives, and storytelling makes explicit what is already there in life" (Guignon, 1998, p. 569). Reality is always mediated through stories. Our ongoing filling of gaps, resolving contradictions, and story revisions reveal our changing perspectives and our ever-unfolding grasp upon the meanings of our lives. A Narrative therapist may ask questions that help clients tell their life stories, listening carefully for events that may help open up alternative stories (Freedman & Combs, 1996; White & Epston, 1990). Narrative therapy and traditional American Indians agree that stories can provoke and affect our lives and if told and reflected upon in the proper context can contribute to our mental health.

Issues of Power

Conversations about political oppression can be very liberating to many American Indians. American Indian people experience discrimination in different forms. Stories abound among Indian people of how they did not receive due consideration for appointments or advancements in employment settings. Many American Indians live in low-cost, self-help projects. Unemployment and public school dropout rates are exceedingly high, and drug and alcohol problems are prevalent (Beauvais, Chavez, Oetting, Deffenbacher, & Cornell, 1996). American Indians are often derided as "drunks" or as being untrustworthy, angry, detached, uncaring, or resistant. In movies they are represented as being either warlike or ridiculously noble. Among American Indians, discrimination takes the form of derogatory labels that often have to do with being mix breeds or full bloods, or of being an off-tribe (a term used to denote any tribal member who is not of one's own tribe).

Postmodernist Michel Foucault (1980) was especially interested in the way dominant social discourses control the way people perceive their reality. He worked to fragment the logocentism of wills to power that claim to be objective truth especially in the areas of sexuality and politics (Foucault, 1980). Combs and Freedman (1996) claim that reality is socially constructed by the powerful in order to perpetuate their own hegemony. Freedman and Combs (1996) believe that "dominant stories can be subjugating of persons' lives . . . stories of gender, race, class . . . are so prevalent and entrenched in our culture that we can get caught up in them without realizing it" (p. 57). Foucault (1980) argues that values and principles are imposed upon us from the time we are born. Similarly, powerful prejudicial points of view have been imposed upon Indians for many generations.

Narrative therapy contends that our psychological problems stem from buying into toxic stories (White & Epston, 1990). One of the writers of this chapter counseled an Indian boy who grew up saturated by overt and subtle messages telling him that his dark skin was ugly. He was adopted into a Euro-

American family and he was especially attached to his very successful stepfather. He did "poorly" in school and other children teased him. He began to interpret his life's experiences according to the basic story line of his "ugliness." He took to trying to rub the "darkness" from his arms and face. It takes an informed and culturally sensitive therapist to help traditional American Indians dig beneath the political oppression to draw upon their strong cultural roots as well as individual strengths.

Strengths and Possibilities

When working with American Indians, therapists should keep in mind that many positive social and political changes are taking place every day that positively affect the lives of American Indians. Tribal governments are working hard to facilitate tribal members to act on new job opportunities that will instill renewed self-confidence and pride. As we write this chapter, the *Native American Times* (2002) lists approximately 400 job opportunities for Cherokees in northeast Oklahoma with the opening of a finishing plant. Choctaw women can read in their tribal newspaper, the *Bishinik* (2002), where to sign up for a workshop on how to start a small business. Strength begins at a grassroots level. Although often living in close proximity with related and nonrelated people, American Indians are developing new and creative ways to cooperate and manage conflicts revolving around limited resources. Traditional views about interdependence have emphasized that relationships must be extensive and entwined beyond blood. American Indian people are an active and involved people in tribal politics and social renewal.

The American Indian Constructionalist Family Therapy Model rejects the deficit model on which many psychological theories are based and emphasizes strengths and possibilities. It attempts to help people deal with the world out of their strengths, not their weaknesses. The goal is to move beyond the focus on internal conflicts and impotent resentments. Although American Indian families experience overwhelming stress as a result of rapidly changing social conditions as well as continued overt oppression, they are not without opportunity and hope, which will help with self and tribal recreation. Certainly there should be attention placed on social oppression as well as tribal mistakes and lapses, but renewal can flow from therapy only if attention is equally focused on strengths and possibilities.

One of the current writer's clients, an elder in his tribe, lost his eyesight. Instead of spending the rest of his life bemoaning his fate, he accepted his new condition and spoke of finding a new balance in his life. He learned how to maintain his vitality even though he was now blind. This attitude toward life consists of not living according to life denying stories but with the attitude that seeming deficits can be used to enhance life. The mystery of life is not a problem to be solved. The telos of this approach is to help clients assume an attitude that accepts life as dynamic.

Interventions

Neither the theory nor the techniques of the American Indian Constructionalist Family Therapy Model are wholly original. There is no need to discard "old" psychological ideas that have had instrumental benefit in analysis or treatment. Nonetheless, older therapeutic approaches are rearranged and extended. For instance, although this approach is fairly nondirective, some situations and issues benefit from directive therapy, as demonstrated in the Talking Feather technique. In fact, American Indians respect and see great value in leaders who are directive in given situations. Also, although the approach does not emphasize the unconscious, the exploration of what is "absent" in stories and the use of metaphor often opens up clients to unconscious contents. Cognitive-Behavioral approaches also have informed this theory through a consideration of irrational self-talk, which is similar to looking for "gaps" in logical structure. Nonetheless, the differences in this and other approaches should not be soft peddled. This approach is radically collaborative. Clients have great power in deciding the direction and organization of therapy. Also, although the clients and therapists deal with unconscious contents, therapists do not provide "expert" interpretations. Further, this approach does not adhere to cause and effect mechanics and beginning-middle-end reduction tyranny. The notion of arriving at an unquestioned telos is too neat. Provisional resolutions, values, and meanings are arrived at only to open up to new vistas.

Talking Feather Technique and the Reflecting Team

Attneave (1985) argued that the most effective delivery agencies for American Indians are traditional community and kinship networks of support. Since the late 1960s, several American Indian therapists and academicians, such as Speck and Attneave (1974) and Red Horse (1982) have advocated for and initiated "network therapy," which mobilizes family, relatives, and friends into a socially interdependent group of support.

The Talking Feather technique is closely related to traditional ceremonial situations, such as blessings and honoring ceremonies that occur in family networks. Before engaging in the Talking Feather technique, family members are instructed that they will be given about 3 to 5 minutes to consider the value that they feel is strongest in guiding their individual life. All reflect in silence. Then, one family member is given the talking feather and asked to relate his or her value and reflect upon it. (There may be customs that restrict persons from holding the talking feather in certain circumstances, such as when a woman is menstruating.) All other family members listen. Next, the feather is passed around to each family member, who may choose to respond to the original speaker's remarks. Last, the feather is returned to the original speaker and she or he is given an opportunity to revise his or her remarks. After each round, the therapist asks questions to help family members compare and contrast values, discuss feelings, examine the way values are passed along and the sources of values, and to discuss what and how differences can be tolerated or not.

The Talking Feather technique draws from the reflecting team technique used by Narrative therapists. Grandesso (1996) argues, "the therapists and team, side by side, permit the coexistence of different versions as equally possible. . . . The validation of a multiplicity of versions of the family's reality undercuts the search for a correct explanation of the problem, moving the family away from a disjunctive either-or logic and toward an additive logic of a both-and type." Clients overhear conversations about their stories spoken nonjudgmentally. They are in positions to listen carefully instead of getting lost in defensiveness. Combs and Freedman (1998) write, "We have found that inviting people to assume a witnessing position to each other's emerging new stories frees them to hear instead of defend. Hearing things differently and giving voice to those differences contributes to transformation" (p. 407).

The social construction of reality is emphasized. White (1995) contends that telling and retelling stories is a way of "thickening" the description to gain more insights. Through hearing others' versions of experiences, clients are liberated from the prison house of their own often-totalizing explanations. As unity of perspective is fragmented by different perspectives, the therapist attempts to proliferate new meanings. Clients speculate on ambiguities or contradictions in their stories. Clients have the opportunity to revise their stories by incorporating other persons' details and explanations. The counselor may ask questions and further call attention to contradictions and oppositions in stories. Multiplicity is held together with tolerance. Listening, family members "can take refuge in an inner conversation. In this way they are free to make their own leaps between levels of meaning" (Andersen, 1987).

Difference

Traditional Indians use words with reverence and awe. Prayers and chants spoken in tribal languages have a mesmerizing influence upon listeners. Momaday (1966) writes, "For her words were medicine: they were magic and invisible. They came from nothing into sound and meaning. They were beyond price; they could neither be bought nor sold. And she never threw them away" (p. 89). For many American Indians there is a psychological connection between being Indian and speaking one's tribal language. Being able to speak the language is directly correlated with participating in tribal ceremonies and the maintenance of customs. Sometimes speaking and translating one's language into English is difficult. Many American Indians do not understand words used by professional helpers but are hesitant to indicate their misunderstandings. This makes it all the more important for both the therapist and clients to utilize "difference."

Difference is a method used by Derrida (1973) to deconstruct language. *Difference*, a French word, refers both to respect (to differ) and contrast (difference). It is a critical technique that is used to look for traces of the opposite in a concept. It is one of postmodernism's most elegant contributions to the exploration of language. Instead of being foreclosed truths, and definite in their meanings, words and principles contain ambiguity and can be explored. Every principle exists in relation to its opposite. Exploring what is absent from a client's peculiar uses of words and comments is a helpful approach to gain insight. It involves focusing on what is missing in a client's remarks. For instance, Indian people often speak of the importance of "respecting your elders." Questioning may encourage the family to discuss the elements of concern and esteem implicit in the phrase or a therapist may carefully discuss both the positive and negative elements that the phrase contains in the context in which it is used. For instance, one of our adolescent clients was told by his parent that he should drop out of a gifted program where he was learning how to use computers. When asked for the reason, the parent responded because "our son should respect his elders." When asked how dropping out of the class would be synonymous with "respecting elders," we were told that computers would take his son from the reservation and cause him to forget tribal ways. When we asked the son what he felt respecting elders was, he said, "participating in the ceremonies and continuing to sing tribal songs." We then explored the possibility of combining the client's definition of respecting elders with his continued study of computers and possible move from the reservation. Difference entails asking questions that help clients bring out the substances of words and phrases.

Supplementation

Traditional ideas and stories related in ceremonies, such as peyote meetings and sweats, are not intended to be immediately understood. The meanings come to a person when one's life has been supplemented by enough relevant experiences to warrant them. For instance, years ago, one of the current authors, when ill, had a strange dream of a corn maiden spirit offering him an ear of corn of many colors. A medicine person told him something to the effect that true healing occurred within communities where differences were respected and honored. Years later the dream and interpretation came back to him in the heat of a bitter conflict at a practicum meeting. Accumulated experiences and reflection allowed him to attain a new understanding of how the growth of the counselors and the healing of the clients depended a great deal on the cohesion and mutual respect of the group of counselors.

Supplement is a technique Derrida (1976) uses to open up interpreted stories to new meanings. Supplement functions as addition and substitution. Often clients offer narratives of profound experiences in only a few sentences. As clients add details to their stories, they open themselves up to new feelings and meanings. After a client offers a skeletal story with few dominant impressions, therapists may ask questions such as: Where and when did it take place? What things do you remember hearing and seeing? Who was there? Who was not there? What were you expecting? What was your dominant impression of the place . . . person? As the new details cause the story to become more vivid, clients often discover new meanings in their stories as well as feel emotions that may be married to certain images. Further, a therapist may facilitate clients to substitute alternative interpretations of their experiences. This technique may involve concentration on missing links in the logical structure of clients' stories and interpretations, helping clients become aware of the assumptions that guide their actions, or calling attention to incongruent feelings. As content is added through new experiences, old beliefs and viewpoints may not have kept up. The contents of one's consciousness and unconsciousness may oblige a new arrangement in one's stories and opinions. A psychologist helps the client to graft new experiences and ideas upon the old body of thought. New viewpoints emerge that may help the client see more profound meaning in their experiences and enable them to cope more effectively with stressful situations.

Derrida (1976) distinguishes between those who decipher stories and those who engage in free play. These categories are helpful when considering our therapeutic styles. Deciphering tries to get at the bottom of things to a place that is ultimately reassuring and safe. In free play the story may be extended infinitely. There is no clinging to right answers that fit within rules. Meaning has no respite; it engages itself endlessly. This does not mean that therapists should not make tentative interpretations, nor that meanings should be abandoned or destroyed. It does mean that meanings should be reinscribed, that is, played with to find new connections and contexts. Clients are not passive recipients of meaning, but participate in the ongoing activity of creating meaning.

Metaphor and Externalization

Duran and Duran (1995) argue that "when working with traditional peoples, the therapeutic method must take into account the way in which traditional healers think . . . symbol functions as the entity that transforms" (pp. 16, 17). They continue, "The Native American psyche searches for an object onto which to project in order to restore harmony and relationship with the world" (p. 143). Ceremonies often entail the use of concrete symbols such as staffs, feathers, and medicine wheels for their healing effects. Therapists too may benefit from the use of metaphors in helping clients to externalize their problems. Narrative therapists utilize a technique called "externalization" (White, 1991). Therapists listen for remarks that cry out to be viewed in a different light. They use externalization to help a client detach his or her identity from a destructive mode of being. For instance, a client who comments, "I am depressed," may be asked, "How is depression affecting you?" The therapist may choose to ask, "If you could see this depression, what would it look like?" The client may say, "A ditch 15 feet deep." After supplementing the description of the ditch with more details, the therapist may ask, "How might you get out of the ditch?" The client may say, "Ask for help," or "Dig out stair steps to the top." Then the therapist may relate the ditch to depression and a plan of action to get out of depression. Through this use of externalization and metaphor, the therapist helps a client transform indefinite feelings into something more concrete and manageable. In addition, because the problem is no longer identified with the client, but externalized, it ceases to encapsulate the client's identity. The client is "affected by depression" rather than "being depressed," an altered perspective that hopefully helps to unfreeze the client's relationship to his or her depression.

Shifting Perspectives

When one comes into a peyote meeting, the leader often directs one to a particular place in the teepee. A person perceived as a future leader may be positioned in a "special place" in order to get a particular perspective of the fire. Different positions offer participants' unique visions. All of the visions from the different positions are valued. Single perspectives limit our understanding. Being receptive to different perspectives can expand one's awareness, sensitivity, and visionary experiences.

This model emphasizes that therapists pay special attention to any limitations of a client's point of view, taking note of gaps and absences, and considering biases. Therapists sometimes ask clients to shift perspectives. The therapist may have the client assume the perspective of another in order to counter a client's limited "frame up" of an issue and open his or her awareness to new perspectives. One of the writers of this chapter has witnessed many Indian clients expand their perspectives by viewing difficult situations from the perspectives of a level headed, respected grandparent.

Narrative therapist Karl Tomm (1998) uses the method of interviewing the internalized other. He asks the client to take the "I" position of another person and to speak from that person's innermost experience. For example, he asks a mother questions as if she were the daughter, even addressing her by the daughter's name. Questions may consist of how well her mother listens, how well they interact, about other relationships in the family and sociocultural context.

Deconstruction of Power

Duran and Duran (1995) argue, "Successful clinical interventions are not possible in a Native American setting unless the provider or agency is cognizant of the socio-historical factors that have had a devastating effect on the (Native

American socio-political) dynamics" (Duran & Duran, p. 11). Foucault (1980) has described how the productions of power can be particularly insidious. Ghostly normalizing judgments dominate our thinking and actions even as we declare our individuality. We assume our morality, aesthetic views, and assumptions are ours when they may have been uncritically adopted. We may even see ourselves as being fulfilled by the dominant illusory truths. Fear and a survival instinct have required many Indians to introject foreign values.

Therapists can help create a context in which clients can converse about imposed accounts of reality as well as their effects by asking questions regarding topics such as racism, colonialization, sexism, and poverty. White and Epston (1990) encourage therapists to help clients externalize these practices of power and internalize responsibility. Therapists may ask questions that help clients identify how these practices may have affected their own and others' lives and to examine the extent and nature of the practices.

Therapists should also be cognizant of power issues that manifest within families. It is not uncommon that a husband who is oppressed on the job plays out his oppression on his wife and children at home. During sessions, therapists should consider who is excluded from exercising power. Efforts should be made to give presence to marginalized persons who exercise little power in the session. Offering persons with less power a position of power can challenge an oppressive family system. Interrupting the flow of conversations with questions directed at marginal members of the family can be helpful. Also making implicit rules that govern marriages and families explicit is a time-honored technique to deal with unfair power issues. A therapist may directly confront an oppressive family member with questions such as: How is your exercise of power in your family related to your concept of husband? How does it connect or disconnect you from other family members? What is an instance when you may have exercised an excess of power?

Reconstruction

The focus of therapy moves from deconstruction to construction. In order for positive changes to occur, clients need liberation from disempowering problem saturated stories. As therapists help clients disempower toxic stories, they are listening for optimistic traces within stories. White (1995) writes of helping clients "reauthor" their stories (p. 27). Therapists look for times when clients have succeeded against a problem's influence. From this trace of hope therapists and clients attempt to reconstruct more productive stories. Conversations gradually focus more on how the client overcame a problem and the means by which others overcame similar problems. Positive stories coupled with new insights come to the foreground of discussions and provide the courage to create and explore new possibilities.

Support groups can reinforce the new stories and changes in clients' lives. Traditional tribal communities and network therapy has taught us that family and community support can be invaluable. Few therapists have not felt the futility that comes from seeing their clients make major strides in therapy only to regress into old dysfunctional stories and patterns of behavior after therapy has terminated. Interaction with supportive people can encourage clients to resist the influence of problems. Therapists can facilitate their clients immeasurably by learning about support groups that meet periodically in their communities. American Indians typically feel deep connections and responsibilities to extended family members. Uncles and aunts may be referred to as mother and father, and cousins as brothers and sisters. Grandparents often play very important roles in rearing their grandchildren. Therapists cannot afford to ignore the support of the extended family for American Indian clients. If extended family members are not available, therapists may initiate support groups. Many therapists have underutilized this aspect of therapy. If one accepts the social constructionist assumptions outlined in the preceding, a support group becomes an integral aspect of one's treatment approach.

Ongoing Evaluation of Therapy and Clients' Life Stories

Therapists who engage in this therapy regularly deconstruct the therapeutic process. They are encouraged to frequently ask how the session went, and what was and was not helpful at the end of sessions. At the beginning of each session the therapist may ask clients how their lives have changed since the last session. Therapy ends when there are few complaints. The last session is often a thorough review of the benefits and problems with the process, relationships, and the outcome. The American Indian Constructionalist Family Therapy Model is founded on the mission of helping clients develop attitudes of acceptance about ongoing development. Yet, there will always be a tension between the desire to reduce one's life to a specific schema of interpretation and development and the desire for a dynamic and complex relation to ever-changing moments. This model offers structures for clients to become aware of their strengths and possibilities, but ongoing inquiry and discussion is required to combat tendencies toward the sclerosis of life-affirming dynamism.

Case Study

The concepts and methods described in the preceding can best be understood when they are given life in an actual case description. The following contains highlights from therapy with an American Indian family and a Euro-American family.

Session 1

Because of a cancellation, I agreed to see a father and a son who came in without an appointment. The father explained that his 15-year-old son had shamed his family by speaking crudely to a girl at school. The son looked at the floor and said nothing.

The father explained that his family had vital roles in their tribe's religious ceremonies and that he had also succeeded in the White community, making $35,000 per year, and served on committees in town. His son also had responsibilities in ceremonies and had maintained a "B" average at school. The father informed me that these double accomplishments were unusual for full bloods. Before launching into the story he again reported how embarrassed he was about what had happened. During class a "White" girl had shown classmates a tattoo on her stomach. His son had remarked, "I'm going to rape you." He was sent to the principal immediately and because of "further defiance," was suspended and required to see a counselor. I expressed my appreciation to the father for his disclosure and to the son for his listening. I then asked the son if he might tell the story as he had experienced it. He supplemented details to fill the gaps of his father's story. He confided that he had had a "one-time attraction" for the girl he had verbally abused. He added that he thought she was showing off for the "cowboys." At this point, I explained that I had another client to see, but would be interested in conversing with them again in 2 days. I asked if there were others they felt might contribute to the discussion. The father suggested his wife (his son's mother). The son suggested his uncle (his father's brother), and then the father suggested the abused girl and her family, principal, and teacher. He said he would extend an invitation to them.

Session 2

The next session, the father, mother, son, uncle, and the girl's father attended. After introducing ourselves, I asked why each person had attended. The mother said she was there to try to help her son. The uncle explained that he was like a counselor in the family and had a special responsibility to help his nephew grow up. The girl's father began by describing the "incident" from his perspective, supplementing his narrative with his daughter's feelings of fear and his own anger, as well as remarks he had gathered from teachers. He remarked that teachers said the young man was quiet and stubborn, yet they expressed surprise about his harassing remarks. Notwithstanding, the teacher who had referred him to the principal said, "it is the quiet ones you have to worry about" and that he seemed to be angry at Whites. I chose to deconstruct this cliché. He asked me if I had ever read *In Cold Blood* (Capote, 1961), which was "a true story." I responded that I had, but asked him how it informed him about the current situation. He said the "rapist" was the quiet character in the story. I asked, "Do you consider the murderer in the novel an Indian?" He asked, "Why?" "Because he is an Indian," I answered. I wondered if quietness looked and behaved the same in "Indian culture" as it did in his culture. He said he did not know what I meant. The young man's father said that silence was more accepted in Indian culture and that he worried more about "the loud ones." The girl's father said he had never thought about that. I asked him if he could associate other instances in his life where quietness might be associated with rape and murder. He said he had never met anyone who had raped or killed anyone. I asked him exactly what it was about the young man that angered him most. He said it was the brutality of the words he had spoken to his daughter.

Next, the young man offered a revision of the story he had told the previous session, filling in gaps and supplementing his story by responding to details of the story he had just heard. He said he was "quiet" but he thought he was a "fairly nice person." He said that he had written some poems for her and a note to tell her that he "liked" her, but she never responded to them. Instead, she was "being friends" with the cowboys, who "constantly put Indians down." He appealed to us that he could not even wear his Indian t-shirts to school because the cowboys would make fun of him and call him racist. They, on the other hand, did not hesitate to refer to Indians and African Americans as "redskins" and "niggers." He said he was taking out a lot of "mad feelings" on her and that he knew she did not deserve his anger. He added that he would never really have raped her. I turned to the young man's mother and uncle. His mother said she felt sorry for the girl and that she had known girls who had been raped and it was not a word to "throw around casually." His uncle said it was not time for his nephew to talk about how he was being bullied when he was bullying someone. The abused daughter's father then commented that he was still wondering about this young man. The young man said that he felt "trapped." I utilized the metaphor and asked if he would help me visualize about how he felt trapped. He said he was like a badger in a cage. "What does the cage look like?" I asked. He described the cage as being small and with steel bars. The badger was angry about not "being free" and at being "teased by people who didn't understand him." He explained that he felt trapped at school. When the cowboys ridiculed him, he bit the wrong person. Later that session, I utilized the shifting perspectives technique. I asked the young woman's father to put himself inside what he felt was the young man's deepest self and to speak in first person. He began by speaking in third person, but I asked him to speak in first person again as though speaking as the young man. He said, "I made a mistake to harass the young woman. I want to be a kind person but racial prejudice causes me to be angry." I asked the young man for a response. He said he thought the young woman's father understood. I then asked the young man to put himself in this man's deepest self. He said, "I love my daughter and would do anything to protect her. I feel angry but am feeling more trust toward the young man." I asked what was and was not helpful about the session. They felt that the discussion had clarified many things, but all expressed an interest in including the daughter in the next session.

Session 3

All participants in the second session returned, with the addition of the young woman who had been verbally abused. After small talk, I began by focusing therapy on the young woman and asked the others to listen to our conversation as a reflecting team. She indicated that she felt stalked when she received the note and poetry and later felt abused when he made his harsh remark. She remarked that her fathers' description of the previous session explained a lot. She said that it was true that some of the cowboys did verbally abuse Indians. But just because she did not have romantic feelings for him and cowboys ridiculed him, did not justify his "attack" on her. The young man said that his emotions had gotten out of control, and he had taken his anger out on her when she did not deserve it. Then he asked her why she had ignored him after his note and poems. She said that it felt like he was "stalking" her. He said that there was nothing "mean" in his letters and poem. She said, "But I really didn't know you." I then utilized difference to explore notions of romantic interaction. I asked the mother what she believed to be the rules and conventions of "courting." She said that a young man should get to be friends with a girl before making romantic advances. The young man said that that was "old fashioned" and that young people don't "court" anymore. I asked the young woman if she felt there were rules of courting anymore. She said she was currently dating a young man with whom she had talked the whole semester before they became romantically involved. I asked the uncle what he felt were the rules of courting. He said that there were not really any rules but it was important to know if a person was interested in you before "invading their space." The young man's father knew his wife was interested in him by the way she laughed with him and grabbed his arm. I asked the young man about his feelings about the young woman. He said that he was not angry with her but still confused. "What are you confused about?" I asked. "I don't know how she feels about me," he said. She responded, "I don't feel romantic feelings for you, but I'm not mad at you anymore because you don't seem so threatening now." He responded that maybe he was more confused about himself than he was about her. He did not understand why he had acted as he did. At this point, the girl said she hoped he would not feel uneasy around her. He said, "I just kind of feel embarrassed right now." Later, I asked the young man how the stories and remarks would effect his future romantic involvements. He said that he guessed he would move a little slower, waiting for hints about how to approach a girl. All said that it was helpful to hear their children's conversation. The two young people said they understood each other better now. Whereas the young man's family said they wished to have another session, the young woman and father said that they felt that they were satisfied with what had taken place and would not be returning.

Session 4

I opened this session with the question, "What brings you back to therapy this week?" They all said they wanted to understand each other better. I asked if it was acceptable if the mother and uncle could act as a reflective team while I had a conversation with the father and son. I explained the notion of the reflecting team. I asked the son what he knew about his father. He said he was smart, did not drink, went to stomp dances, and was a "great man," but he did not understand why his father was a "suck up" to White people. I asked him to give me an example of what he was talking about. He offered a sketchy story about his father embarrassing him. "My dad was all smiling and stuff talking to this really phony businessman." I asked him questions to supplement his story. "How long ago? What time of day? Where was the encounter? What was he going to do during the meeting? What did the businessman look like? Tell me as much of the conversation as you can remember?" I interspersed questions about his dominant impressions throughout the story. He carefully elaborated on each of his responses. He explained that his father knew that the man was greedy and phony. But his father stood there laughing even when the businessman addressed them with, "How's my redskin friends?" The young man said that he "couldn't stand looking" at his dad and "the phony man." Hoping to move in the direction of deconstructing power, I asked what the story meant. He said that his dad was too "hung up" on "what pleases White people." He added that he wanted his father to care about him, not what the school administration thought about their family. The father patiently listened and showed no visible reaction, then he said it hurt him for his son to think of him as a "suck up." He said his son was wrong if he thought that he cared more about the opinions of others than he cared for his family. His son's immaturity caused him to see friendliness with Whites as "suck up" behavior. He explained, "to make it in this world, you have to let some things run off your back." I asked the mother and uncle to talk to each other about the conversation they had overheard. The mother said it was difficult for her to see her husband and son at odds knowing how close they had been. The father had taught their son stomp dance songs. She wanted them to "get back together." The uncle agreed. He said that he and his brother had gone different ways in some respects. He said he had joined the American Indian Movement (AIM), but his brother had not approved. They had been angry at each other for years, but were able to reunite, although never fully agree, especially on politics. I asked him how they had "reunited." He said that they both "came from the same place," and understood each other even though they were different. I asked, "Where did you come from?" He said they came from "a place where things didn't come easy." They had to learn to feel good about who they were even when others thought they were "dirt." He said he learned that his brother's "putting up with things" was done so he could help his family live better. He said that his nephew should not forget that his father had endured a lot for him and he had cared enough about traditional ways to teach him tribal songs and bring him to Green Corn ceremonies. I let the young man sit in silence in order that he might freely choose whether or not to graft these comments onto his perspective. Next, the father and son responded to the overheard conversation. The father said he wanted to be more supportive of his son. I asked the father what he felt about his son being ridiculed at school. He said that "kids" can be "cruel," and some things they say should be ignored, whereas others shouldn't. He said that he was going to inform the principal about the cowboys' remarks. The son retorted that he did not want his father to call the principal because he could handle the situation himself. The father said that he would like his son to tell him when the cowboys ridiculed him. The son said he was glad his father was "on his side" and when things got "really bad" again he would tell him. I asked the family what they felt they were getting from therapy. They said they understood each other better. They agreed that they wanted to come back the next week.

Session 5

I began the session thinking about helping the family to move more in the direction of reconstruction by helping everyone to have an equal opportunity to express opinions in session. The son responded that his mother had not said much. The mother said that it was not unusual. At this point, I explained the "Talking Feather Technique," which, if utilized would allow everybody an equal opportunity to be heard and wondered if they would be willing to participate. The father told me that his older brother should take the talking feather first. Affirming traditional hierarchy, the uncle said it was "their way" for older men to speak first but efforts should be made for women to be respected too. The mother agreed. After several minutes of silence to allow time to think about their values, the uncle was given the talking feather first. He said that "being fair" was the primary value that he tried to live by. He explained that his parents had taught him "to expect fairness." I asked him to expand on his story of fairness. He said he remembered how his mother and father always gave equally to him and his brother. I wondered how "fairness" looked in other contexts. He said that he had gone to Wounded Knee to support the people there and that he had taken his idea of fairness into that situation. Fairness was not just expecting your share, but also supporting fairness for all people. He said that fairness looked brave at Wounded Knee because it was a dangerous situation. The talking feather was passed around to each person for a response. Each person responded but the father, the uncle's brother, was especially moved. He said that even though he and his brother had often argued about issues revolving around Wounded Knee, he had been proud of his brother's action. His brother took the feather again and responded that his brother had gotten an education to promote greater fairness for Indians in his own way. I asked if it would be appropriate if the mother speak next in an effort to address her marginality in our counseling sessions. The mother said "the family" was her parent and her own most cherished value. Her parents went through hard times but always provided sufficient food for the children. She always felt loved. She and her son had had a hard time recently when her mother died. The son motioned for the feather next. He was like his mother in that he was close to his grandmother. The uncle said that it was a good thing to be "tender-hearted." We agreed to continue the activity next session.

Session 6

The father took the talking feather and said, "Pride is my value." "What does pride mean?" I asked. He said, "doing what you do well . . . it's also having people respect you for what you do." He said that one of his uncles used to come to their house drunk, crying, asking for money and causing conflict. One morning he saw him passed out on the main street of a nearby town. He said he felt sad for him but also "embarrassed." While looking down on his inebriated uncle, he told himself he would not drink and that he was going to college. His parents were proud that he went to college. He explained that "in the Indian way" you represent your people and family with your actions. I asked, "How does enduring slander relate to pride?" He said that in order to have real pride you sometimes had to humble yourself. Because he endured it without retaliation, he believed he was now in a position to bring about change through his example. Other reflecting team members offered similar and contrasting views about pride. The uncle worried that enduring too much harassment might cause such a loss of pride that a person might never get it back. The mother worried that pride could cause one to think one was better than others were. The father responded by saying there was a definite limit to the "negative remarks" he would endure. I asked what the limit was. He said he learned to not react impulsively but to take time to think before he reacted. He then said that he did not want any of us to think he believed his uncle was not as good as he. Nonetheless, he believed his uncle could have offered more support to his family if he had not drunk so much. When the son took the feather, he said "being an Indian" was his "main value." Again, I looked for difference in this concept. I asked him if he could tell me his story about his "being Indian." He replied that he had gone through the scratching ceremony during Green Corn Ceremonies and that the experience united him with other tribal members. He explained that an elder told him that when he endured the scratches down his back, he was to reflect on the pain other tribal members have endured through history and consider that he would die someday like all other earthly creatures. After a pause, he said, "I am proud to be an Indian." Later, I asked him if he had ever seen an instance when someone "acted too Indian." Everyone laughed. He said he knew a man who thinks he's more Indian than anyone else is. He was always correcting everybody about Indian things. I asked the young man how he was the same or different from this man. He said that sometimes he was a "know it all." I said, "So you know the one and only Indian way sometimes." He laughed. He explained that he had to "catch himself" from being a "know it all" at school sometimes. The others had also been scratched during "Green Corn" ceremonies and spoke of how proud they were of the young man and that they were glad it meant something to him. We talked at some length about an unassuming Indian identity and striking a balance between affirming traditional values and being proud of their heritage and at the same time allowing people the space to "go in their own directions even if they seem like White directions." The uncle looked at the young man and added that sometimes it was justified to point out that it was a White direction that some Indians were taking. During the last 30 minutes of this hour-and-a-half conversation, we concentrated on empowering stories. I asked what they specifically had heard during the conversations that would help their future interactions. The mother said that she respected her son's anger about being ridiculed by the "cowboys" and intended to offer her support to him. His father said that even if he and his son did not agree about some things, he respected his pride and intended to try to understand it better. The uncle said that he was most pleased with the remarks about respecting one another. The young man said that he did not feel so alone and angry as before. The uncle told the young man, "You'll make other mistakes with women, Romeo. I hope you don't make the same ones again." Before leaving, we discussed setting up biweekly counseling with the school counselor for the young man. We discussed his greater involvement in his school's Indian club. Both parents said they intended to become more involved in the Johnson O'Malley Indian program at the school.

Case Conceptualization

The preceding case study demonstrates the possibilities of the American Indian Constructionist approach with an American Indian family suffering from acculturative stress. The family members were distressed over the lack of kinship they experienced in an oppressive and alienating society. Each of them believed that the attainment of solidarity within their family would act as a bulwark against external oppression. Each of them told stories about how they had been marginalized from different forms of power by being labeled, ignored, and discriminated against. They had tried to fit into mainstream society and—being rejected—felt rage, embarrassment, and emptiness. They also bore some of the responsibility of reacting to oppression with dysfunctional thoughts and behavioral patterns. Their greatest distress came from their realization that estrangement had invaded their family. Loud oppressive discourses of dominant society had drowned the voices of their hearts and had been directing their behaviors. The therapist tried to help them to hear and understand these voices of dominant society that governed their thinking and actions. The therapist tried to help them to become more critically conscious of society's oppressive dominant stories, and reconnect them to their own and their tribal life stories, beliefs, actions, experiences, and interactions. These sessions involved invoking a wide gambit of traditional and postmodern rituals and techniques to combat the lies of oppressive society, forces of alienation, feelings of resignation, and impotent rage. They helped to bring about transformation and renewed feelings of kin-ship. The constructionist perspective provided a gateway for those outside the typically insulated counseling room who may have been affected by the problem to enter and partake in the healing process. Externalization and metaphor helped the young man invoke his identification with the badger's essence. The Talking Feather Technique helped family members listen to the values of their deceased parents and grandparents. The use of difference helped the family members to honor the warriors within themselves. And the deconstruction of power ap-proach helped family members to hear the dominant stories that pressured their thoughts and behaviors. The open-ended questions and quasi-nondirectional nature of the interventions offered clients the freedom and space to proceed in ongoing meaning-making activity rather than arrive at resolutions that some-times may be equated with premature closure.

Considerations

When presenting this approach at conferences, participants express several con-cerns. For some, the radical democratization of therapy is objectionable. But let us be clear, we do not deny a provisional authority from which to interpret, criticize, decide, and act. It is true that we are skeptical of the expert role that many psychologists assume. We associate expert absolutism with reductionism in therapy that limits the richness of meaning. Still, we affirm that although this approach attempts at further democratization of therapy, it is somewhat direc-tive. Therapists should be careful before abandoning directive techniques that could challenge damaging hierarchies. Questions are used to guide clients to bring forth traces that can help alter toxic narratives and create new life stories. American Indians have long utilized directive rituals to promote mental health and know their value.

Nonetheless, as demonstrated in the preceding case example, when appro-priate and possible, allowing persons to arrive at their own thoughts and feel-ings through an egalitarian process is likely to be more profound than if imposed from on high. Collaborative decisions concerning a client's therapy is a funda-mental idea of this approach, although it is rarely attained. Even with a collabo-rative perspective, therapists must be vigilant to guard against unconsciously participating in alienating practices of power. Therapists must be careful not to lead clients in directions they think they should go, lest they are guilty of marginalizing clients from their own stories. For instance, a therapist may make oversimplified assumptions about an American Indian family. As discussed, persons living in American Indian cultures may not place the same boundaries around a family as do other cultures. Herding families into something that is called a "normal" family is equivalent to colonialization in this context. It is crucial to look at our assumptions about families and be careful not to colonize our clients' realities by imposing our views on them.

Some criticize the American Indian Constructionalist approach for lacking definable behavioral goals. It is true that it is not uncommon for beginning therapists who base their work on postmodernist principles to open clients up to multiple meanings but leave them adrift in regard to provisional resolutions and behavioral change. Inherent in the postmodern dismantling of authority and efforts to avoid reductionism is the problem of how to help clients in the area of intentional action. Collaboration may end in discourse instead of action. This does not have to be the case. Most Narrative therapists, for example, work very hard to water the seeds of change found in troubled persons' narratives. Therapists need to take one more step to move from insight to strategies for action. The emphasis on multiple perspectives and provisional resolutions need not preclude a plan and an implementation of behavioral change.

Some critics of this approach say that clients want "answers" and definite resolutions to their problems. They ask, "Won't ongoing questioning contribute to our clients' dehabilitating feelings of self-doubt?" Certainly, a therapist must be cognizant of his or her clients' limits for inner exploration. But the more serious danger is that a therapist contributes to a client's premature closure to self-exploration. Doubt opens us up to new perspectives. Accepting the indeterminacy of life, yet resolving to decide and act anyway is the goal of this therapeutic approach. Intrigue with life's mysteries is viewed as more healthy than assuming final enlightenment. The basis of this approach is that it promotes renewal in the most radical fashion. The character of resolutions is that they are provisional. They are open-ended and subject to renegotiation and reinterpretation through discourse.

Conclusion

This chapter has been an attempt to combine American Indian notions of healing and postmodernist ideas to explore the possibilities of generating greater psychological health for American Indian families without getting lost in colonialization logic. It has been an attempt to accept the American Indian experience of ongoing hybridity as a state of possibility. For generations, it has been the lot of American Indian people to carefully sift through foreign tools and machinery, horses, food and drink, governmental systems, and interactional patterns. It is crucial to carefully sift postmodern and postcolonial thought through unique American Indian modes of being and thinking. Too often psychologists working with American Indians utilize approaches that are thoroughly enclosed in colonialist discourse that usurp tribal histories and cultural identities. The American Indian Constructionalist Family Therapy Model attempts to undermine the authority of colonialist narratives by offering space for American Indian individuals to explore the social dimension of their individuality. Some may see postmodern thought simply as an another form of Western psychology's ongoing colonialization. Certainly it cannot be accepted unconditionally and our synthesis of it with American Indian ideas about healing involved sifting it of its corruptions. We have attempted a thoroughgoing evaluation of our theory's assumptions. For us, it appears to offer a relentless criticism of oppressive socially constructed realities, something that cannot be said of many Western psychological models. We described the American Indian Constructionalist Family Therapy Models as succinctly as we can and welcome ongoing revisions that may lead to a model even more helpful to American Indian families.

Discussion Questions

1. Social constructionism has been criticized for placing too much emphasis on controlling discourses embedded in institutions and structures and not enough on individual volition. This therapy model incorporates postmodernism's emphasis on difference, and deconstruction that emphasizes individuals' powers to undo social discourses. Discuss the extent to which the authors effectively struck a balance and the therapy's usefuleness with clients?

2. What are some assumptions of other family therapies that this approach calls into question and may even be in conflict with?

3. The case study describes families who experienced domination in areas such as race, sex, social oppression, and civil rights, as well as other forms of subordination. How might this approach be more or less effective when treating families who experience multiple systems of domination?

4. What are some societal messages that members in the family have received? How does the approach facilitate awareness of the influence of these messages, and help them to want, reject, or modify them?

5. How does this approach attempt to be both respectful to American Indian traditions and yet challenge subordination struggles that may occur between women and men?

6. How does this approach address lateral oppression, or the oppression of American Indians toward other American Indians? How may the fairly relativistic perspective of this model make these types of issues difficult to deal with, or does it?

7. Describe some family problems with which you feel this approach may not be so efficacious?

References

Andersen, T. (1987). The reflecting team: Dialogue and meta-dialogue in clinical work. *Family Process, 26,* 415–428.

Attaquin, H. (1987). There are differences. In R. G. Carlson (Eds.), *Rooted like the ash trees* (pp. 20–23). Naugatuck, CT: Eagle Wing Press.

Attneave, C. (1974). *Family networks.* New York: Vintage Books.

Attneave, C. L. (1985). Practical counseling with American Indian and Alaska Native clients. In P. Pedersen (Ed.), *Handbook of cross-cultural counseling and therapy* (pp. 135–140). Westport, CT: Greenwood Press.

Beauvais, F., Chavez, E. L., Oetting, E. R., Deffenbacher, J. L., & Cornell, G. R. (1996). Drug use, violence, and victimization among white American, Mexican American, and American Indian dropouts, students and academic problems, and students in good academic standing. *Journal of Counseling Psychology, 43,* 292–299.

Bishinik (Durant, OK), January 2002 (p. 4).

Capote, T. (1961). *In cold blood: A true account of a multiple murder and its consequences.* New York: Random House.

Combs, G., & Freedman, J. (1998). Tellings and retellings. *Journal of Marital and Family Therapy, 24*(4), 405–408.

Derrida, J. (1973). "Difference" and "form and meaning: A note on the phenomenology of language." In D. B. Allison (Ed. & Trans.), *Speech and phenomena and other essays on Husserl's theory of signs* (pp. 107–160). Evanston, IL: Northwestern University Press.

Derrida, J. (1976). *Of grammatology* (D. Chakravsity, Trans.). Baltimore: Johns Hopkins University Press.

Descartes, R. (1960), *Discourse on method and meditations* (L. J. Lafleur, Trans.). Indianapolis: Bobbs-Merrill Company. (Original work published 1641).

Duran, E., & Duran, B. (1995). *Native American postcolonial psychology.* Albany, NY: State University of New York Press.

Foucault, F. (1980). *Power/knowledge: Selected interviews and other writings, 1972–1977.* (J. Faubion, Ed., C. Gordon, Trans.). New York: Pantheon.

Freedman, J. & Combs, G. (1996). *Narrative therapy: The social construction of preferred realities.* New York: W. W. Norton.

Gergen, K. J. (1994). *Realities and relationships: Sounding in social construction.* Cambridge, MA: Harvard University Press.

Grandesso, M. A. (1996). *The Marriage Clinic: A scientifically-based marital therapy.* New York: W. W. Norton.

Guignon, C. (1998). Narrative explanation in psychotherapy. *American Behavioral Scientist, 41,* 558–577.

Laclau, E., & Mouffe, C. (1985). *Hegemony and socialist strategy.* London: Harvestor Press.

LaFromboise, T. D., & Rowe, W. (1983). Skills training for bicultural competence: Rationale and application. *Journal of Counseling Psychology, 30,* 589–595.

Lefley, H. (1986). Why cross-cultural training? In H. Lefley & P. Pedersen (Eds.), *Cross-cultural training for mental health professionals* (pp. 90–104). Springfield, IL: Charles C Thomas.

Momaday, N. S. (1966). *House made of dawn.* New York: Harper & Row.

Native American Times (Tulsa, OK), January 15, 2002 (p. 1).

Red Horse, Y. (1982). A cultural network model: Perspectives for adolescent services and para-professional training In S. M. Manson (Ed.) *New directions in prevention among American Indian and Alaska Native communities* (pp. 173–184). Portland, OR: Oregon Health Sciences University.

Silko, L. (1977). *Ceremony.* New York: Penguin Books.

Speck, R.V., & Attneave, C. (1973). *Family networks.* New York: Pantheon.

Tomm, K. (1998). A question of perspective. *Journal of Marital and Family Therapy, 24*(4), 409–413.

Watts, A. (1958). *Nature, man and woman.* New York: Vintage Books.

White, M. (1991). Deconstruction and therapy. *Dulwich Centre Newsletter, 3,* 21–40.

White, M. (1995). *Re-authoring lives: Interviews and essays.* Adelaide, Australia: Dulwich Centre Publications.

White, M., & Epston, D. (1990). *Narrative means to therapeutic ends.* New York: W. W. Norton.

Chapter 3

NTU Psychotherapy and African American Youth

Laurence E. Jackson
Henry Gregory
Maisha G. Davis

This chapter describes NTU psychotherapy, an approach based on African philosophy that emphasizes spirituality. The relationship between the client and therapist is central because the therapist is viewed as a conduit for healing. NTU psychotherapy is structured into five phases and aims to facilitate a change in the client's perspective, which creates new possibilities, and formulate solutions. All behavior is considered to be based in positive intention and clients' strengths are emphasized. The case study demonstrates the approach with an at-risk African-American adolescent male suspended from school.

Limitations of Traditional Western Approaches

NTU psychotherapy is a treatment model that emphasizes the significance of culture, and particularly the role of spirituality in the lives of those being treated. In much the same way that Kuhn (1970) described the process of scientific revolutions, this approach grew out of a frustration with prevailing traditional Western approaches to mental health treatment, which essentially ignored cultural dynamics in both conceptualization and treatment of African Americans and their prescription for mental health treatment. Regarding the mental health and treatment of African Americans, several noted scholars and practitioners (Akbar, 1981; Boyd-Franklin, 1989; Nobles, 1980, 1986; Parham, White, & Ajamu, 1999; White, 1980) challenged traditional approaches that largely characterized Black families as pathological or, the ostensibly less negative view, culturally deprived. Black families were typically characterized as lacking insight, inherently psychologically deficient, and ultimately not responsive to treatment

(White, 1980). An increasing number of scholars began to challenge the appropriateness of traditional approaches until it became widely accepted that treatment approaches based on one set of cultural phenomena, in this case treatment approaches based on European values and world views, are at best limited in their application to "different" cultural dynamics (McGoldrick, Pearce, & Giordano, 1982). This is akin to what Kuhn (1970) describes as a paradigm shift. That is, when a prevailing model or theory can no longer adequately explain a phenomenon, new models evolve.

African Philosophy and the NTU Model

NTU psychotherapy is an alternative treatment model that is based on an African philosophy. Unlike most traditional models, its values and philosophical assumptions are explicitly stated. In a seminal article on NTU psychotherapy, Phillips (1990) takes considerable care in discussing the core principles and assumptions on which this model is based. Much like Minuchin's (1974) structural family therapy model, the NTU model developed from direct clinical experience with predominantly urban, African American families.

The NTU approach is particularly relevant for African Americans because historically, spirituality has been an extremely important dimension in the lives of African Americans. Traditional approaches to mental health focus almost exclusively on the mind and body dimensions. Moreover, academic institutions tend to view spirituality in strict religious terms, thus avoiding its inclusion in training curriculum. According to Boyd-Franklin (1989), "training in the mental health fields largely ignores the role of spirituality and religious beliefs in the development of the psyche and in its impact on family life. In the treatment of Black families, this oversight is a serious one" (p. 78).

The word "NTU" (pronounced "in-to") originates from the Bantu peoples of central Africa (Phillips, 1990). In an in-depth analysis of African philosophy, Jahn (1961) describes NTU as the cosmic, universal force from which all of life emanates. Phillips (1998), the primary architect of NTU psychotherapy, envisioned a treatment model that emphasizes spirituality, because from an African world view, at core humans are spiritual beings. Phillips (1998, p. 359) states that

> NTU is a force, a spiritual energy, an inner vigor that is ubiquitous. It manifests itself in man, beast, thing, place, time, beauty, etc. and is both immanent and transcendent. The perspective of human beings as energy and spirit is not merely an academic discussion, but has significant implications for mental health healing, and the practice of psychotherapy.

Thus, the NTU model, in sharp contrast to most Western approaches, begins with the assumption that the most fundamental construct or dimension to humans is a spiritual force. Based on this assumption, our "spirituality," then, becomes the platform for both the conceptualization and development of treatment methods. NTU psychotherapy utilizes our spiritual essence as the primary vehicle for healing.

Culture and Context

There are six major characteristics of the NTU approach: (a) Spiritually oriented, (b) Family Focused, (c) Cultural Competence, (d) Competency-Based, (e) Holistic/ Systemic, and (f) Values-Driven. Each characteristic represents and frames a dimension of the client's life that may be considered during the therapeutic process. Although few clients stay in treatment long enough to directly approach each issue, the skillful NTU therapist/counselor assesses the client along these dimensions and negotiates goals to be worked on with the client from this repertoire.

Spiritually Oriented

Acknowledgment that there is a primal, creative, sustaining force in the universe.

- Does the client express an applied reference or respect for some universal force, that is, God, nature, life relationships?
- What is his or her idea of that force?
- What is the nature of his or her relationship with that force?
- How does the client feel about his or her relationship with that force?
- Is the client behaving in a manner consistent with his or her idea of proper behavior?
- How does the client feel about his or her behavior?
- Is the client aware of his or her (spiritual) purpose?

Family-Focused

The entire family, including both biological and psychological members, is the focus of treatment, whether they are present or not.

- Who is in the family?
- Who is absent, unavailable, or has a difficult or toxic relation with the client?
- What are the relationships like between the client and family members?
- How does the client feel about his or her relationships?
- How does the client act out his or her feelings about the relationships?
- What does the client want of and in the relationships with family members?
- How can the client get more of what he or she wants in relationships with family members?

Cultural Competence

An awareness and appreciation for the unique characteristics of a group bound together by common beliefs, attitudes, and/or behaviors.

• What cultural groups (race, ethnicity, gender, social activity, religion, socio-economic class, profession, etc.) is the client a member of?
• What beliefs and assumptions do these groups promote?
• What beliefs and assumptions are primary in the client's life?
• How do these beliefs and assumptions affect the client's behavior?
• What feelings are associated with the group memberships for the client?
• Where is the client in his or her identity-formation process?
• Who does the client want to be in the future?
• What must he or she do to claim the future identity?

Competency-Based

An awareness, and support and reinforcement of strength, competence, capacity, and resiliency as opposed to pathology.

• What does the client do well?
• What does the client like about himself or herself?
• What do others like about the client?
• What does the therapist/counselor appreciate about the client?
• What adaptive skills does the client possess?
• How does the client's pathology work for him or her?
• What are the client's intentions?
• What does he or she do that is consistent with his or her intentions?
• What healthy ways does the client use to take care of herself or himself?
• What healthy ways does the client use to change his or her mood when the mood is not pleasant or desirable?
• What is the client's predominant learning style?
• Which of the seven basic intelligences does the client use to negotiate his or her world?
• In what positive way does the client manifest power?

Holistic/Systemic

Recognition that all life is interconnected both internally (body, mind, and spirit) as well as externally.

• What is the status of the client's physical health and health habits (eating, resting, exercising, hygiene, etc.)?

- What is the client's mental status (cognitive and emotional functioning)?
- Is the client spiritually grounded—actualizing his or her spiritual values?
- Are the client's body, mind, and spirit in harmony?
- Is the client able to identify and utilize help and assistance?
- Is the client able to see the relationship between his or her behavior and his or her circumstance?
- Can the client take responsibility for his or her own actions and issues in relational interactions?
- Is the client connected to others in his or her family and community?
- Does the client possess relational and interpersonal skills?

Values-Driven

Behavioral commitment to a set of values that are life enhancing for the individual, family, and community.

- Unity: Does the client work well with others?
- Self-Determination: Does the client take care of himself or herself? Does the client think for himself or herself? Is the client aware of and resistant to societal programming?
- Collective Work and Responsibility: Does the client do his or her fair share? Does the client contribute to family and community welfare? Does the client value service?
- Cooperative Economics: How well does the client manage money? Is the client meeting his or her earning potential? Does the client contribute to the economic well-being of the family and community?
- Creativity: Does the client contribute to the esthetics of the community, thereby making a more nurturing, growth supporting environment for everyone?
- Purpose: Does the client accept a purpose for his or her life that enhances humanity?
- Faith: Does the client believe in himself or herself, his or her family, his or her community and God?

Core Principles

The NTU model subscribes to four principles that reflect African philosophy and establish the core tenets from which to understand health and healing (Phillips, 1990). The four principles are: (a) Harmony, (b) Balance, (c) Authenticity, and (d) Interconnectedness. Optimum health is a reflection of the extent, or measure, of the manifestation of these principles in one's life.

Harmony

Harmony is created when we move in concert with the universe. Everything in the universe pulsates, from individual cells to the solar systems. Each of us has a note, a rhythm, and a pace that is uniquely ours. Individual harmony is supported physically when we eat nutritiously, exercise regularly, rest appropriately, and practice good hygiene. Mental harmony is supported when we learn to observe and process the functioning of our minds and ultimately make choices that program positive mental responses into our experiences. Spiritual harmony is supported when we acknowledge a relationship with a Higher Power and affirm this understanding behaviorally.

Central to African philosophy is the belief that humans are a manifestation of divine energy and, by design, function optimally when they are in "harmony" both with their environment and within themselves. In this regard, harmony is more a "state of being." When one is in harmony within (self) and without (environment), one experiences positive health. To achieve a state of harmony, one's internal system must operate properly. A good working car requires that multiple levels of systems work in concert—the engine, transmission, air pressure in tires, wheel bearings, electrical system, etc. Likewise, the human organism requires uniformed operation among its multifaceted physical, emotional, and spiritual systems, which results in harmony when operating in concert. Similarly, from an African world view, the same energy or force creates both humans and everything living in the environment. The environment is an extension of us, and we are an extension of it. This suggests the need for positive relationships with both humans and nature. We are in harmony when both our internal and external constructs are working together. In this context, perhaps one of the most profound examples of harmony is love—only when we love ourselves (internal) are we able to love others (environment). The human organism is designed to experience harmony when it is in confluence with life's internal and external forces.

Balance

Balance is said to be the cousin of harmony. Although harmony refers to a state of being, balance refers to the "process" of achieving harmony. To function optimally, the human organism requires a balance of seemingly opposite functions. Proper muscle development, for example, requires both tension and relaxation. To be alert, one must get adequate rest and sleep. The holistic health movement also illustrates the importance of balance, with its emphasis on attending to physical, mental, and spiritual health.

From a clinical perspective, Phillips (1998) discusses how a therapist can act to balance the energy of a client from a NTU framework.

When an organism is not in balance, it oscillates at a different or less-harmonic frequency. Since we each have a biofield (energy field) which surrounds and penetrates the physical body, a person, particularly a NTU therapist skilled in energy work, can knowingly and divertly experience the unstable energy of another person (client) which provides invaluable assessment information. Since energy is not bounded by the physical skin we are always in contact with the biofield or "vibration" of others. (p. 16)

The principle of balance, therefore, involves an ongoing dynamic and interactive process of regulating seemingly competing functions in order to achieve "harmonious" health.

Interconnectedness

The principle of interconnectedness refers to the African (Bantu) belief that all elements in the universe are connected, as stated earlier, by a creative, divine force (NTU). Thus, as Phillips (1998, p. 360) points out, "human beings are more than flesh and bones, cells and protein; rather we are composed of the same stuff of the universe and are in dynamic equilibrium with a universe of energy. We are connected to all life and from an African world view, connected across time and space in the spirit world." As a measure of optimum health, then, interconnectedness has clear implications for the quality of human relationships. Simply, we need each other. Similarly, Phillips (1998) defines good mental health as the extent to which a person is and feels connected to others. He further suggests that love is simply interconnectedness intensified.

The principle of interconnectedness is perhaps readily familiar because its basic premise, that we are all of the same substance—we are all the same—is a precept in most world religions. Perhaps because the concept of love is so strongly associated with religious dogma, most models of therapy have steered clear of it. In the traditional psychoanalytical model, the therapist is instructed to keep distant from the client. In behavioral approaches, the significance of the relationship between the therapist and client is minimized and, instead, emphasis is on achieving objective tasks.

The principle of interconnectedness is particularly germane to the client–therapist relationship. If one's health is related to the quality of his or her relationship with others, then the client–therapist relationship is seen as a vehicle to promote healing. In sharp contrast to approaches that prescribe distance, the NTU approach encourages closeness. Although it is recognized that problematic "countertransference" issues can arise, attunement to the spiritual "sacredness" of the relationship serves as an internal guide for therapeutic direction and boundaries (Phillips, 1998).

Authenticity

The principle of authenticity refers to the extent to which we manifest our true selves. It is both a state and a process. When we are authentic, we are attuned to our divine nature and are regulated by it. Yet, largely because we live in a culture with strong material influences, the "process" of achieving authenticity is often difficult. From an NTU perspective, our authentic self reflects our natural divine state—one in which we feel connected to our Creator and relate to our environment (e.g., other people) in the same manner that our Creator relates to us. When we are authentic, we are our very best. Authenticity, then, much like the principle of harmony, is something that we strive for intuitively and affectively, more so than cognitively; we "know" we are being authentic. It also simply "feels" right. When we are authentic, we operate out of a sense of wholeness and confidence. We feel inner-directed, attuned to our spiritual selves, and less directed by outside influences. When we are faced with life problems while in an authentic mode, we are able to "respond" based on spiritual insight. This is not to say that we are shielded from tragic occurrences or pain; rather, it means that when attuned to our real selves, our divine selves, we know that we will endure life's greatest challenges.

Role of the Therapist

The role of the therapist, as with most models of therapy, is a critical variable in the NTU model. The emphasis on spirituality, particularly as it pertains to the actions of the therapist, distinguishes NTU psychotherapy from most Western approaches. The most fundamental differences can be seen in four areas: (a) the emphasis on the relationship between therapist and client, (b) the notion of *vessel* versus *causal* agent, (c) the use of therapeutic techniques, and (d) the health of the therapist.

Phillips (1990) maintains that NTU psychotherapy assigns a "premium" on the relationship between the client and therapist for two important reasons. The first is the belief that psychotherapy, from an Africentric perspective, is a spiritual and therefore sacred process. The relationship, in this sense, is bigger than two individuals; rather, the relationship establishes a divine context for healing to occur. Ideally, then, the therapist recognizes that the relationship is "sanctioned" by the Creator and, therefore, should be revered and authentically valued. The second point Phillips makes is that in an Africentric value system, the "person-to-person orientation" is key; that is, how the client "feels" about the therapist is key. Similarly, Boyd-Franklin (1989) stresses that when working with Black families, therapists must actively work to "join" each family member. Therapy cannot effectively begin until the client feels good about the relationship.

The notion of vessel versus cause refers to the attribution the therapist assigns to what or who causes healing. The NTU model teaches that the therapist, in essence, is a vessel or conduit, for the NTU force (healing energy). Healing, then, occurs "through" you, not "by" you. This is a very important distinction because it creates powerful dynamics in the way the therapist relates to the client, and vice versa. A personal story can help clarify this point. During one writer's clinical internship at a hospital, he was required to attend an orientation with all of the incoming medical doctors who were beginning their internships at the hospital. A speaker, himself a physician and faculty member of the hospital, said, "always remember that you are the equivalent of God to your patients, you have the skills to determine life or death." Although I trust that he was attempting to reinforce the seriousness of their new jobs as physicians, his comments, I believe, foster a dynamic of doctor as powerful and patient as powerless. In sharp contrast, the NTU model presupposes that all people are equally valued. More specifically, the therapist has been "called" to remind the client of his or her innate self-healing potential and attempts to "share" energy with the client system in order to reignite the flame.

In so doing the NTU therapist works with each family/client from a strength-based perspective. Rather than seeking to remedy deficits, the therapist seeks to facilitate health by way of identifying and building upon existing family and individual strengths, some of which often are not acknowledged by the family/client. The therapist must also be able to view each family/client objectively and nonjudgmentally. In order to be a conduit for healing he or she must be discerning of these qualities within the client/family that are essential for the therapist to connect with to facilitate healing and must be continuously working on his or her own counseling issues and concerns.

In the use of therapeutic techniques, the therapist relies more on his or her intuition, and less so on prescribed steps. This is not to minimize the importance of knowledge and skills pertaining to specific techniques. Rather, knowing "when" and "how" to use techniques is the key issue from an NTU perspective. The timing and use of techniques should be driven by a spiritual process. As described by Phillips (1990, p. 66):

> As the therapist becomes more attuned, the spiritual forces that allow for intuition and inspiration or, what Gestalt therapist Fritz Perls described as the "Ah-ha" experience, are more readily available and likely to occur within the client's system. Similarly, when the therapist is more attuned, then she or he is more spontaneous and more accurate in her or his selection of effective and operative therapeutic techniques. The therapist just "seems to know" when to utilize this or that technique as opposed to rigidly following a prescribed plan. In the parlance of athletes, the therapist is "operating in the zone."

The health of the therapist is an unavoidable factor in the NTU model. If the therapist is seen more as a "vessel," then it follows that optimum functioning occurs when the vessel is clear and clean. This, then, suggest that therapists should actively practice health-enhancing behavior, proactively working on their mind, body, and spirit. Because NTU relies on the therapist's ability to attune to the client, the therapist functions best when "centered" and free from distractions. As most clinicians learn in their training, "countertransference" occurs when we are not aware of our own issues.

NTU Applications with Adolescent Populations

Progressive Life Center (PLC), a service agency that serves at-risk adolescents and their families, foster children, substance-abusing individuals, and other subgroups, utilizes the NTU approach widely. Coupled with the NTU approach, Rites of Passage is the main group treatment modality used with the adolescents. A description of the application of each of the four principles in working with adolescents follows.

Harmony has a dual designation in the NTU approach (Gregory & Harper, 2001). First, it is a principle that refers to the union among body, mind, and spirit that is required to experience optimal health. Second, it is the first stage/phase of intervention in the five stages of the NTU interview process. As part of the interview, its purpose is to create a union between the interventionist and the client system.

Connecting with youth and establishing a relationship in the harmony phase is frequently a matter of verbally demonstrating appreciation and interest in issues of interest and value to the youth. Music, sports, fashion, and peers are some of the common themes to which we expose the youth to begin an interaction. For youth who are remanded to our service and consequently resistant, the harmony process of necessity may begin with empathetic expressions that acknowledge the youth's feelings and concerns relevant to his or her forced participation. Many times the experience of feeling heard and acknowledged is enough to at least get a youth's attention.

We ritualize as much of our interaction with youth as possible, particularly the group interactions. Rites of Passage is a psychoeducational process purposed to provide guidance and support to youth who are transitioning from one stage of development to another; that is, from late childhood to adolescence or from adolescence to adulthood. Youth who participate are required to complete a series of developmental and therapeutic tasks to demonstrate their readiness to transition to the next stage of their development. The components of Rites of Passage are orientation, rite of separation (retreat), rites group, naming ceremony, and graduation/transformation. All rites groups start with a harmony-creating ritual, the unity circle that facilitates intrapersonal and interpersonal bonding and connection. In the unity circle we may use affirmations, visualizations, guided meditations, and nondenominational prayers to assist youth in becoming still enough to hear the "small voice within" that offers nurturance and guidance to the listener. We refer to the Rites of Passage throughout this chapter.

Balance, the second NTU principle, refers to the state of equilibrium that we experience when we behaviorally balance the effect of apparent opposites that exist in a continuum. Life is diunital (Nichols, 1976), not dichotomous. Opposites are complimentary, not competitive. Every opposing force or energy is validated by its opposite. This is an important issue because it is a major characteristic of traditional African logic that remains part of the psyche of many people of color. Everything is relative and contextual from this point of view. There are no absolutes. There is no finite White or Black, right or wrong, male or female; there are only degrees of each. The constructivists (Efran, Lukens, & Lukens, 1990) say that our labeling of experience in finite terms is more a matter of social agreements than the nature of the phenomena. Are not who is White and who is Black a matter of political designation; are not right and wrong relative; and are there not degrees of male and female?

One of the primary balance issues with adolescents is the balance of their dependency with autonomy needs. These seeming opposite needs are actually complimentary, expressing the appropriate priorities of both the youth and the parents. This experience of conflicting priorities is an opportunity to teach our youth to negotiate with their parents. Within the context of family therapy we frequently facilitate a negotiation of decision-making powers by having the adolescent and parents make offers and counteroffers to each other. Most youth see autonomy as an all-or-nothing process. When they are assisted in an ongoing negotiation around issues such as curfews, allowances, dating, and so on they become empowered. The parent(s) in this negotiation usually is concerned about responsibility and accountability, the issues that are the foundation of autonomy. The key to the negotiation is keeping the communication flowing by focusing on intentions using relabeling and reframing to emphasize the positive intent of the requests and responses.

A more subtle balance issue common to adolescents is that of gender roles. Many innercity youth have skewed and exaggerated ideas of what is appropriate male and female behavior, particularly in relation to dating. Promiscuity and abuse, both verbal and physical, can result from this skewed perspective. Compounding this unbalanced view and value of gender differences is their lack of affective knowledge or emotional competence and a preference for a predominantly cognitive style of knowing. The NTU approach, acknowledging that people of African descent are generally predisposed to an affective orientation, emphasizes learning to read, process, and respond to feelings in one's self and others as necessary for healthy productive relationships. This emphasis is promoted in all therapeutic interactions. The most effective way to calm a distraught adolescent is to get him or her out of his head by reflecting and processing his or her feelings.

Interconnectedness acknowledges that all experience, whether internal or external, is related and linked. Sophisticated, mature thought is characterized by an understanding of the connection between thought and action, behavior and consequence, effort and achievement, the welfare of self and others, etc. Separation or lack of connection to self or others is the source of most dysfunction. The NTU approach recognizes the foundational need that adolescents have to experience interconnectedness.

This need for interconnectedness is often seen in our experience with youth in foster care. Many of these youngsters who have been abused and neglected by members of their biological families, nearly always pursue relationships with their original families. Similarly, youth who are victims of sexual abuse and molestation frequently pursue relationships with the abuser, and foster care youth who abscond actually often go home to their biological families.

There is no way to make a young person (or an old one for that matter) do anything he or she does not want to do. We have found that the key to obtaining the cooperation of youth is to exploit their innate desire to get the approval of their parents or caretakers. Of course, this desire is neither conscious nor obvious to most youth. The NTU interventionist assists the youth by facilitating positive communications that frequently start with direct communication and acknowledgment of the love and/or concern between the youth and parents. Sometimes this process must start with encouraging parents who may feel angry, guilty, and overburdened to give positive feedback to youth who are used to hearing criticism and disappointment from their parents. The rule of thumb is: The more difficult it is for family members to directly express love to one another, the more important it is to pursue the expression.

In Rite of Passage we support the interconnectedness of the youth through the libation ritual. Libation is a ritual in which ancestors are acknowledged and honored for their contribution to the lives of participants. During libation, participants call out the names of departed loved ones in a call-and-response format. Sometimes participants contribute short stories about the deceased or acknowledge and share the deceased's attributes with the other participants. This is an acknowledgment of what the participant has learned from the deceased. Libation offers the youth the opportunity to acknowledge the loss of their loved ones and connect with their memory and the lessons learned from the lives of the deceased. It is an excellent tool for working through the grief process.

Authenticity refers to the practice of being present and genuine in interactions with youth. Consistent and committed workers who continually work on their own therapeutic and developmental issues promote authenticity. Being genuinely authentic requires one to "walk the talk." Youth know when they are being offered textbook interventions that lack relevance and when the interventions come as the result of the personal and professional knowledge and experience of the workers. NTU interventionists participate in ongoing training that develops along parallel tracks that emphasize both the personal development of the clinician as well as acquisition of skills. Our intention is ensure that the clinicians are first applying NTU to their own lives and that they are using NTU to intervene in their clients' lives. Training includes a variety of instructional modes such as lecture, didactic, role-plays, case reviews, and practical experience under direct supervision with ongoing feedback. It is this combination that encourages staff's authentic presentation to youth.

Authenticity is an important principle when working with youth, who frequently can be obsessively concerned with "being real." This may include abandoning the role of authority that sometimes puts workers in the position of defending systems and behaviors that are indefensible. We lose our credibility with youth when we defend programs, agencies, parents, and institutions that do not merit defense. A more therapeutic and authentic response to such tests is to acknowledge the youth's critique and encourage the youth to have an appropriate response to what may be inappropriate behavior by a program, agency, parent, or institution.

Youth who are required to attend human service and juvenile justice programs can be reached emotionally when we avoid arguments and confrontations. A valuable technique in this regard is the "Yes, but" method that encourages accepting their critiques. The NTU process refines this popular response further by advocating behavior and speech that "adds but does not subtract" from the youth's contribution. Reflections and reframing are used to acknowledge the youth's comments but not to discredit their contributions. "Adding, not subtracting" as an attitude and technique work very well in the group process where heavy confrontation of youth can be counterproductive.

Interventions

NTU psychotherapy and counseling is structured into five phases: (a) Harmony, (b) Awareness, (c) Alignment, (d) Actualization, and (e) Synthesis. Each phase has its unique objectives. The phases represent the micro- and macro-presentation of the therapeutic process. The micro-presentation of the NTU phases occurs within the therapeutic hour or its equivalent. The macro-presentation occurs in the duration of the treatment process.

Harmony Phase

The first phase begins with a greeting. The purpose of this phase is the building of relationship between the adolescent and interventionist. In this phase connection is established, bonds developed, and joining facilitated. Each person (adolescent, family members, probation officers, social workers, etc.) in the session is individually attended to in this phase. Participants often sabotage therapy when therapists try to solve problems before solid connections are formed. Adolescents can be joined around issues of interest to them such as music, sports, peers, movies, clothing, shopping, school, etc. The joining preferably occurs around issues that are not related to the problem. The exception to this rule occurs if the adolescent is distressed. Then the joining process becomes one of empathizing with the adolescent. The harmony phase should continue until the adolescent and interventionist begin to relax and feel more comfortable with each other. Body posture, voice tone, and facial expression are some of the cues to the adolescent's state of comfort. This joining process may happen quickly when the therapist and client have an ongoing relationship and more slowly when the relationship is new.

The skilled NTU interventionist returns to harmony whenever she or he meets resistance from the adolescent. In this manner the client is comforted and reminded of the relationship before being refocused on the difficult tasks that may be encouraging the resistance.

Awareness Phase

Awareness is the phase where all who are present identify strengths, challenges, and intentions. Each person present is encouraged to clearly state his or her perception of the problem(s). In this phase the adolescent is encouraged to tell his or her story. The therapist uses reflective listening, relabeling, reframing, and tracking to follow and understand the client's perception of the situation. The therapist begins in this phase to reconstruct the story to put into a workable framework from which it can be processed. For instance, absolutes may be reframed as relatives, negatives relabeled as positives, and intentions clearly identified and given adaptive meaning. Techniques such as "peel the onion (progressively pushing for deeper meaning)" and "worst fear (identifying the person's core fear)" may help to identify the adolescent's foundational concerns. The awareness phase should end with a clear statement by the interventionist that designates the issue to be immediately worked on.

Alignment Phase

Alignment is the most challenging and generally the longest phase of NTU. It is also the phase that provides the most opportunity to facilitate change. It is this phase of the work that most frequently determines the outcome of the session. The purpose of the alignment phase is to facilitate a change in the client's perspective and shift in consciousness, thereby making room for behavior change. Each of us holds our lives together with a world of beliefs, assumptions, and ideas. This world of mental constructs structures our problem-solving behavior by setting limits on our choices. These constructions define, defend, and justify our behavior. Using NTU we attempt to attack the foundational assumptions that create the adolescent's problems. When even a slight shift in perspective is accepted it creates new possibilities. Reframing and relabeling are the techniques that are used most often in the alignment phase to change how the client perceives her or his situation. Relabeling can be as simple as redefining a situation from impossible ("I can't") to possible ("It's difficult"). Reframing can be as simple as redefining "the teacher doesn't like me" to "you're finding it hard to develop a good relationship with your teacher."

Problems to a large extent are a product of how we see and define circumstance. People in general and adolescents specifically create problems for themselves by the things they believe and the way they talk with one another. In those conversations, issues of cause, blame, and intent can represent pitfalls. Helping people talk straight is at the heart of the therapeutic venture; the therapist should set the example.

In NTU the focus of the intervention is the person's intentions, which are always assumed to be positive. When we accept the adolescents' intentions as being positive, we tap into their motivation to achieve their goals and avoid power struggles that are so easy to fall into with youth. Many times we activate motivation that may have been dormant previously.

Once the intention is identified the task is to revoke existing discrepancies in the relationship among the adolescent's thoughts, feelings, and behaviors. When this alignment is off, the client's balance is corrupted. Alignment occurs differently in individual and family interventions. In the individual intervention the alignment is an internal process. It is the encouraging of consistency in what is thought, felt, and done by the individual that engenders alignment in the individual. For example, if a client complains of being upset and angry (feelings) at mother, and she thinks (thoughts) that she is being mistreated, she will not be fully present in her experience and available to the harmonious flow of NTU (life energy) that is the foundation of health and vitality until she acts (behavior) in a manner that is consistent with her thoughts and feelings. The effort with the adolescent is to align thoughts with feelings; feelings with behavior; or thoughts with behavior. Challenging and confronting cognitive, affective, and behavioral discrepancies and inconsistencies in the adolescent's story create alignment. Frequently, the adolescent will become uncomfortable in this phase, creating the need to reestablish harmony. This alignment also must be in harmony with the client's larger intentions.

In family interventions, alignment includes family members talking directly to one another. In the family intervention, alignment is a product of having family members experience the same or compatible feelings, thoughts, or behaviors at the same time. Connections are reinforced and healing is facilitated when family members experience the same mental, emotional, and spiritual spaces together. For instance, if an adolescent is complaining about the way he is being treated by his mother, alignment may occur when the mother allows herself to feel his pain (feelings), understand his thinking (thoughts), or respond to his issues (behavior). Too often conflict is not resolved in families because family members are allowed to spend time in the therapeutic session defending themselves and accusing others, as opposed to responding to and experiencing each other. When family members experience each other through their vulnerability without defenses, the natural healing power of NTU (love) can flow and a deeper level of connection and relationship becomes possible. Defenses are emotional blocks that inhibit the flow of NTU, and create dis-ease and disharmony in the client system. Although defenses are necessary their extreme expressions destabilize systems and disrupt equilibrium.

Actualization Phase

Actualization is the problem solving/solution building stage. Novice counselors frequently make the mistake of entering this phase too quickly. They move to suggest solutions to the adolescent rather than have the adolescent work through the issues in the alignment phase. Solutions only work when the client is ready and readiness is a matter of aligning thoughts, feelings, and behavior, thereby removing obstacles and impediments.

In this phase the youth is assisted in formulating solutions and developing plans. Once the formulations and plans are made the youth and interventionist may practice the solution via role-play, role reversal, empty chair, etc. If this is a session involving another person (parent, teacher, probation officer, etc.), then this phase is an opportunity for enactment. The enactment may include mediation or negotiation where the interventionist's responsibility is to facilitate effective communications between the participants.

Actualization also should include the development of home assignments to reinforce the therapeutic process and actualization plan beyond the therapeutic hour. The assignments should be relevant to the problem that has been worked through and supplement or enhance the enactment or practice that occurred in this phase. Home assignment should include a role for each participant in the session.

Synthesis Phase

Synthesis offers the opportunity to clarify what the adolescent has gleaned from the sessions. It should include some evaluation of the therapeutic process and its relevance or value. The adolescent should be able to see the connection between the work in the sessions and improvement in his or her circumstance. This phase also offers the opportunity to assess the therapeutic relationship. It is important to remember that all efforts were for the benefit of the client and the client should be able to see and feel improvement as a result of the intervention.

In this final phase the client is required to repeat his or her assignments and make sure the assignments are clear. The NTU interventionist should by all means attempt to determine whether or not there is genuine commitment to completing the assignments, and if not seek to cultivate that level of interest. This phase ends with a scheduling of the next appointment.

It should be noted that although phase one (harmony) and five (synthesis) generally begin and end the therapy sessions, it is acceptable and sometimes necessary to revisit, during the session, the three middle phases to address new issues through awareness, alignment, and actualization. Success in therapy requires that the therapist address one issue at a time and not fall into the trap that many therapists fall into by trying to handle several issues simultaneously.

Case Study

Background

The Department of Juvenile Justice referred Charles to Progressive Life Center's Youth Diversion Program (NJIA), for a second-degree assault charge. Charles is a 16-year-old, African American male, enrolled in the 11th grade. He does well in school and has goals of successfully graduating high school and attending college. In addition, Charles is very respectful and has a good relationship with his parents and family. Charles possesses an infectious sense of humor and joins very easily with others. From the very beginning Charles and his family maintained that Charles is a good youth who very rarely participates in delinquent behavior. Based on the family's contention and the family counselor's initial assessment, the counselor decided to focus on assisting Charles in developing his strengths as a major treatment goal. Although participating in the treatment portion of the program, Charles was assigned to our summer leadership-training program because we felt he would excel as a group motivator and a leader.

Despite his strengths, Charles continues to be a 16-year-old male who deals with the pressures of school and peers, and who seeks to balance his adolescent urges with his family loyalty. After a short period of interaction, the counselor learned that Charles participates in many of the activities that youth his age indulge in, including smoking marijuana, having sex, going to parties, and occasionally fighting. Therefore, throughout the remainder of the intervention, we focused on aligning Charles' feelings and goals (intentions) with his behaviors. We worked to encourage Charles' strengths and self-determination and discourage negative behaviors.

Charles successfully completed the intensive portion of the program as well as the summer leadership program. After termination, Charles continued to regularly, voluntarily attend the groups that we offer, maintained consistent contact with the counselors, and occasionally sought assistance when he was confronted with difficulties. Because of his leadership potential and continued involvement, Charles was offered a paid position with the program as a peer counselor.

The following session took place with Charles, after his completion of treatment and during his employment as a peer counselor. It was scheduled as a result of a request made by Charles' mother. She called Charles' original family counselor and explained that Charles was suspended from school for verbally threatening another student. She expressed some concern for this incident as well as Charles' apparent frustration with the school setting. She felt that some intervention on our part would assist Charles' in refocusing and resolving any underlying issues. The counselor agreed and scheduled a time and date to meet with Charles.

NTU Phases and Interventions

Upon Charles' arrival to the center, he portrayed his usual, upbeat, entertaining, and welcoming attitude. However, once I reminded him that we would be meeting soon, his demeanor quickly changed, becoming anxious and guarded. I immediately attempted to put Charles at ease by promoting the harmony that already exists between us and assuring him that the session would not be long. During the session, Charles was obviously much more reserved than normal. However, he was able to speak openly and honestly once he became comfortable.

Charles and I met in a therapy room. Because he was obviously uncomfortable and somewhat tense, I sought to engage him around something humorous and tap into his comfort zone. To do this, I brought up the subject of his upcoming 17th birthday and lightly teased him about being an "almost adult." He relaxed almost instantly and joked along with me about the subject. As this conversation tapered off, I then joined with Charles by conducting an informal ritual that we often used while he participated in active treatment. I asked him to tell me something good he did for himself and for someone else over the past week. Because I am aware of Charles' cognitive and emotional strengths, I was confident that this ritual would be appropriate and solicit a genuine and appropriate response from him. Additionally, I was seeking to "set the stage" or prepare Charles for the issues at hand. By having Charles acknowledge some good behaviors, I attempted to highlight his strengths and accentuate the balance that he generally possesses, despite his current difficulties. The information he shared through the ritual can be used later in the session to identify the incongruencies in Charles' behavior or to illuminate his intentions.

After establishing harmony and feeling confident that Charles' anxiety had decreased, I entered the awareness phase by reminding Charles that his mother made me aware of his suspension and had expressed concern for Charles' recent attitude toward school. At that time, Charles verbalized his version of the situation, which included him threatening physical harm to a young man that made advances to Charles' girlfriend. Charles further revealed that he already dislikes the youth because on a previous occasion, the young man refused to assist Charles in cheating on an assignment. Although these two issues had obviously upset Charles, I recognized that they were merely surface issues that masked some deeper concerns. With the use of some reframing and reflection, Charles was able to identify that he was angry because of the other youth's disregard for Charles' need for help and his relationship with this young lady. Feelings of disrespect and inadequacy were also identified. I helped Charles admit that he has been experiencing a lack of success recently in school and that the young man's behaviors worked to emphasize Charles' frustrations in this area.

In the alignment phase, I wanted to guide Charles in managing his true feelings of frustration and unsuccessfulness. I sought to assist him in recognizing that he is responsible for his own difficulties in school and that his anger and negative behaviors toward the opposing young man were misplaced. Utilizing reflection and relabeling, it became clear that Charles' anger was unwarranted. For example, in referring to the other youth's unwillingness to cheat, Charles stated, "it's not like I never helped him before." To refocus the attention to Charles' level of preparedness I relabeled this statement by saying, "So, you are usually prepared for tests and other school assignments." Of course he agreed, which allowed me to explore with Charles why this had not been the case recently. Confrontation or "care-frontation" about Charles' unrealistic expectations of this other youth initially made Charles uncomfortable. Recognizing his lack of ease, I shifted and sought to reestablish the harmony that we had obtained early in the session. I reminded Charles of our ritual and restated the positive behaviors he had boasted about earlier. I then utilized encouragement and validation to emphasize his strengths. Charles relaxed and appeared to approve of the verbal support. In order to help Charles find his power, I encouraged him to compare for himself, his positive actions with the actions that warranted this meeting. At this time, Charles was able to draw parallels, which allowed him to acknowledge that his reaction to the young man was unnecessary. He further agreed that the threat was directly related to his feelings about the previous situation (receiving help) and less reactive to the current one (the girlfriend).

Through introspection in the actualization phase Charles verbally acknowledged that his decreasing school success had really frustrated him and was more of a problem than he had originally admitted to himself. Using brainstorming, Charles identified other means by which to handle these situations. He acknowledged his need to be prepared with his own school assignments and expressed that he could not seek to blame his lack of preparation on other students. Together, we prioritized his school responsibilities and developed a more feasible study plan. Charles then explored other options to utilize when he feels disrespected or disregarded by another. He admitted that he does have the tendency to take his frustrations out on others and agreed to make efforts to avoid that defense mechanism. Through role rehearsal and other demonstration techniques, for example "the empty chair," Charles showed exactly how he could handle similar situations in the future.

In the synthesis stage, we reviewed the contents of the session. We first restated the original problems and the original reasons for the threats. We then agreed on the underlying issues that led to this incident, including Charles' lack of preparation and feelings of inadequacy in school. At that time, I had Charles reiterate to me his plan to improve his school performance. Additionally, Charles reviewed some of the skills that he developed during the role-plays to manage frustrations brought on by others or situations. I further validated Charles' insightfulness and his willingness to change his behavior. I closed by suggesting that we meet again soon to review his success with the study plan and his use of alternatives for appropriate conflict resolution.

In terms of prognosis, overall, I propose that Charles is insightful. Despite his insecurities, he has the capability to make healthy life choices. However, it is imperative that he is continually reminded of his goals and encouraged to remain task-focused. The hope is that through his continued training and efforts as a peer counselor, Charles will become able to identify many tools that can assist him in facing adversity with consistency and appropriateness.

Conclusion

NTU is an evolving treatment model and clinical framework that is built philosophically on an Africentric understanding of human behavior. Developed from observation of clinical practice with people of color, it challenges many of the assumptions of traditional Western approaches to mental health. Traditional Western approaches support the hierarchical idea of the therapist as expert and change agent. The traditional Western therapist seeks to change the client system to what the therapist thinks is a better level of functioning. This process has become very outcome-driven as a result of the economics of managed care.

NTU views the therapist as a conduit of the universal energy (NTU). Change from the NTU point of view is a natural process that can be assisted, shaped, and directed but not created. From an NTU perspective, positive results and outcomes come from the positive and skillful interaction in the NTU intervention, but the results cannot be controlled or predicted. They can only be encouraged and inspired, allowing for appropriate respect of client choices and avoiding the common tendency to use therapy as a vehicle for manipulating the person(s) being served. The NTU interventionist looks for competence that already exists on some level and is frequently overlooked because of cultural bias and preferences. Traditional Western approaches, with their emphasis on pathology, promote a unitary standard and label much of everything else as deficient for not fitting within its rigid boundaries.

NTU is a treatment model that provides a culturally competent, family-focused, competency-based, spiritually oriented, wholistic/systemic, and values-driven framework that is based on universal principles of harmony, balance, interconnectedness, and authenticity. NTU focuses on raising the energy (NTU) vibration of client systems by supporting, teaching, and promoting healthy habits and interactions. The central question in traditional ego-centered treatments is, "What do you (client) really want?" From the NTU perspective the central question is, "What does God (life, nature etc.) want of you?" This question defines the goal of treatment as one of submission to a divine, universal force as opposed to mastery over one's environment.

NTU acknowledges the reality that most of the people required to provide therapeutic interaction vocationally are not psychologists or social workers with years of training in theory and practice, but case managers, advocates, probation officers, counselors, group home workers, etc., who may have minimal training but are responsible for working regularly with the most clinically needy clients in our society.

Discussion Questions

1. How does the NTU therapist address resistance in the therapeutic relationship? Discuss specific tools that a therapist might utilize to engage a resistant teenager.
2. Compare and contrast NTU psychotherapy with traditional Western approaches. How do the characteristics of the NTU model distinguish this from other approaches?
3. Briefly outline how a therapist might navigate through the NTU phases with a 13-year-old female client who demonstrates aggressive behaviors toward male classmates.
4. Integrating spirituality into the treatment process is a key feature of the NTU model. What are some pros and cons to explicitly addressing spirituality in the treatment process?
5. How is the variable "culture" conceptualized in the NTU model?
6. The NTU model focuses on strengths rather than pathology. What is gained from this approach, and does focusing on strengths have disadvantages?

References

Akbar, N. (1981). Mental disorders among African Americans. *Black Books Bulletin, 7*(12), 18–25.

Boyd-Franklin, N. (1989). *Black families in therapy.* New York: Guilford Press.

Efran, J., Lukens, R., & Lukens, M. (1990). *Language, structure and change.* New York: Norton.

Gregory, H., & Harper, K. (2001). The NTU approach to health and healing. *Journal of Black Psychology, 27,* 304–320.

Jahn, J. (1961). *Muntu: An outline of new African culture.* London: Faber & Faber.

Kuhn, T. S. (1970). *The structure of scientific revolutions.* Chicago: University of Chicago Press.

McGoldrick, M., Pearce, J., & Giordano, J. (Eds.). (1982). *Ethnicity and family therapy.* New York: Guilford Press.

Minuchin, S. (1974). *Families and family therapy.* Cambridge, MA: Harvard University Press.

Nichols, E. (1976). *The philosophical aspects of cultural differences.* Ibandan, Nigeria: World Psychiatric Association.

Nobles, W. W. (1980). African's philosophy: Foundations for Black psychology. In R. L. Jones (Ed.), *Black psychology* (pp. 22–36). New York: Harper & Row.

Nobles, W. W. (1986). *African psychology: Toward its reclamation, reascension, and revitalization.* Oakland, CA: Black Family Institute.

Parham, T. A., White, J. L., & Ajamu, A. (1999). *The psychology of Blacks: An African-centered perspective.* Englewood Cliffs, NJ: Prentice-Hall.

Phillips, F. B. (1990). NTU psychotherapy: An Afrocentric approach. *Journal of Black Psychology, 17*(1), 215–222.

Phillips, F. B. (1998). Spirit energy and NTU psychotherapy. In R. L. Jones (Ed.), *African American Mental Health* (pp. 357–377). Hampton, VA: Cobb & Henry.

White, J. L. (1980). Toward a Black psychology. In R. L. Jones (Ed.), *Black psychology* (pp. 5–12). New York: Harper & Row.

Structural Ecosystems Therapy with Hispanic Adolescents Exhibiting Disruptive Behavior Disorders

Michael S. Robbins
Seth Schwartz
José Szapocznik

This chapter highlights Structural Ecosystems Therapy (SET), a family-based intervention developed at the Center for Family Studies. SET recognizes that adolescent behavior problems are a function of factors both within and outside the family (cf. Szapocznik & Coatsworth, 1999). As such, intervention strategies specifically target patterns of interaction, within the family and between the family and other systems (e.g., peers, schools) that influence the development or maintenance of behavior problems. The goal is to create new and adaptive patterns of interaction within the family to promote prosocial adolescent behavior. Although SET has been developed for both African American and Hispanic populations, this chapter exclusively focuses on the application of SET with Hispanic adolescents and their families. The case study demonstrates the application of SET with a drug abusing adolescent and her family.

Culture and Context

Adolescents with disruptive behaviors represent one of the most difficult treatment populations (DiGiuseppe, Linscott, & Jilton, 1996). Conduct problems are remarkably stable over time and are characterized by escalations as the child moves into adolescence (Patterson, 1993). Nonetheless, reviews of the treatment research literature have noted the success of family-based interventions in improving adolescent problem behaviors (cf., Alexander, Holtzworth-Munroe,

& Jameson, 1994; Liddle & Dakof, 1995a, 1995b; Stanton & Shadish, 1997). These reviews have included studies conducted with adolescents and family members from a variety of racial, ethnic, and cultural backgrounds, suggesting that the mechanisms involved in family-based interventions operate across demographic boundaries.

One program of clinical research highlighted in this literature is the work of José Szapocznik and colleagues at the University of Miami's Center for Family Studies. Guided by the clinical and self-identified needs of Miami's Hispanic community, this research team has developed, refined, and evaluated family-based interventions for Hispanic youth with disruptive behavior problems (see Szapocznik & Williams, 2000). This program of clinical research has provided strong support for the impact of family interventions with a diverse group of Hispanics in Miami.

The 1970s witnessed the first wave of increase in the number of Hispanic adolescents exhibiting behavior- and drug-related problems in Miami. In response to this problem, the University of Miami Spanish Family Guidance Center (the precursor to the Center for Family Studies) was established to provide treatment within the local Hispanic community (which at the time was almost exclusively of Cuban origin). The first challenge encountered was to develop a culturally appropriate and acceptable treatment intervention for Cuban youth with behavior problems. To develop a better understanding of Cuban culture and how it resembled, and differed from, mainstream American culture, a comparative study of value orientations was conducted. This study determined that a family-oriented approach in which therapists take an active, directive, present-oriented leadership role matched the expectations of the Cuban immigrant population in Miami (Szapocznik, Scopetta, & King, 1978).

An important problem identified in these early studies was that, in Hispanic families, the acculturation process often created disruptions within the family. Adolescents tended to learn English and adapt quickly to American culture, achieving a balance of Americanism and Hispanicism. In contrast, parents tended to hold onto the values of their culture of origin, and compared to their children, adapted much slower to American culture. Combined with normative parent–adolescent differences, the stress of acculturation tended to produce exaggerated intergenerational differences and exacerbate intrafamilial conflicts (Szapocznik & Kurtines, 1980). In turn, this greatly increased the likelihood of behavior problems in the adolescent.

As a consequence of the value orientation study, the Center for Family Studies adopted structural family therapy as its core approach (Szapocznik et al., 1978; Szapocznik & Williams, 2000). Through a series of clinical research studies, the structural approach has been refined to include treatment methods that are strategic (i.e., problem-focused and pragmatic) and time-limited. In doing so, the structural approach evolved into Brief Strategic Family Therapy (BSFT), which includes both structural and strategic interventions. SET essentially evolved from

BSFT. In fact, the within-family interventions in SET are identical to those in BSFT. However, SET moves beyond the family to include a systematic focus on the adolescent's and family's social ecology. The ecological components of SET are based on the same structural and strategic principles and intervention strategies that underlie BSFT. Thus, SET is best considered as BSFT plus ecological interventions. In this section, a brief review is presented to: (a) outline the core principles of SET, and (b) present the intervention framework for working within the family (i.e., BSFT) and in the adolescent's and family's social ecology (i.e., SET).

Core Principles of Structural Ecosystem Therapy (SET)

SET is a family-based intervention designed to help to reduce behavior problems, including alcohol and substance abuse, in children and adolescents. To improve a youth's behavior problems, SET attempts both to change family interactions and reduce the deleterious impact of cultural/contextual factors that are critically related to the youth's behavior problem. The within-family component of SET is based on the assumption that the family is the "bedrock" of child development (Bronfenbrenner, 1986). That is, the family is viewed as the primary context in which children learn to think, feel, and behave.

SET is also heavily influenced by research identifying multicausal pathways in the development of adolescent behavior problems (Dishion, French, & Patterson, 1995; Hawkins, Catalano, & Miller, 1992), as well as our own clinical work with behavior-problem adolescents. For example, increased recognition of the role of peers in the evolution and maintenance of antisocial behaviors has prompted the development of interventions to systematically target adolescents' relationships outside the family. This expansion into the wider ecosystem is consistent with BSFT theory, which explicitly recognizes that the family itself is part of a larger social system and—as a child is influenced by her or his family—the family is influenced by the larger social system in which it exists. In SET, the basic principles that have guided BSFT to modify within-family interactions have been systematically extended to directly target interactions between the family and its larger social ecological context. The emergence of this integrated family and ecological approach is particularly appropriate for Hispanic families that tend to be close-knit and to rely on one another and the larger context (e.g., extended family, informal networks) as they negotiate their daily lives (Szapocznik et al., 1997).

The organizational framework for SET is based on the theoretical work of Urie Bronfenbrenner (1977, 1979, 1986). Consistent with Bronfenbrenner's organization of the social ecology, SET focuses on four levels of systems that impact youth's developmental trajectories: microsystems, mesosystems, exosystems, and macrosystems (Fig. 4.1). *Microsystems* refer to systems that include the youth directly. The most prominent of these systems for youth with behavior problems are the family, peer, school, and juvenile justice. *Mesosystems* represent relationships between the microsystems in which the youth participates. In SET, the primary mesosystemic relationships involve parents' interactions with the youth's peer, school, and justice systems. *Exosystems* are those systems that include a member of a microsystem, but that do not involve the youth directly. For drug-using youth, exosystems may include a friend who is in a gang or the social support network or stress and burden of a parent. Both of these exosystems, through their impact on the friend (gang members support the anti-social behavior of friend) and on the parent (parent receives support from friends/extended family or is under considerable external stress), respectively, may have an indirect impact on the youth through interactions between the youth and the other person. *Macrosystems* are defined by the broad social forces and systems that have the most widespread impact, such as the law, as well as by the cultural blueprints that pervade a family's social environment, such as the belief that parents are less valuable to society because they do not speak English. At this broadest level, SET recognizes the role of cultural factors in the development and maintenance of behavior problems, such as the differential levels of acculturation among parents and children in immigrant families.

The framework presented in Figure 4.1 captures the complex set of relationships that influence youth and their families. However, to understand the influence of these contextual influences on the development, maintenance, and treatment of adolescent behavior problems, and to understand how treatment in SET is designed around these contextual influences, it is necessary to understand three central constructs that underlie the process (e.g., interaction) focus of SET: system, structure, and strategy (Szapocznik & Kurtines, 1989). Based in BSFT theory, these constructs have been expanded to capture the complex set of interactions that occur in the adolescent's and family's social ecology.

System

A *system* is an organized whole comprised of parts that are interdependent or interrelated. A family is a system comprised of individuals whose behaviors necessarily affect other family members. As such, family members become accustomed to the behaviors of other family members, because such behaviors have occurred many times over many years. These behaviors synergistically work together to define a family's system. Systems explain the interdependency between the "parts" of a family. In SET, the concept of systems is widened to include the adolescent's entire ecology, of which the family is one part. The adolescent's peer network, school context, and juvenile justice involvement, along with the parents' relationship with each of these contexts, are seen as an organized whole and as interdependent with one another. Just as the various members of a family interact repeatedly and establish interrelationships, so do the components of the adolescent's social ecology. Bronfrenbrenner's organization of the social ecol-

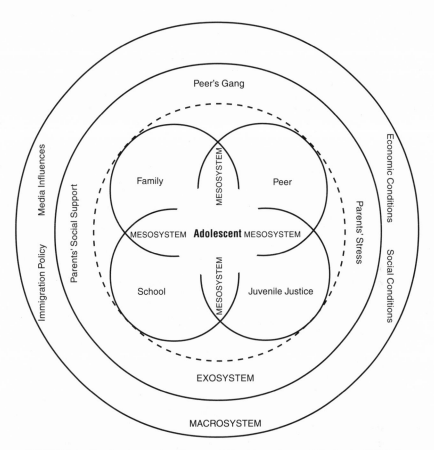

FIGURE 4.1. Structural ecosystem theory: relationships among ecodevelopmental levels.

ogy illustrates how these systems work together to produce the adolescent's and family's reality.

Structure

The set of repetitive patterns of interactions that are idiosyncratic to each family system is called the family's *structure*. Structure refers to the patterns of interactions that emerge and become habitual among the "parts" of the family. A maladaptive (poorly functioning) family structure is characterized by repetitive family interactions where family members repeatedly elicit the same unsatisfactory responses from each other. From a systems perspective, a maladaptive family structure is viewed as an important contributor to the occurrence and maintenance of behavior problems. Likewise, once the maladaptive family interactions have been corrected, the adolescent's behavior problems are likely to decrease. In

SET, structure is expanded to include patterns of interactions among the systems in the adolescent's social ecology. The primary emphasis is on maladaptive patterns of interaction between the family and outside systems, such as parents' lack of monitoring of peer activities, or lack of involvement in the adolescent's school system. These maladaptive repetitive family–ecological interactions result in family members repeatedly experiencing the same unsatisfactory and unproductive exchanges with the social environment.

Strategy

The third fundamental concept of SET, *strategy*, is defined by therapeutic interventions that are practical, problem-focused, and deliberate. Practical interventions are selected for their likelihood to modify family and ecological interactions, and therefore to decrease or eliminate adolescent problem behaviors. One important aspect of practical interventions is choosing to emphasize one aspect of a family's reality (e.g., that a drug-abusing youth is in pain) as a way to foster a parent–child connection, or another aspect (e.g., "this youth could get killed or overdose at any moment") as a way to heighten the parent(s)' sense of urgency. In the service of maintaining the problem focus and brevity of the model, this positive or negative reframing is done in lieu of portraying the entire reality of a situation.

The problem-focused aspect of SET refers to targeting only those family and ecological interaction patterns that are the most directly relevant to the symptomatic behavior of the child. Although families usually have multiple problems, targeting only those patterns of interactions linked to the symptomatic behavior contributes to the brevity of SET. For example, working with parents to help them to facilitate testing and appropriate placement in school of their child or increasing the couple's ability to parent are primary targets because these issues are directly linked to problem behaviors. However, focusing on the couple's sexual problems in their marital relationship might not be targeted in this brief therapy model.

Interventions

All therapist interventions in SET emanate from the three BSFT general intervention components: joining, diagnosis, and restructuring. Each of these components is implemented at several levels.

Joining

Joining the Family System

Joining occurs at two levels in the family. First, at the individual level, joining involves establishing a relationship with each participating family member. Second, at the systemic level, the therapist joins with the family system to create a "new" therapeutic system in which the therapist is both a member and its leader. Thus, joining requires both a sensitivity and ability to respond to the unique characteristics of individuals as well as the ability to quickly discern the family's hierarchy and leadership structure.

The first step in working with a family is to establish a therapeutic alliance with each individual family member. In doing so, therapists must be sensitive to the fact that family members often enter treatment with competing and conflicting demands and may be hypersensitive to which family member's side the therapist is going to take. Thus, it is critical for therapists to respond to each family member directly and attempt to foster in each the belief that she or he has something to gain by participating in treatment. Likewise, therapists must remain cognizant of the family's power structure and characteristic pattern of interaction, and they must join the system through these established patterns. By identifying the family's most powerful member, the therapist can strategically focus on her or him early in treatment and enlist her or his help in bringing other family members to treatment.

Joining the Ecosystem

The process of joining ecosystems is similar to joining the family in that the goal is to establish a therapeutic relationship in which the therapist is both a member and a leader. Joining ecosystems involves connecting both with individuals and the systems to which they belong.

The first step in joining the ecosystem involves gaining family members' approval to contact members of the ecosystem. The second step in engaging the ecosystem is to identify the most influential members of the adolescent's ecosystem (e.g., peers, probation officers), and to obtain their permission and willingness to participate in treatment in support of the parents. This involves assessing the system's power structure, and entering the system with the permission, approval, and sanction of the power structure—without alienating individuals that may resent the power structure.

Peers

One of the most difficult challenges in working with behavior problem adolescents is gaining access (either direct or indirect) to the child's peer world. Youth are reluctant to discuss peer relations, particularly when the peer group is engaged in antisocial activities, and they only rarely permit the therapist to gain direct access to their peers. Therapists often only can indirectly access and influence peer interactions through discussions with the youth and her or his parents. However, there are several strategies that therapists can use to increase the likelihood that interventions can influence the family's/parent's ability to minimize the negative impact of the peer group on the youth's behaviors. First, the therapist must recognize that the adolescent is the key to engaging the peer network. If the adolescent does not trust the therapist's motives, the chances of introducing peers as targets of intervention in treatment is nonexistent. Therapists must avoid the "trap" of blaming the adolescent's problem behaviors on peers, which can be particularly difficult when a parent is criticizing the youth's friends in the session. Any support of the parent's statements must be countered by reframing the family's negativity about peers and shifting the focus onto the youth's appropriate needs for social connectedness (e.g., connection with peers results from a desire to feel accepted rather than as an indication of rebellion). This reframing creates a new context where the adolescent may not feel threatened about discussions of her or his peers. Such discussions shed light on what the child derives from her or his peer relationships, and thereby create an opportunity to connect with the adolescent at a deeper level of understanding. In turn, this creates an opportunity for orchestrating a meeting with the child, her or his parents, and her or his peer group.

Second, therapists should attempt to schedule meetings with the adolescent on her or his turf, either in the home or the community. Some adolescents are even comfortable having the therapist "hang out" on the street corner or go to the basketball courts with them. Although this is not always easily accomplished, these opportunities represent an excellent opportunity for meeting the child's friends and observing what the child may get out of interactions with her or his peer group. At a minimum, these experiences provide an excellent reservoir of information about the day-to-day life of the adolescent.

Third, therapists should focus on peer relationships that may support the goals of treatment. Clinical experience in implementing SET has demonstrated that therapists have a relatively easier time engaging the adolescent's boyfriend or girlfriend into treatment, and that the youth's romantic interest often shares the same concerns as the therapist and family members. In many SET cases, positive outcomes have been facilitated by capitalizing on the youth's and family member's connection to a prosocial, romantic partner.

Finally, because deviant peer systems tend to be rigid and closed from outside influences, SET therapists work hard to help parents connect their child to other peer networks (basketball leagues, church groups) and work to help integrate the child into these informal networks.

Schools

Joining interventions in the school system typically involve direct contact with either a teacher or school counselor. However, the ultimate goal of joining the school system is to create an opportunity for parents and school representatives to meet and work together to meet the needs of the behavior problem child. The therapist's role is simply to remove barriers that may prevent parents and the schools from working together in a collaborative manner. Joining requires sensitivity to the family's and school's power structure. For example, when joining with a school counselor, therapists gain the approval of the parent and adolescent as well as permission of the school principal. Once permission has been obtained, the therapist works with the counselor to develop collaborative goals for what may be accomplished with the adolescent and her or his parents. Such work may be particularly difficult when there is a history of negative interactions with the child and her or his family (e.g., lack of parent involvement, youth expulsions from school). Simultaneously, the therapist works with parents and the adolescent to empower them with respect to the school system. Anger at the school is reframed (usually to focus parents on the school's positive goals for their child) and parents are coached and provided with information about how to effectively negotiate with the school system to make sure that parents are involved with critical decisions that schools make about their child. By joining both systems, the therapist is able to create an opportunity for parents and teachers/counselors to meet and work together in a more effective manner.

Juvenile Justice System

Joining interventions in the juvenile justice system are quite similar to schools. For example, the therapist often works directly with the juvenile justice system (e.g., Public Defender, case manager) separately to prepare the terrain for a meeting with parents, while working with the parents to increase their understanding of the juvenile justice system. Parents, particularly recent immigrant Hispanic parents, usually feel powerless in the face of the judicial process, and do not realize the important role they can play in facilitating an outcome that is in their child's best interest (cf. Coatsworth, Pantin, & Szapocznik, 2002). Thus, rather than trying to achieve changes by working solely with the juvenile justice system, SET therapists are focused on developing skills in the parent that will facilitate their ability to work with the justice system. The therapeutic goal is to prepare the family to work with the justice system (as well as the school system, peers, etc.), and then organize meetings with parents and members of the justice system so parents can interact effectively with the juvenile justice system to influence the judicial decision-making process.

Diagnosis

Diagnosing the Family System

Diagnosis refers to identifying family interactional patterns that allow or encourage the adolescent's problematic behaviors. In other words, what are the interactions that contribute to the family's failure to eliminate the youth's problems? To diagnose the family's problems, therapists carefully examine family interactions along five interactional dimensions: Organization, Resonance, Developmental Stage, Identified Patienthood, and Conflict Resolution (see Table 4.1).

TABLE 4.1. Dimensions of Family and Ecological Functioning

Organization	Resonance	Developmental Stage	Identified Patienthood	Conflict Resolution
Family Microsystem (BSFT)				
Hierarchy/Leadership	Enmeshment	Parenting	Negativity	Denial/Avoidance
One parent is more active than the other.	Psychological emotional, or physical boundaries between family members are excessively close.	Parent is immature.	Family members are critical about and negative toward the identified patient.	Family members deny/avoid conflict.
Child is more powerful than parents.	Disengagement	Children	Centrality	Diffusion
Lack of collaborative parental leadership.	Psychological emotional, or physical boundaries between family members are excessively distant.	Child is treated as or acts too young (e.g., overly restricted, low requirement/opportunity for responsible behavior, or no negotiation allowed).	Identified patient is almost always the central topic of conversation.	Family members jump from conflict to conflict without achieving any depth regarding one particular issue.
Decision-making subsystem is absent.		Child is treated as or acts too old (e.g., exhibits parent like behavior or is overloaded with adult tasks).	Family members are organized around the identified patient and his or her problem behaviors.	Emergence Without Resolution
Behavior Control		Extended Family	Support	Family engages in an in-depth discussion about a particular conflict but is not able to resolve the problem.
Parents not engaging in behavior control when needed or behavior control is ineffective.		Extended family usurps parental power or treats parent as a child.	Family members protect or support the identified patient.	Negativity/Conflict
Guidance/Nurturance				Family interactions are openly critical or hostile.
Parents not nurturant or are poor role models.				
Spousal Subsystem				
Marital relationship is poor.				
Sibling Subsystem				
Relationship between siblings is poor.				
Triangulation				
Child stuck in conflict between adults.				

Communication
Family lacks direct communication.

Ecological Interactions

Inappropriate or ineffective collaborative leadership effort (e.g., parent–teacher, parent–case worker).

Lack of collaborative leadership subsystem.

Problematic monitoring and/or supervision of activities (e.g., peers, school, justice).
Indirect and/or poor communication with other subsystems.

Overconnected/ Overinvolved with other subsystems.

Lack of connectedness or uninvolved with other systems.

Problems adjusting to developmental milestones (e.g., traumatic event, immigration, transition from middle to high school).

Other subsystems are critical and negative about the identified patient (e.g., school).

Parents blame other systems.

Parents are blamed or criticized (e.g., peer, school, justice).

Highly conflicted/ negative interactions with other systems.

Organization consists of leadership, hierarchy, and communication flow. Resonance identifies the degree of connectedness among family members, ranging from enmeshment (overinvolved) to disengagement (underinvolved). Developmental Stage refers to the degree to which the adolescent is parentified or infantilized within the family, as well as the degree to which extended family members usurp parental roles and responsibilities (e.g., grandparents undermining parent's rules). Identified Patienthood assesses the degree to which the adolescent's problems are centralized within the family. Conflict Resolution identifies the family's characteristic manner of resolving differences of opinion.

Diagnosing the Ecosystem

Therapists must also systematically assess each of the ecosystems targeted by SET (family, peer, school, juvenile justice, family–peer, family–school, family–juvenile justice, family support network) to identify interactional patterns that are linked to the youth's problem behaviors. Diagnosis for each of the ecosystems occurs along the same five dimensions as the within family component (i.e., Organization, Resonance, Developmental Stage, Identified Patienthood, and Conflict Resolution). Common problems assessed in the ecosystem are noted in Table 4.1.

Organization focuses on the leadership by parents across systems, such as the degree of parental monitoring and supervision of adolescent activities and the nature of the communication across systems. Resonance is the extent of parent and adolescent involvement (under to over) with the youth's microsystems. Developmental Stage assesses family members' (and external systems') adaptation to the adolescent's developmental milestones. Identified Patienthood assesses the extent to which the adolescent, the parent, or other systems are labeled as problematic by family members and members of the ecosystem. Conflict Resolution identifies the style of addressing differences of opinion between family members and specific components of the ecosystem.

Restructuring

As therapists diagnose the within family patterns of interaction and interactions of the family with its social ecology, they also determine the relationship between the family's and the family–ecology's patterns of interactions on the one hand, and the youth's problem behaviors on the other. Based on these systemic diagnoses and their relationship to the adolescent's presenting problem(s), therapists develop an intervention plan. The implementation of the treatment plan is called *restructuring*. Restructuring interventions allow therapists to orchestrate opportunities for families and ecosystems to interact in new, more adaptive ways. Some of the most important restructuring techniques in SET (like in BSFT) fall within three broad categories: Working in the Present, Reframing, and Working with Boundaries and Alliances.

Prior to discussing the implementation of these categories, it is important to note that SET is not like case management, where the therapist achieves changes in the ecosystem by working directly with the social ecology. Rather, in SET, family members (usually parents) are central in almost every ecosystem intervention and the thrust of interventions designed to change ecosystemic interactions is focused on helping parents bring about change (e.g., attending parent–teacher conferences, monitoring youth's activities with peers). That is, ecological interventions in SET work largely at the mesosystem level, rather than at the microsystem level.

Working in the Present

Although some types of counseling focus on the past, SET focuses primarily on the present. The focus is not on hearing stories about the present, but rather the present interactions that occur between family members or that occur between family members and members of the ecosystem (e.g., parent–teacher, parent-peer) during therapy sessions or telephone calls. This focus on observing interactions is critical because stories are generally told from each storyteller's point of view, and various individuals may be in conflict about their version of the story. It is only through watching the family interact with each other and the ecosystem that the therapist can truly understand what is happening and can intervene to correct the maladaptive interactional problems that she or he has observed.

Enactments are a critical feature of SET. In within-family therapy sessions, enactments occur as the therapist encourages, helps, or allows family members to interact with one another in their characteristic manner, that is, as they would naturally behave if the therapist were not present. During the enactment, whenever family members attempt to centralize the therapist, she or he redirects the communication to the person(s) being referenced in the communication. Enactments are important because they provide the therapist with the opportunity to both observe and transform maladaptive family interactions. Frequently, this transformation is best accomplished by allowing the family to interact, and then intervening in the midst of these interactions (e.g., blocking, reframing, reorganizing alliances, etc.) to facilitate the emergence of a different, more adaptive set of interactions. For example, if the mother begins to tell her son Benny that he never listens to her, but then the grandmother intervenes and insists that the mother should leave Benny alone, the therapist can block the grandmother's interruption by distracting her, thereby allowing the mother to interact with her son. Repeated over time, this type of transformative therapist intervention is one way to produce changes in the family's pattern of interactions. Similar enactments can be facilitated within the adolescent's ecosystem.

In SET, therapists are not interested in having the family and its ecosystem simply "talk about" behaving differently. Rather, they are interested in having the family and its ecosystem behave differently within and following the intervention sessions. This requires that the therapist remain decentralized. The therapist needs to make every effort to make sure that interactions occur among family members and between family members and the family ecosystem (and not just with the therapist). The family and the family–ecosystem are encouraged to practice the behaviors that will be helpful to them in their daily life rather than merely discuss them with the therapist. This is true for changing both within-family interactions as well as interactions with the social ecology. As such, therapists create opportunities for family members, particularly parents, to interact in new and more adaptive ways with individuals from the ecosystem.

Reframing

Perhaps the most powerful technique in SET is *reframing*. Reframing denotes creating a different sense of reality by providing individuals with an opportunity to perceive their interactions or situation from a different perspective. Reframing serves two important functions. First, it is a tool for changing negativity and apparent "uncaring" into positivity and caring. This is achieved, for example, by redefining anger and frustration as the bonds that tie a family together: "Of course you are angry, because you care; and because it hurts you so to see your daughter in this condition; and it hurts when she acts that way toward you. It hurts you so deeply because you care so deeply." Such an intervention removes the focus from the parent's anger and refocuses on the parent's deep sense of concern for the youth. In the family–ecosystem relations, reframing negativity is critical because teachers, school administrators, parole officers, etc. on the one hand, and adolescents and parents on the other often perceive each other in a negative light.

The other important function of reframing is to shift the focus that exists on blaming and castigating the identified patient (i.e., usually the troubled adolescent) to a team feeling: "We are here because we care, and because we are willing to do whatever it takes to help Juan, even if it means that each of us has to do something differently." In family therapy sessions, a reframe such as this is utilized to diffuse the family's negativity toward the adolescent and suggest that the adolescent is not the family's sole "problem." Additional reframing may be implemented to illustrate that the problem belongs to the entire family. The goal of such reframes is to prompt family members to accept some degree of responsibility for the problem, and therefore some of the responsibility to change it. In ecological interventions, this type of reframing is critical to move parents and ecological representatives toward working together collaboratively to achieve a common goal. For example, decreasing negativity may help parents and teachers see that they both share a commitment to the child's education.

Working with Boundaries and Alliances

Boundaries are the "social walls" that exist around groups of people who are allied with each other; and that stand between individuals who are not allied with each other. Shifting boundaries then, refers to changes in alliance patterns among other things.

Boundaries and Alliances in the Family System

A common pattern with drug-using youth involves parent-youth alliances that cross generational lines and work against the effective functioning of the executive parental hierarchy. For example, there may be a strong bond between the youth and her or his mother figure and—whenever the youth is punished by the father figure for inappropriate behavior—the youth uses the strong bond to the mother figure to solicit sympathy and support, and ultimately uses this bond to undermine the father figure's authority and remove sanctions placed on the youth. In many cases of single parents, it may be the grandmother who overprotects the youth and undermines the mother's efforts to discipline the youth. Shifting boundaries thus involves creating a more solid boundary around the parental subsystem so the parental figures become mutually supportive and demonstrate it by making executive parental decisions together. This shift of alliances from parent-child to parent-parent decreases the child's influence and ability to undermine the executive parental subsystem.

Boundaries and Alliances in the Ecosystem

In implementing the ecological component of SET, two kinds of boundary shifting interventions are typically used: those intended to enlarge positive informal social support networks and linkages with formal service delivery on the one hand, and those intended to discourage damaging relationships on the other (e.g., antisocial peers, drug using parents). Interventions aimed at enlarging systems are frequently accomplished by creating and assigning tasks to create a history of successful shared experiences on which more substantive experiences and relationships can be built. Interventions aimed at discouraging damaging relationships may utilize blocking and limit setting. Because SET emphasizes building the system's (in this case, the family-ecology systems) inner capacity to conduct and maintain changed behaviors, the therapist best accomplishes these kinds of interventions by allying with and strengthening those subsystems that have the competence, power, and interest to undertake the limit setting.

The most prominent ecological interventions involve creating mesosystemic relationships, particularly parents' relationships with the systems that directly contain the adolescent (i.e., peer, school, and justice). In the peer system, for example, interventions systematically address parent supervision and monitoring of peer activities. Parents are encouraged to meet the child's friends as well as the friends' parents, and are coached and supported in setting up procedures/ rules for tracking their child's daily activities. Likewise, parents are coached on how to effectively negotiate with the school system. Parent–teacher conferences are conducted (with the therapist present), and plans are developed for maintaining consistent parent investment in the youth's school activities. Similarly, parents and adolescents are encouraged to interact to discuss the youth's current criminal charges, and a plan is developed for interacting with the justice system that will maximize the likelihood that the family's goals will be met. Parents are coached on how to interact with the justice system, and the therapist attends these meetings to work with parents and juvenile justice representatives to facilitate interactions that ensure that the parent is able to have some influence on the judicial decision-making process. A benefit of conducting sessions with parents and justice system representatives is that a new pattern of interaction is established in the family–juvenile justice mesosystem. A secondary benefit of these types of intervention is that parents learn valuable skills that they may generalize to future interactions within important microsystems.

Exosystemic interventions typically include enhancing or supporting the connection of parents with a supportive extended network. The focus of interventions in this domain is to facilitate the enlargement of boundaries to establish a parent support system. With such supports, parents are better able to carry out their leadership and nurturing role within the family. This may involve enlisting the support of extended family, friends, employers, and in instances where a parent figure (or figures) has a history of drug abuse, therapists may encourage the parent(s) to attend appropriate support groups.

Cultural Issues Addressed by Structural Ecosystems Therapy

The core principles and interventions strategies reviewed in the preceding section were specifically developed and refined for Hispanic adolescents and families. However, beyond these core principles, there are several cultural issues that are frequently encountered in the implementation of SET. The most common cultural issues are briefly reviewed in the following section.

Culturally Based Risk Factors: Immigration

Given that many Hispanic adolescents in the United States are immigrants or the children of immigrants, the experience of immigration is a critical focus in SET. Immigration, whether voluntary or dictated by political or economic pressures, can create challenges as young people and their families confront a new culture, language, and value system as well as the loss of their support network. This transition may leave immigrants feeling overwhelmed and isolated from critical resources that they need to effectively manage their and their families' lives and often prevents Hispanic immigrants from seeking support in their new environment.

Three consequences of immigration have been systematically addressed in SET: extended immigration-related separations between parents and children, parents' lack of knowledge about the new culture, and differential levels of acculturation between parents and their adolescents (Mitrani, Santisteban, & Muir, in press; Coatsworth, Pantin, & Szapocznik, 2002).

Extended Immigration-Related Separations

Many families do not immigrate to the United States as a unit and in a single step. Rather, the parents enter the country first, secure housing and employment, and send for their children at a later point in time. In some instances, this pattern may be reversed; children may be sent to live with relatives in the United States while parents remain in the country of origin, continuing to work to support the family, while attempting to arrange for a job and other necessities in the United States (Suárez-Orozco & Suárez-Orozco, 2001). In either case, children are separated from their parents for extended periods of time, sometimes as long as 4 or 5 years (Mitrani et al., in press).

When the family is finally reunited in the United States, parent–child relationships once characterized by warmth and closeness can become awkward and conflicted. Parents who left a child behind in the country of origin may find themselves reunited with an adolescent who looks like an adult. Children and adolescents, who have since bonded with the family members or friends who cared for them following their parents' (or their own) departure, may view their parents as strangers who abandoned them. As such, immigration-related separations may lead to conflict that arises from unrealistic expectations on the part of both parents and children when the family is reunited.

SET adopts a bridging approach to correcting the awkwardness and conflict between formerly separated parents and adolescents. The therapist focuses on connecting the adolescent to an extended-family member to whom she or he already feels somewhat close (this may be the individual who cared for the adolescent during the period of separation, if this individual is available to participate in treatment). This dyadic relationship is then used as a bridge for reconnecting the adolescent with her or his parents. That is, the therapist works through the "intermediary" to facilitate reconnection. It is important to note that the therapist must ensure that the extended family member supports the treatment goal of reconnecting the parent and child. Otherwise, any attempts to reestablish the parent–child relationship through the extended family member are met with subtle and overt resistance. Reframing interventions may be used to expand the youth's and parent's understanding of each other's experiences prior to and during the separation and following reunion. Equally important are reconnecting interventions in which affective bonds are searched for and highlighted from the past experiences of both the parent and child. This is one of the few times when SET focuses on the past as a tool for changing present interactional patterns.

Lack of Knowledge

Many Hispanic immigrants have little or no working knowledge of English or American ways. These language or cultural barriers prevent immigrants from involving themselves sufficiently in their community and its institutions. The longer Hispanic immigrants remain without learning English, the more they remain marginalized from American society (Baptiste, 1993). The parents' inability to communicate in English often results in a reversal of normative parent–adolescent roles, where adolescents serve as translators, authorities on the local culture, and vital links to the outside world. As a result, parental authority is undermined, adolescents are left without parental guidance, and youth are placed in roles for which they are developmentally unprepared (Szapocznik, Robbins, Mitrani, Santisteban, & Williams, 2002). For example, in some SET cases, the adolescent, who was in trouble for fighting in school, had to translate between his parents and teachers during a disciplinary meeting. Not surprisingly, the parents and teachers were both left to wonder whether their words had been translated accurately.

Equally and sometimes more important, Hispanic immigrants also may lack knowledge about the systems and workings of American society (Leon & Dziegielewski, 2000). This is the case even in highly Hispanic cities like Miami where peer, school, and juvenile justice systems are still primarily American. Parents' lack of familiarity and knowledge about their new host culture serves to isolate them from their children's social environments. This, in turn, prevents the isolated parent from learning about and intervening in the contexts that their adolescents confront (cf. Szapocznik & Kurtines, 1993). Two areas in which this is particularly apparent are the peer and school systems. For example, immigrant parents are generally not aware of the responsibility that American culture places on parents to monitor teens' behavior and school performance. With respect to friends, immigrant parents often fail to provide adequate supervision and monitoring of peer activities and many times have little or no connection to the parents of their child's friends. With respect to schools, immigrant parents often remain disconnected from the school system because they expect the school to provide the structure and support necessary to ensure their child's successful school performance. Unfortunately, many immigrant parents do not recognize that schools rely heavily on parents to support the school in educating their children. This lack of understanding often results in a lack of connection to the school system as well as an inappropriate scapegoating of parents by representatives of the school system that see the parent as nonsupportive of the child's academic performance.

Therefore, SET works to connect Hispanic parents to their adolescents' peer, school, and juvenile justice microsystems. A therapist often begins by serving as an intermediary between parents and outside systems (peers, teachers, probation officers), but—as therapy progresses—the therapist starts to back away and allow the parents to interact directly with representatives of outside systems. In doing so, the therapist assists in helping parents begin to acquire the necessary knowledge about how to parent effectively in the United States.

Differential Acculturation

Hispanic immigrant parents and adolescents differ markedly in their degree of exposure to American culture. Whereas parents often reside in largely Hispanic areas and associate mainly with other Spanish speakers, adolescents are quickly introduced to American customs in school, through their peers, television, and other media (Szapocznik & Kurtines, 1993). As a result of these differences in cultural exposure, cultural incompatibilities between the host culture and the immigrant's culture of origin are brought to bear on the family system. Immigrant children and adolescents have a tendency to acculturate quickly to the host culture, whereas parents tend to hold on to their culture-of-origin beliefs and—compared to their children—are much less likely to quickly adopt the values of the host culture (De la Rosa, Vega, & Radisch, 2000). This phenomenon, known as *differential acculturation*, may lead to heightened levels of family conflict by compounding cultural incompatibilities onto normative parent–adolescent disagreements. For example, adolescent immigrants may begin to internalize individualistic "American" behaviors, attitudes, values, and habits soon after arriving in the United States (Baptiste, 1993). Parental authority, which is generally considered to be beyond question in Hispanic cultures, is undermined by this individualistic and self-directed orientation (Leslie, 1993). Traditionally oriented parents may perceive their adolescent's individualistic value system as a rejection of Hispanic values and of themselves, while in turn the acculturated adolescent may perceive her or his parents as overly demanding and controlling (Kurtines & Szapocznik, 1996).

Through the distance it creates, differential acculturation increases the likelihood that adolescents will turn to peers, rather than parents, for advice (cf. De la Rosa et al., 2000; Szapocznik & Kurtines, 1993). Conflicts surrounding cultural issues drive parents and adolescents apart and can prompt adolescents to seek out deviant peers as a way of rebelling against the obedience and deference required in traditional Hispanic families (cf. Szapocznik et al., 2002). In turn, overreliance on peers serves to increase the youth's drug use and other problem behaviors (cf. Fuligni, Eccles, Barber, & Clements, 2001).

SET addresses differential acculturation through its focus on restructuring maladaptive family interactions. Reframing, attending to developmental stage, focusing on executive leadership, and shifting boundaries are all intervention strategies that may be utilized to address the intergenerational differences that are exacerbated by the differential acculturation process. A primary focus of these restructuring interventions is to disrupt within family conflict by: (a) expanding both the parent's and youth's views about American and Hispanic culture, and (b) focusing on the underlying fears and concerns that family members have for one another.

Case Study

The Hernandez family had immigrated from Colombia 3 years prior to their referral for family therapy. The family consisted of mother (38 years old) and two children (daughter, age 15; son, age 12). The family was referred by the public defender following the daughter's (Isabelita) third arrest, this time for drug possession.

In the first telephone contact (initiated by the mother), the therapist heard screaming and fighting in the background. The mother sounded overwhelmed. When the therapist explained why he was calling, Ms. Hernandez angrily stated that she could never get Isabelita go to therapy. The therapist asked Ms. Hernandez for permission to come to the home, during a time in which she and Isabelita were both likely to be home. Because Ms. Hernandez worked during the day, the appointment was set for the next evening. When the therapist arrived at the home, the mother was alone with her 12-year-old son. Ms. Hernandez explained that Isabelita often stayed out with her friends, and she could not predict when she would be home. The 12-year-old son quickly confirmed his mother's story, adding that Isabelita was always upsetting his mother and that he wished she would just go away.

Joining: Establishing the Therapeutic System

The therapist began to join with Ms. Hernandez by listening to the story of her hardships in this country and with Isabelita. Ms. Hernandez expressed how overwhelmed she felt by Isabelita's behavior and that she did not know what she could do. In fact, she said that, "It is all in God's hands now." It appeared from the story that Ms. Hernandez did not have well-established rules or consequences for Isabelita's behavior. Likewise, she had no knowledge of Isabelita's activities outside of the home. Communication between daughter and mother was characterized by anger, blaming, and fighting. Ms. Hernandez stated that they could argue for hours about the same thing, and the next day they would have the same argument all over again.

After an hour, Isabelita arrived. Her gait was unsteady and her speech was slurred. She went straight to the kitchen. When Ms. Hernandez said to Isabelita, "Come here, there is someone here who has come to see you about your arrest," Isabelita answered, "F---k them, I am hungry." Ms. Hernandez went to the kitchen to serve Isabelita her dinner, screaming at her, "Your food is already cold. You are late again. We had dinner two hours ago." The screaming between mother and daughter continued for another 10 minutes before the therapist came to the kitchen to attempt to introduce herself to Isabelita—as a way of extending the joining process.

Diagnosis and Treatment Plan

Organization: Family Microsystem

There is a clear problem with this family's hierarchy and leadership. In particular, there is an inverted power structure where the daughter is in a powerful position, whereas the mother is powerless and feels overwhelmed. This inversion is exacerbated by the lack of rules or consequences for the daughter's behavior. In addition to problems with hierarchy and leadership, there is also no sibling subsystem, and the son is triangulated between mother and daughter. A major focus of treatment is to transfer power back to the mother by enhancing her leadership role in the family.

Resonance: Family Microsystem

Mother and daughter are enmeshed in a conflictive relationship, and the mother and son are emotionally overconnected. The focus of treatment is to reframe the daughter's behavior to reduce the negativity, and to block the son from getting involved in mother–daughter conflicts.

Developmental Stage: Family Microsystem

The daughter's behavior is inappropriately infantile and demanding. The son is playing a "mother's partner" role, and the mother does not assume appropriate parenting roles. The focus of treatment is to help the daughter express her feelings in an age-appropriate manner and to help the mother elicit and validate the daughter's feelings. Again, the therapist must block the son and help the mother develop the skills to block the son from getting involved directly in mother–daughter interactions. Interventions must also help the mother get the son involved in age-appropriate social activities.

Acculturation differences are compounding normative parent–adolescent disagreements and are exacerbating the distance between mother and daughter. The therapist must reframe disagreements in this light to help the two of them to "get on the same page" in their interactions. The mother must develop skills for effectively monitoring and supervising the daughter's activities in the peer and school systems, thereby increasing the mother's leadership role in the family.

Identified Patienthood: Family Microsystem

The daughter is designated as the source of the family's problems. This rigid, centralization of the daughter must be addressed by expanding the focus to the entire family.

Conflict Resolution

The mother and daughter tend to shout at and insult one another with no resolution. Interventions must reframe negativity and family members must be redirected to stay on topic and resolve issues without leaving the room or resorting to personal attacks.

Resonance: Exosystem

The mother and son are socially isolated. Interventions must help the mother by creating opportunities for her to become familiar with the American culture, particularly with those systems that may provide her with direct support (e.g., church group). The mother needs to be encouraged to support and provide opportunities for her son to associate with same-age friends.

Resonance: Family–Peer Mesosystem

The daughter is overinvolved with high-risk peers. The mother does not have a connection to the adolescent's peers or their parents. She also does not monitor or supervise her daughter's peer activities. Interventions must address the mother's ability to communicate with her daughter about her activities and acquaintances without belittling her daughter or her friends. As interventions are successful in transferring power back to the mother, the daughter's peer selection must be brought up, and the mother needs to encourage the daughter to evaluate the interpersonal consequences of peer selection.

Resonance/Conflict Resolution: Family-School Mesosystem

The mother does not recognize the role she can play in influencing the daughter's school attendance and performance, and has thus remained uninvolved with school personnel. This lack of involvement has been interpreted by teachers and counselors as a lack of investment on the part of the mother. Interventions must focus on increasing the mother's awareness of the role she can play with the school, decreasing the school personnel's negative interpretations of the mother, and organizing a meeting with the mother and school personnel to create a family–school system that plans, monitors, and supervises Isabelita's school attendance and performance.

Case Conceptualization

In the Hernandez family, the mother is overwhelmed and is unable to manage her daughter's behavior. The daughter, in turn, has distanced herself from the family and spends the majority of her time with sexually active and drug-using friends. When the daughter is home, she and her mother fight constantly, with the brother intervening to take the mother's side against his sister. The brother's triangulation further isolates the daughter from the family.

The therapist must start by joining the mother, then joining the daughter, and then joining additional systems. It is important very early to work to restructure the dysfunctional family hierarchy. By supporting the mother, the therapist needs to help her break the cycle between herself and her daughter so that the mother can begin to recapture some control. The brother's attempts at triangulation need to be blocked, allowing the mother and daughter to resolve their issues in a dyadic manner. This would also permit the brother to engage in more age-appropriate activities. Isabelita's disobedient behavior and the mother's anger need to be reframed in more positive terms to change the affective tone of her relationship with the mother, and thus to permit more positive interactions between them.

Cultural issues also need to be taken into account in diagnosing the Hernandez family. Upon their arrival in the United States from Colombia 3 years earlier, the members of this family began to drift apart from one another. Isabelita began learning English and associating with Americanized peers, whereas her mother remained socially and culturally isolated. Ms. Hernandez had become increasingly uncomfortable with Isabelita's behavior and choices of friends, but the widening chasm between mother and daughter discouraged Ms. Hernandez from addressing these issues with Isabelita. By the time Isabelita was referred to treatment, the family's maladaptive interactions had become rigidly entrenched, and Ms. Hernandez had ceded nearly all of her power and authority to her daughter.

Restructuring

During the second session conducted 1 week later, the same incident reoccurred with Isabelita coming home late, clearly on drugs. Having established a therapeutic relationship with the family, while the therapist sat with Ms. Hernandez waiting for Isabelita to show up, the therapist used the time to discuss with Ms. Hernandez how she could respond differently to Isabelita when she arrived late (i.e., a reversal), coaching her to remain calm and not to let Isabelita engage her in a screaming match. Upon her arrival, Isabelita bolted to the kitchen and demanded food as usual. Ms. Hernandez, encouraged by the therapist to do so, continued to sit in the living room, which in their small home was just next to the kitchen. Isabelita came into the living room and began shouting at her mother about the food. The mother yelled back to Isabelita, "You are a drug addict," and this began a new cycle of blaming and recrimination. The therapist intervened by saying to Ms. Hernandez, "You need to stay calm, and not let her control you with her fighting." After several such interventions, Ms. Hernandez finally looked at the therapist and said, "I am trying to do it, but it is very hard." This statement represented Ms. Hernandez's initial step in using the therapist as an aid to help her detach from the conflict with her daughter. Furthermore, when the son stepped in, the therapist encouraged the mother to hold him back as well.

Isabelita continued to scream at her mother without a response for another 15 minutes before storming to her bedroom in a fury. Having been unsuccessful in engaging either her mother or brother in a fight, she was frustrated and gave up. After the therapist gave the mother ample support and praise for having controlled the situation and avoided a fight, the therapist moved the conversation to the next step by discussing with the mother other ways in which Isabelita would "push her mother's buttons," and gave Ms. Hernandez the task of using the newly learned skills on these other occasions.

This was a great gain for a single session, and it was clear that the gains from this session needed to be followed up and extended as soon as possible. The therapist told Ms. Hernandez that "we can keep making things better if we meet again in a few days." After getting Isabelita to rejoin the discussion, the therapist pointed out to her that ". . . these fights between you and your mom don't have to happen. If you'll agree to have me here again next week, we can keep working toward having peace in your life." As a result, both Ms. Hernandez and Isabelita agreed to hold another session.

At the beginning of the next session, the therapist followed up on the previous week's gains by reviewing how Ms. Hernandez and Isabelita had made progress around the issue of fighting. The therapist intervened to block the brother's attempts to triangulate himself into interactions between Ms. Hernandez and Isabelita. Throughout the session, the therapist praised Ms. Hernandez whenever she avoided a fight, and empathy when she did not. ("I understand how hard it is, but I know you tried.") The therapist also praised Isabelita amply for her ability to follow her mother's lead in avoiding fights that are "so upsetting to you." Hence, both mother and Isabelita received credit and praise for accomplishing changes in their relationship. The therapist also helped the mother to block her son's attempts to interrupt her interactions with her daughter, and provided support to the mother as she controlled her son's behaviors. Having made a major accomplishment in placing the mother in control of the interactions, the therapist was now ready to move to the next level—negotiation of rules and consequences. The therapist also began to reinforce changes in Isabelita's behavior. The therapist took an active role in helping Ms. Hernandez to move into a more appropriate parental role by gradually praising each of the mother's attempts to guide or set limits for her daughter. Isabelita's disrespectful behavior was reframed as her way of showing her own frustration and pain.

At the same time, the therapist began to expand the mother's leadership role in the school, peer, and juvenile justice systems. The therapist provided information to Ms. Hernandez to increase her understanding of these systems, particularly about the important role that she can play in influencing how these systems treat her daughter. Working with Ms. Hernandez, a meeting was scheduled with one of Isabelita's teachers and her school counselor. Prior to this meeting, the therapist contacted the school counselor to gain information about her experience with Isabelita. During this meeting, it was very clear that the teacher held negative beliefs about Ms. Hernandez because she had not attended any parent–teacher conferences. These beliefs were reframed as a lack of knowledge of school procedures rather than a lack of parental investment. During a meeting with Ms. Hernandez and the school counselor, the therapist validated Ms. Hernandez's and the counselor's efforts to set up a plan for monitoring Isabelita's attendance and homework, but otherwise tried to permit the interaction to occur with as little interference as possible, thereby permitting Ms. Hernandez to gain valuable experience negotiating with the school on her own behalf.

Ms. Hernandez also worked directly with the justice system to be directly involved in monitoring the terms of Isabelita's probation. This connection with the justice system further elevated Ms. Hernandez's leadership role, and provided tangible support for her as she set up and enforced rules.

The therapist also worked at three levels to address peer relationships. First, the therapist worked with Ms. Hernandez to increase her understanding of the critical influence that peers play in the lives of adolescents in the United States, and to develop skills for monitoring and supervising peer relationships. Ms. Hernandez was encouraged to meet Isabelita's friends and their parents. Second, at the family level, the therapist worked with both Ms. Hernandez and Isabelita to improve their ability to discuss peer relationships. Ms. Hernandez was coached on how to be more supportive of her daughter's needs for social connectedness and to not be overly critical of her friends. As she focused more on her daughter's needs and decreased her negativity about peers, Isabelita became more open to discussing both her positive and negative experiences with her friends. Finally, at the level of the ecosystem, the therapist worked with Isabelita, Ms. Hernandez, and the school to place Isabelita in an after school program that involved teaching kids a variety of skills, including arts and music. This program was excellent because it: (a) decreased the amount of time that Isabelita was unsupervised,

(b) decreased the amount of time she spent with her peers who were involved with alcohol and drugs, and (c) increased her involvement with peers involved in prosocial activities.

Gradually, over time, Isabelita's externalizing behavior and drug abuse decreased. Ms. Hernandez learned to befriend her daughter and show affection (i.e., a reversal) whenever Isabelita threw a tantrum. Isabelita began to phrase her complaints in the form of respectful disagreements rather than hostile attacks. The brother, sensing that the tension between his sister and mother was decreasing, backed away from the triangulated relationship with his mother. The mother was encouraged to provide opportunities for the brother to engage in his own social activities. This was accomplished by encouraging Ms. Hernandez to enroll the son in a youth group at her church. An additional benefit of connecting the son to this youth group was that Ms. Hernandez was able to increase her interactions with other parents who were struggling with raising children in America. These interactions with other parents served to further decrease Ms. Hernandez's isolation and provided her with knowledge and support for her effective parenting attempts.

It is important to note that although the present example involved a single-parent family, SET is appropriate with many types of family constellations, including two-parent (biological, blended, alternative, foster) and extended family households (e.g., grandparent). The goals and focus of treatment in two-parent households are quite similar to the example presented in the preceding section; however, interventions often involve creating and supporting a parental leadership subsystem where power is shared and balanced between the parental adults.

Conclusion

SET is a family-based intervention that has evolved from 30 years of clinical work with Latino children and adolescents and their families in Miami. Based on family systems theory and therapy (BSFT), SET consists of structural and strategic interventions that are intended to reshape family interactions. The within-family components of SET target aspects of family functioning that have been shown to be directly related to adolescent behavior problems. Thus, the primary focus of interventions is to create new and adaptive patterns of interaction within the family that engender prosocial adolescent behaviors. Five patterns of within-family interaction are addressed: Organization, Resonance, Developmental Stage, Identified Patienthood, and Conflict Resolution.

Recognition of the critical importance of the full context of influences on the adolescent, SET extends the family systems focus to target other systems that directly or indirectly influence adolescents. In doing so, SET provides a comprehensive framework for organizing and implementing interventions across all of the adolescent's "worlds." Specifically, interventions are implemented to target the microsystems (peer, school, juvenile justice), mesosystems (family–peer, family–school, family juvenile justice) and exosystems (family support networks) that directly and indirectly influence adolescent behavior. Finally, SET is particularly effective in addressing processes that arise among families of recent immigrants. In particular, SET is sensitive to identifying and addressing problems associated with immigration-related separations, lack of knowledge of American culture, and differential acculturation within the family.

Although the within-family components of SET have been extensively examined in research investigations, the efficacy of the full ecological model has yet to be established. Although research in this area is currently underway, there is a clear need for additional studies of SET and its component parts.

Discussion Questions

1. Is SET more effective than alternative, or already established, interventions?
2. What sort of training or clinical skills are needed to successfully implement SET interventions?
3. Are community agencies receptive to the SET philosophy, and more important, are agencies structured in a way that makes the implementation of SET feasible in a real-world setting?
4. Are the additional resources required in SET (e.g., intervening in multiple systems) more cost effective than other intervention alternatives?
5. Can SET be adapted to integrate the array of services provided by interdisciplinary providers to address adolescent behavior problems in a more systematic and case-specific manner?
6. What are the most effective strategies for engaging members of the adolescent's ecosystem into clinical interventions? How can this be achieved while maintaining a trusting, confidential relationship with adolescents and their family members?

Acknowledgment

The work presented in this chapter was supported by the National Institute on Drug Abuse (DA 10574, José Szapocznik, principal investigator).

References

Alexander, J. F., Holtzworth-Munroe, A., & Jameson, P. B. (1994). The process and outcome or marital and family therapy: Research review and evaluation. In A. E. Bergin & S. L. Garfield (Eds.), *Handbook of psychotherapy and behavior change* (pp. 595–630). New York: Wiley.

Baptiste, D. A. (1993). Immigrant families, adolescents and acculturation: Insights for therapists. *Marriage and Family Review, 19*, 341–363.

Bronfenbrenner, U. (1977). Toward an experimental ecology of human development. *American Psychologist, 32*, 513–531.

Bronfenbrenner, U. (1979). Contexts of child rearing: Problems and prospects. *American Psychologist, 34*, 844–850.

Bronfenbrenner, U. (1986). Ecology of the family as a context for human development: Research perspectives. *Developmental Psychology, 22*, 723–742.

Coatsworth, J. D., Pantin, H., & Szapocznik, J. (2002). Familias Unidas: A family-centered ecodevelopmental intervention to reduce risk for problem behavior among Hispanic adolescents. *Clinical Child and Family Psychology Review, 5*(2), 113–132.

De la Rosa, M., Vega, R., & Radisch, M. A. (2000). The role of acculturation in the substance abuse behavior of African-American and Latino adolescents: Advances, issues, and recommendations. *Journal of Psychoactive Drugs, 32*, 33–42.

DiGiuseppe, R., Linscott, J., & Jilton, R. (1996). Developing the therapeutic alliance in child-adolescent psychotherapy. *Applied and Preventive Psychology, 5*, 85–100.

Dishion, T. J., French, D. C., & Patterson, G. R. (1995). The development and ecology of antisocial behavior. In D. Cicchetti & D. J. Cohen (Eds.), *Developmental psychopathology, Vol. 2: Risk, disorder, and adaptation. Wiley series on personality processes* (pp. 421–471). New York: Wiley.

Fuligni, A. J., Eccles, J. S., Barber, B. L., & Clements, P. (2001). Early adolescent peer orientation and adjustment during high school. *Developmental Psychology, 37*, 28–36.

Hawkins, J. D., Catalano, R. F., & Miller, J. Y. (1992). Risk and protective factors for alcohol and other drug problems in adolescence and early adulthood: Implications for substance abuse prevention. *Psychological Bulletin, 112*, 64–105.

Kurtines, W., & Szapocznik, J. (1996). Family interaction patterns: structural family therapy in contexts of cultural diversity. In E. Hibbs & P. Jensen (Eds.), *Psychosocial treatments for child and adolescent disorders: Empirically based strategies for clinical practice* (pp. 671–697). Washington, DC: American Psychological Association.

Leon, A. M., & Dziegielewski, S. F. (2000). Engaging Hispanic immigrant mothers: Revising the time-limited psycho-educational group model. *Crisis Intervention and Time Limited Treatment, 6*, 13–27.

Leslie, L. A. (1993). Families fleeing war: The case of Central Americans. *Marriage and Family Review, 19*, 193–205.

Liddle, H. A., & Dakof, G. A. (1995a). Efficacy of family therapy for drug abuse: Promising but not definitive. *Journal of Marital and Family Therapy, 21*, 511–543.

Liddle, H. A., & Dakof, G. A. (1995b). Family-based treatment for adolescent drug use: State of the science. In E. Rahdert & D. Czechowicz (Eds.), *Adolescent drug abuse: Clinical assessment and therapeutic interventions* (pp. 218–254). Nida research monograph No. 156, NIH Publication No. 95-3908. Rockville, MD: National Institute on Drug Abuse.

Mitrani, V. B., Santisteban, D., & Muir, J. A. (in press). A family treatment module for Hispanic behavior-problem adolescents reunited with their mothers following an immigration-related separation. *American Journal of Orthopsychiatry.*

Patterson, G. R. (1993). Orderly change in a stable world: The antisocial trait as a chimera. *Journal of Consulting and Clinical Psychology, 61*, 911–919.

Stanton, M. D., & Shadish, W. R. (1997). Outcome, attrition, and family-couples treatment for drug abuse: A meta-analysis and review of the controlled, comparative studies. *Psychological Bulletin, 122,* 170–191.

Suárez-Orozco, C., & Suárez-Orozco, M. (2001). *Children of immigration.* Cambridge, MA: Harvard University Press.

Szapocznik, J., Hervis, O., & Schwartz, S. J. (2002). *Brief Strategic Family Therapy for adolescent drug abuse.* Rockville, MD: National Institute on Drug Abuse.

Szapocznik, J., & Kurtines, W. (1980). Acculturation, biculturalism and adjustment among Cuban Americans. In A. Padilla (Ed.), *Psychological dimensions on the acculturation process: Theory, models, and some new findings* (pp. 139–159). Boulder, CO: Westview.

Szapocznik, J., & Kurtines, W. M. (1989). *Breakthroughs in family therapy with drug abusing and problem youth.* New York: Springer.

Szapocznik, J., & Kurtines, W. (1993). Family psychology and cultural diversity: Opportunities for theory, research and application. *American Psychologist, 48,* 400–407.

Szapocznik, J., Kurtines, W., Santisteban, D. A., Pantin, H., Scoppetta, M., Mancilla, Y., et al. (1997). The evolution of structural ecosystems theory for working with Latino families. In J. G. Garcia & M. C. Zea (Eds.), *Psychological interventions and research with Latino populations.* Boston: Allyn & Bacon.

Szapocznik, J., Robbins, M. S., Mitrani, V., Santisteban, D., & Williams, R. A. (2002). Brief Strategic Family Therapy with behavior problem Hispanic youth (pp. 83–109). In J. Lebow (Ed.) & F. Kaslow (Series Ed.), *Integrative and eclectic psychotherapies: Comprehensive handbook of psychotherapy,* vol. 4. New York: Wiley.

Szapocznik, J., Scopetta, M., & King, O. E. (1978). Theory and practice in matching treatment to the special characteristics and problems of Cuban immigrants. *Journal of Community Psychology, 6,* 112–122.

Szapocznik, J., & Williams, R. A. (2000). Brief strategic family therapy: Twenty five years of interplay among theory, research and practice in adolescent behavior problems and drug abuse. *Clinical Child and Family Psychology Review, 3,* 117–135.

Part II

International Applications

Chapter 5

Essentials of Good Practice
The Making of a Cultural
Psychiatrist in Urban India

Vasudeo Paralikar
Mohan Agashe
Mitchell G. Weiss

The authors describe a cultural approach to psychotherapy that encourages patients to examine and experiment with different local (emic) formulations of their illness. The limitations of Western diagnostic categories and frames of reference are discussed within the context of cultural and family systems in middle-class, urban India. An emic assessment framework derived from cultural epidemiological research that focuses on illness-related experience, meaning, and behavior is presented. Case extracts drawn from experience in psychiatric practice in Pune, India illustrate an approach to culturally sensitive mental health care.

A freshly graduated psychiatrist in India may be well equipped with an armamentarium of diagnostic and therapeutic skills appropriate for practice in Western societies, but these may nevertheless require extensive modification for practice in urban India. To make these skills useful locally, there is still much to learn, unlearn, and adapt for the two essential tasks of helping patients and facilitating professional survival. In this chapter we consider this process of cultural recalibration, a framework to guide it, what it entails, and its value for clinical practice. At the outset, it is useful to examine the local practice setting, characteristics and expectations of patients, and the orientations of practitioners.

With a strong family system and rich cultural traditions, the local approaches to identifying and managing psychological and interpersonal problems in middle-class urban India constitute a context that shapes the needs and expectations of mental health services. We shall consider how a cultural perspective generally, and a particular emic framework that has emerged from research in cultural epidemiology, may guide a locally appropriate clinical practice. Clinical applications and implications of this cultural orientation are reviewed and illustrated with examples from experience in the private practice of psychiatry in urban Pune. In deference to that clinical setting, which experience discussed here is based on, the terms psychiatrist, therapist, and doctor are used interchangeably in the text.

Urban Setting and Psychiatric Practice

Pune is India's eighth largest city with a population of 3.75 million (Census of India, 2001). It is also widely acknowledged as a cultural center for education, theater, and art. It is the home of the country's national Film and Television Institute of India, and it is also a center for computing and software development, not only for many private companies but also the national Centre for the Development of Advanced Computing on the campus of Pune University. The city is located 160 km southeast of Mumbai, the state capital, and the state of Maharashtra is widely regarded as a progressive state with the largest number of psychiatrists and inpatient psychiatric beds. Psychiatric services include a large state-run mental hospital, an academic institute and private hospital departments of psychiatry, and many private psychiatrist practitioners.

Based on the standard training in psychiatry, rooted in the European and American traditions, in clinical practice one expects to be able to diagnose patients with relatively "pure" disorders (that is, disorders that clearly meet standard diagnostic criteria for a single category). Such patients are the ones typically recruited in trials to test the efficacy of new pharmaceutical drugs. In the reality of clinical practice, however, experience in academic and private practice settings shows that patients who typically come for treatment have complex problems that may not readily fit into the neat categories of disorder outlined by the major diagnostic systems—the *International Classification of Diseases*, 10th edition (ICD-10; WHO, 1995) and the *Diagnostic and Statistical Manual of Mental Disorders*, 4th edition (DSM-IV; APA, 1994). The match and mismatch of patients' problems and international categories of disorder is more complex than standard training in the field suggests, not only in India but also in the West (Guthrie, 2000), but cultural differences in the roots of psychiatry and the setting of psychiatric practice highlight the mismatch. Moreover, inasmuch as psychiatry is rooted in a biopsychosocial model, at least in principle, its scope is broader than other branches of medicine. As a result of this complexity, the insights learned during practice may seem amorphous compared to those learned in academia, which are generally crystallized and crisp. By acknowledging such ambiguities and promoting a model of medicine that extends beyond biology, psychiatry serves a unique function in linking medicine to various other domains, including culture, sociology, spirituality, and religion (Horacio, 2000).

Biopsychosocial and Cultural Perspectives

From a biological perspective, it is necessary that we understand the origins and manifestations of patients' suffering in terms of brain and behavior. The psychiatric practitioner has to be a physician first, to be able to diagnose the condition, to understand the physical processes responsible for the emotional and behavioral manifestations of his or her patient, and to investigate or refer the patient appropriately. The ability to detect and handle the medical condition responsible for a patient's obvious psychiatric symptoms is the basic prerequisite of good psychiatric practice.

Also, the pharmacological treatment and monitoring of the psychiatric and physical condition of the patient are essentially biological aspects of psychiatric treatment. Thus, a psychiatrist has to be "physician plus," a doctor as well as a counselor. This is necessary not only for medical and ethical reasons, but also for one's professional survival. Patients may not understand the value of this, but referring physicians feel more secure in the psychiatrist who has good clinical acumen and thus would not miss an organic condition that is often associated with or even causing the psychological symptoms.

The psychosocial approach contributes to the counseling component of a psychiatrist's professional identity. An understanding of psychological development, deviations from the "normal" development, the methods and contents of inquiry, and the nonpharmacological management of the diagnosed condition define this identity of the psychiatrist. Because psychiatric disorders do not occur in a vacuum, but always have a psychosocial and cultural context, one has to be conversant with the distinctive as well as the common characteristics of her or his own psychosocial and cultural development and that of the patients in her or his own community. The so-called normal development is rich in different nuances of the live process of human development. Naturally, the manifestations, course, and outcome of psychiatric disorders are different in each culture. Discerning these nuances of a patient's thinking, feeling, behavior, and personality, various stressors, and the internal and external resources, facilitates charting of the ever-changing dynamic of a patient's mental life in health and disease. Each experience and expression of a patient, whether verbal or otherwise, is then available for assessment. Putting these in perspective is essential for management.

Attention to cultural factors typically is overlooked in training curricula and left for the individual to deal with from experience. Various reasons may account for that, including the volume of biomedical information and predominance of a biological approach. An already packed curriculum and the need for uniform standards in medical education that leaves little room for consideration of local cultural issues are additional factors. Readiness to conform to the values of the dominant Western culture and the influence of pharmaceutical interests and perks also contribute to the priority of biological models in educa-tion and practice.

The Role of Arts and Festivals

The structural changes in the brains of musicians, the functional changes in the brain during the telling of truth and lies, and various neurochemical changes in the brain associated with aggression (Kale, 2002) are all proofs of how percep-tion, feeling, thought, and behavior are important in mental health and disease. Arts, festivals, and other manifestations of culture also play a significant role in shaping the environments of well being, distress, health, and illness (Agashe, 1984). Festivals, arts, and literature also provide a myriad of characters and scripts, and as we examine, identify, and emulate them, they define a set of cultural experiences and meanings in various aspects of personal and social life. Their symbolism enriches the life of our inner worlds with numerous introjects ema-nating from and enriching collective local cultures. Cultural traditions in India are very old and heterogeneous, and the characters and scripts produced over the course of this cultural history are innumerable, eminently engaging, and highly relevant to the interests of mental health and illness (Shamasundar, 1993; Weiner, 1997).

Psychiatric Practice Setting and the Demands of Therapy

Therapy transpires on an island in time and space through a highly abnormal relationship with unique rules and language. These must be learned not only by therapists but also by patients. With various kinds of therapy, professionals know how difficult it is to restrict practice to a single pure type to meet the needs of a given patient. Consequently, therapy may proceed as a process of reverse engi-neering, in the sense that the therapist has to decipher the mechanisms and rules of functioning that account for verbal and nonverbal expressions, and in-dicate the nature of the patient's personality. Subsequently, the therapist aims to help the patient learn about those mechanisms and rules and to correct or change maladaptive ways. Thus, the therapeutic task is a live process of collabo-rating, learning, reflecting, doing, modifying, adapting, and relearning.

Counseling and psychotherapy are integral components of psychiatric prac-tice in urban India. Some patients may ask, What is the difference between a psychologist and a psychiatrist? The subspecialties among psychiatrists and coun-selors are known to very few, and are specifically sought after by fewer. Ques-tions about the professional concepts of disorder, however, may be more substantial. Some people do not regard emotional suffering as a diagnosable disorder even after they become patients and seek professional help for such problems. In psychiatric practice in India, it is rare for a patient to be told a diagnosis, even after recovery at the end of treatment; this lack of authoritative information may render patients more vulnerable to stigmatizing stereotypes and attitudes (McGorry & McConville, 1999).

Psychiatrists in general are explicitly or implicitly regarded as doctors who give shocks or electroconvulsive therapy (i.e., ECTs) to the lunatics. There is a lurking fear in the minds of almost all patients seeing a psychiatrist that a doctor might label them as mad and prescribe or actually give ECTs against their wishes. This is invariably associated with a fear of being permanently stigmatized as an incurable lunatic, someone to be avoided and despised. The scene is changing rapidly and many lay people and doctors in other specialties are becoming fascinated by psychology and psychiatry. We also see many psychologically minded patients who refer themselves for counseling and therapy, and who would like to participate actively in the treatment process.

In the West, for those who can afford it, or where subsidized services are available, psychotherapy is not solely considered treatment for mental illness; it is also regarded as a means to promote mental health and self-actualization. In urban India, however, acknowledging a need for psychiatric treatment suggests irreparable damage to the personality or a moral failing with social consequences, making one the target of stigma (Weiss & Ramakrishna, 2001). In any case, one of the doctor's responsibilities is to discover a patient's views about psychiatry and psychiatrists, his cultural beliefs related to mental health and illness, and to make sense of the patient's illness experience. It is also a clinical duty to assess the problems that bring a patient to treatment, decipher the pathology, and to treat and/or refer. In the course of this work, the psychiatrist must establish a therapeutic relationship based on trust of the patient and family. A doctor who is aloof and too coolly professional may be able to prescribe medicines, but is unlikely to engage patients in psychotherapy. Of course, this facilitates the formations of transferences and makes it easier to understand and interpret the dynamics of the patient's condition. This naturally poses greater responsibility for the therapist to always be aware of her or his role in a particular doctor–patient relationship.

Although with some exaggeration, it may be instructive to note that in clinical practice, it may sometimes be appropriate to proceed with therapy first and explain what transpired only in retrospect. The discussion that follows about therapeutic relationships, contracts for treatment, and consent provides further insight into expectations, fears, and process. Ideally, therapy may be considered a laboratory to create and break various fantasies and expectations, feelings, thoughts, attitudes, and experiences, all with relative impunity. Attaining this level of communication may be realized or verbalized by the patient or therapist; or it may be there without either one noticing it. Lyrons-Ruth and coauthors (cited in Gabbard, 2000) view these moments in therapy as a form of implicit relational knowing when something emotionally reparative transpires without involving the realm of insight or cognitive understanding. Such moments are a crucial element in the mode of therapeutic action.

It takes a lot of reflecting by the therapist to reconsider the formulation and identify the pivotal statements in therapy sessions. This depth of rapport is reached when both the therapist and the patient resonate with empathy; significant communication then may not take the customary full clock hour for therapy to proceed. What patients remember from successful therapy may be completely unexpected by therapists, as is documented. Therapists are often disappointed when they see former patients and ask them what they feel was of most benefit to them during the years they were in psychotherapy. Much to the dismay of the therapist, patients often do not remember any of the psychodynamic formulations or interpretations that the therapist carefully constructed to provide insight. Instead, they remember a joke the therapist told, a belly laugh they shared, a moving moment of emotional connection, or a glance exchanged when a special form of closeness was felt (Gabbard, 2000).

To facilitate the desired process, it is often important to avoid stigmatizing words such as psychiatrist, psychotherapy, or mental illness. Even though the nature and type of therapy may not be discussed in detail at the outset, the therapist has a responsibility to keep track of the aims and course of therapy. He or she should examine the plan and structure of the therapeutic process, critically consider the rationale, and carefully consider how the process may be improved.

Professional Identity as Psychiatrist and Therapist

In India 90% of trainees in psychiatry eventually opt for private practice and only about 10% pursue academics (Kala, 2000). The present curriculum does not address the needs of psychiatrists who are in private practice. The selection of candidates opting for undergraduate or postgraduate medical courses is based on their academic merit as judged by examinations. A fixed percentage of trainees, are from designated backward castes. Teachers are unable to pay attention to the cultural roots of an individual trainee, nor the way in which the changing cultural values and the concurrent professional development influence their development as individuals. Knowingly and unknowingly, students of psychiatry and psychology undergo a change in their own personality and values, often in proportion to their individual sensitivity and ability to introspect. The perceived meaning of their own experiences changes their worldview and self view. Thus, their professional identity often dominates their personal identity—in one's pursuit of the upwardly mobile, elitist culture exemplified by their peers in the Western world. Achieving a comfortable degree of confidence in the professional identity as a psychiatrist and therapist requires time and experience, and the interrelationship of personal and professional growth that is required make this particular enculturation process unique.

As trainees and young psychiatrists develop in their field, questions of confidence and satisfaction arise frequently (Rouff, 2000). It is common to hear colleagues commenting wistfully: "We should have had anesthesia training, since we so often have to give thiopentone or diazepam to our patients," or "We should have had more structured teaching programs, the other institute offers it so well," and so on. Some students arrange and pursue opportunities for training abroad to cultivate the type of practice they want, and to obtain some degree of career stability early on.

Becoming disillusioned or experiencing burnout occurs all too frequently in the course of training and practice of psychiatry. Does anyone ever improve? Why bother? Who listens? Make money! These are the themes of many cynical comments and jokes about psychiatry and its professionals. Overidentification with the patient or becoming alienated from religion, tradition, family, and other medical colleagues is also the fate of some professionals at the other extreme. Perceived lack of authenticity and humanism, failure to understand psychotherapy as a human endeavor, rigidly critical attitudes toward the culture of origin or toward the culture of psychiatry, or ambivalent feelings about both cultures are common. Eventual resolution of these conflicts may lead to an integration of cultures that serve the interests of the aspiring psychiatrist and patients. But failure to resolve the contradictions of these conflicting worlds may result in persistent indecision, discomfort, and dissatisfaction.

Bringing Culture into Psychiatry

The biopsychosocial perspective guides a healing process that extends beyond symptom removal; it aims to bring about lasting psychotherapeutic change. In reality the practice of psychiatry is often reduced to pigeonholing patients' problems into a limited number of diagnostic categories and meting out tranquilizer prescriptions. The patient continues to narrate the somatic complaints, and a Western-trained psychiatrist goes on diagnosing depression! It is evident that the concepts and approach of cultural epidemiological research must be implemented in the clinical practice of psychiatry, and must routinely be incorporated in the teaching curricula of psychiatry, psychology, and medicine.

Clinicians who are mainly interested in clinical practice may be somewhat averse to the term epidemiology. It may connote to them a sense of being far removed from the clinical and useful. A common misconception about culture is that we do not really have a distinctive culture left with us any more; in all modern societies it is the Western culture that is pervasive. Culture is to the society what personality is to the individual; it is a community's way of thinking, feeling, and behaving. Inescapably, it affects all of our individual choices and actions. Culture plays an important role in the concepts, attitudes, and stigma attached to mental illness (Razali, Hasanah, Aminah, & Subramaniam, 1998).

When individuals have a chronic illness it is only understandable and common that they engage in some kind of alternative medicine regime, a religious activity, or astrological prediction, or at least think about a probable explanation that is not contemporary or purely scientific. Such attitudes, beliefs, and practices become more prominent when we are concerned about intimate events in our life cycle, such as marriage. Culture shapes and often contains the psychiatric illnesses. The way we understand and explain our illness, and the manifestations, course, and outcome of the illness are all influenced by culture. Hence, it is necessary to understand the role of culture and epidemiology of cultural representations in the health and disease of a community (Sperber, 1996; Weiss, 2001).

All psychiatric disorders are behavioral in nature and have a social interpersonal dimension in their manifestations. Their outcomes vary according to culture. Therefore, Western diagnostic categories are frequently inadequate in guiding the management of emotional suffering in other cultures (Weiss, 2001). Concepts of anxiety and depression reflect a cultural bias of Western history to some extent. One might reasonably expect to find that some other cultures may be more concerned instead with different emotion, such as greed or envy (Wig, 1983). The prevailing trend in some countries toward limiting psychiatry to the already established diagnostic groups reflects the so-called threshold psychiatry defined by the diagnostic manuals, namely ICD and DSM. This tendency often generates a lot of NOS (Not Otherwise Specified) categories (Weiss, Raguram, & Channabasavanna, 1995). Angst (1997) has focused on these NOS categories and argues for the insufficiency of the threshold psychiatry and shows that the so-called subthreshold syndromes are frequent and clinically relevant. The distinction between threshold and subthreshold syndromes is evidently an artifact of the operational definition of psychiatric diagnoses. The congruence of the same conclusions, arrived at by cultural epidemiological studies and clinical psychiatric studies, is a strong argument in favor of the relevance and significance of subsyndromal disorders. Wherever the biological criteria for diagnoses are weak, the diagnosis becomes more and more culture-specific.

The tools and the power of professional concepts and techniques of psychiatry are not universally applicable. For example, professionally valid concepts such as psychotherapy as a growth-enhancing endeavor, autonomy and its pursuit, individuality over group loyalty, privacy, and confidentiality may not be accepted as such in other cultures. The domains of family interactions and their impermeability, power equations in family and of religious and spiritual activities are quite different in various communities. Hence the local cultural vetoes have to be considered before applying global international concepts to a local setting. For example, psychotherapy may have to be begun without formal contracting to circumvent the stigma about psychiatric intervention. Or the religious and spiritual activities, and pursuit for autonomy of a patient have to be understood in the context of the patient's culture before labeling the disorder.

Intrapsychic constructs such as narcissism, dependency needs, ego functions, and so on may be valid across cultures, albeit with differences in the shades of meaning (Wig, 1996). Tools and techniques for clinical assessment, such as diagnostic systems, interview schedules, and scales for measurement have to be adapted to suit local needs before they can be used.

The value of criteria-based diagnoses for research must be acknowledged as contributing to the scientific basis of psychiatry. Limitations of nosology, however, rapidly become clear with experience in clinical practice. The diagnosis has to be effective in guiding the management of the psychiatric disorders. Because many of the diagnoses are based on criteria that become culture-specific, the nosological understanding has to be complemented by a cultural understanding based on patients' experiences and beliefs, which give meaning to their problems. The limitations of nosology widen the gap between the training and practice of psychiatry, as readily perceived by a junior practitioner. A paradoxical feature concerning the match or mismatch of the clinical complexity of patients and the clinical experience of practitioners is worth noting. Patients with severe mental morbidity generally reach the senior practitioners when the high levels of stigma attached to visiting a psychiatrist can no longer postpone or avoid a psychiatric consultation; but patients with less serious conditions generally choose junior or fresh practitioners. These milder and less dramatic cases are more likely to have subthreshold syndromes, for which indicated treatment is less straightforward. Therefore, the juniors have a particularly difficult task with higher expectations of a successful outcome. The norms for the management of subthreshold disorders are less clear-cut; and the less dramatic presentations are not necessarily the easier to treat.

Moreover, to a freshly qualified psychiatrist it is difficult to understand and accept the ways of functioning of a senior practitioner. He feels that the senior is wrong on many counts and that practice is all about doing things wrongly. With the passing years he slowly imbibes the principles and techniques of practicing based on the needs of his patient–community and his theoretical orientations. Most of this training after graduation takes place inadvertently or unconsciously, often prompted and shaped by the practitioner's survival needs. One of the important lessons is that knowledge about crisp descriptions of clear disease categories as described in the book is not enough for diagnosis and management. One needs to understand the cultural differences in the presentations and course of the disorders. And one needs to supplement and modify the ways of inquiry and of delivering therapy to suit the patient and his suffering. Many of the issues that have to be modified and supplemented are cultural in origin. Hence, there is a need for a mix of anthropological and clinical psychiatric methods.

The relationship of these complementary orientations may be analogous to purported differences in cerebral hemispheres. The analytical, verbal, and factual aspects of the psychiatric methods are like left hemispheric functions; whereas the synthetic, nonverbal, and traditional or intuitive elements of practice are like the right hemispheric functions. It is essential to integrate both approaches. To treat patients effectively as whole persons, it is useful to diagnose and classify their problems, but it is also necessary to learn how they make sense of their suffering, its impact, its basis, and anticipated approaches to recovery. In the context of therapy we encourage patients to examine and experiment with different formulations (i.e., explanatory models) of their illness in the context of their lives.

Emic Framework for Research and Practice

Cultural Epidemiology

Cultural Epidemiology is an interdisciplinary field for research that integrates frameworks and methods of epidemiology and anthropology. Research in the field is concerned with the distribution of cultural representations of illness with reference to categories and narratives of experience, meaning, and behavior. This approach enhances the anthropological inquiry by taking research a step beyond ethnographic identification and description of cultural categories to consideration of their distributions, comparisons, and implications of these categories. It enhances clinical epidemiology by considering the local relevance of illness categories. Basic epidemiological interests in the distribution of disease and disorder are complemented by cultural epidemiological interests in the distribution of illness-related patterns of distress, perceived causes, and help seeking (Weiss, 2001).

As a link between professional and local concepts and priorities, cultural epidemiology has begun to serve as an effective guide to international health policy and multicultural health programs. The Explanatory Model Interview Catalog (EMIC) framework and various locally adapted EMIC interviews were developed as instruments for cultural epidemiological research. Experience with these EMIC interviews began with clinic-based studies of mental illness and infectious diseases (Weiss et al., 1992). Research in cultural epidemiology currently aims to support clinical psychiatric practice by providing local data to aid interpretation of explicit cultural assessments, such as the cultural formulation of DSM-IV (GAP, 2002).

Clinical diagnosis focuses on symptoms, signs, and assessment protocols to generate guidelines for prognostication and management. This is the professional's perspective (etic), intended to provide directions and care based on the diagnostic categories. Psychiatric epidemiological research facilitating the diagnostic assessment is embodied in tools such as DSM or ICD. Similarly, cultural epidemiological research has generated or crystallized certain values, concepts, and techniques the use of which is supposed to guide the cultural formulation of a case. This framework is embodied in locally adapted EMIC interviews, previously identified collectively as the Explanatory Model Interview Catalog. EMIC interviews are instruments used for cultural epidemiological study to determine the distribution of categories of experience, meaning, and behavior in selected clinic and community populations. The emic assessment framework that these interviews are based on is sensitive to the local formulation, which complements the diagnostic assessment frameworks of the ICD and the DSM. Cultural epidemiological research with emic interviews typically include narrative accounts of illness, and data sets maintain extensive qualitative components that are keyed to categorical data for integrated quantitative and qualitative analysis.

EMIC Framework for Clinical Assessment

The concepts "emic" and "etic" evolved from the terms "phonemic" and "phonetic." The emic signifies the subjective, personal, and an insider perspective. The etic signifies the objective, professional, and outsider perspective (Pike, 1966). These terms from the field of anthropology have enhanced the clinical perspective. A study of the experience, its meaning, and behavior (which are to some extent analogous to the scientific tasks of description, reduction, and interpretation of data) complements diagnostic assessment and constitutes a component of clinical evaluation that helps to guide treatment. Operational components of this framework include patterns of distress, perceived causes, and help-seeking behavior. Experience is represented by patterns of distress; perceived causes indicate the meaning for the patient, and assessment of help seeking indicates relevant illness behavior. This particular emic assessment framework emerged from research in cultural epidemiology (discussed in the next section).

In adapting the framework for research to clinical practice, it should be noted that the aim of the clinical consultation is not just to elicit symptoms, perceived causes, history of doctors visited, or treatments taken, but rather to elaborate a history and sequence of events from the onset of the suffering. The process of reviewing this history provides an opportunity to examine explicit or implicit ways of reasoning of the patient and of others who play a significant role in caring for the patient and finding help. The patient's explanatory models are constructed and reconstructed by the patient with the help of the clinician. Meticulous attention to the processes, rather than events, is facilitated by the clinical application of the emic assessment framework.

Application of a Cultural Approach in Clinical Practice

First Session

We allow the patient to speak freely, preferably the patient first and alone, according to the tenets of clinical teaching. But one should not hesitate to adjust if the patient or the family desire otherwise. A patient speaking freely and confidentially with the therapist, without the involvement of the family, is many times perceived as an insult by the close-knit and interdependent family. One may have to let the patient decide the actual setting of the therapy. Taking responsibility for the decision to see a therapist and actually carry it out is a big decision for the patient and his or her family in Indian culture, mainly because of stigma and misconceptions about psychiatry, psychology, and ideas about practitioners in those fields. Many times the patient is utterly dependent on the family or its dominating member. The guilt ensuing from such a rebellious act—that is, talking to a doctor (who is an outsider or stranger) about what happens in the family, is unthinkable. The therapist can be persecuted or blamed for encouraging the free expression of the patient, or the patient may later become defensive about his or her confidential communication. If the family or community does not understand the significance of the therapy process, the therapist may experience pressure from relatives to share with them what the patient has divulged. Patients may suffer for that later, because the family will look down on them. We need extreme tactfulness and patience in allowing the patient and the accompanying person(s) to decide the way they want to seek help. After several such "meetings" (they need not be called "consultations"), the situation is clearer and the therapist can then explain his or her understanding of the case and suggest ways to begin addressing the problem.

Consent of the patient for treatment is likewise implicit at the beginning and continues to be presumed until formalization of some kind is required as for hospital admission. Trying to obtain a written consent may lead to more misunderstanding than clarification. Patients become very defensive, may give false names and addresses, or they may even leave a research interview rather than sign, even if they readily agree to participate if they do not have to sign. Some patients fear that "giving away consent" empowers the doctor to do absolutely anything, including surgical removal and sale of body parts. "You can't complain about anything once you sign," one patient's wife explained, before convincing her husband to leave a research interview. Although this was an extreme example, the general fear of and aversion to consent or written communication is common. It may result from the expectation that a relationship with the doctor is supposed to be one of trust and faith, in which the doctor should offer unlimited patience and benevolence without requiring a signature in a transaction.

Diagnostic Process

Apart from noticing the symptoms, and systematically considering diagnostic categories based on our study of clinical psychiatry and counseling, we need to keep track of another concurrent process that is happening in the therapeutic setting. As the patient or family is speaking freely with as little interruption as possible, the therapist can continue to classify inwardly what is being said, whether experience, meaning, or help-seeking behaviors are being narrated. Reconstructing the history of events as the narrative unfolds, one should keep an eye on the processes that led to these events. Confusing issues often arise when patients start speaking about religious themes or superstitions and altered states of consciousness. Is the patient experiencing dissociative states, delusional experiences, or actually hallucinating? Are we missing epilepsy or other brain disorders?

Our tentative diagnosis and the patient's emerging explanatory model must be compared and synthesized continually, and both require consideration in preparing an explanation for the patient and family. Psychiatrists rely on word of mouth for acceptance and patronage in the community, and the positive regard of patients and their families is especially important, perhaps more so for psychiatrists because of the greater stigma associated with psychological disorders compared with general medical problems. Consequently, practitioners feel they must try to keep their patients satisfied. To establish an effective clinical alliance, a clinician must help patients understand their problems in a way that will be helpful. To do that, it is often useful to integrate the professional concepts and local formulation of the problems, but in a manner that recognizes both the responsibilities of clinical care and the ways that patients make use of their explanatory models.

The danger also should be recognized, however, that a seemingly empathic regard for a patient's explanatory model may be used exploitatively. For example, an unscrupulous doctor may refer back to the patient's account as evidence of a need for unnecessary investigations and treatment. "Oh yes, you do have weakness from deficiency of blood, or from overwork, or from sexual experiences, just as you say. This needs to be corrected with intravenous fluids and tonics, which are expensive."

Negotiating the Therapeutic Relationship

A completely new, uncertain, undifferentiated, and partially defined first encounter with the patient is a potential relationship that can take any form and feature in the days to come. The complexity of the relationship is even greater when the patient and therapist meet outside the consulting room or hospital setting. A therapist is shorn of his identity as a specialist in a particular branch of medicine or a particular school of psychotherapy. The terms "psychiatrist," "psychotherapist," "mental illness," and so forth are best avoided to minimize uncomfortable concerns for the patient about stigma. The identity of the therapist is not necessarily hidden, but usually it is mentioned only when necessary. Distancing from these terms is one of the commonest ways for the patient and family to minimize stigma. "Doctor," as a term of address, on the other hand, is a mark of status and a convenient title in local vernacular language. It is uncommon, although not exceptional, to see a patient who does not feel stigmatized or who does not avoid the formalities in the setting of psychotherapy and counseling. The patient–therapist contracting is thus more informal, more time consuming, more thorough (although without "labels"), and more flexible. One may see a patient throughout the course of therapy without ever contracting formally! Psychiatry and psychotherapy are more stigmatizing for a doctor who comes for psychiatric help as a patient, than for any other patient. In our opinion, doctors invariably feel slighted when referred for psychiatric treatment; they take it as an insult to their intellect.

For some patients it may be necessary to identify a responsible relative or other person who can manage the practical affairs of care taking, such as appointments and financial matters. In that sense adult patients are relieved of the responsibilities of other adults and are looked after by the family, like children. Such relinquishing of responsibilities may be acceptable to both patients and families, more so than in cultures where autonomy is a more compelling ideal. Patients may appreciate the opportunity to recover from emotional problems without having to bother about the practical issues that are managed by the family and therapist. Surya and Jayaram (1996) pointed out that patients in Indian culture want a personal relationship with the therapist. Many astute patients effectively extract this desired personal relationship from doctors who are reluctant to offer it. The therapist may need to accept some cultural adjustments in the nature and boundaries of the therapeutic relationship, recognizing that it may vary from the paradigm of a professional relationship according to Western psychotherapeutic standards. Insisting on too much distance will invariably be perceived by patients at best as emotionally sterility, and often as outright rejection.

A cultural perspective helps the therapist temporarily suspend or even unlearn some of the tenets of psychotherapy, learned from Western paradigms, and to enter into the patient's world of perceptions. He or she empathically listens to the patient's experiences with unconditional positive regard and a nonjudgmental attitude. Clarifying the spectrum of the patient's experiences, meanings, and behaviors helps the therapist to be helpful. Even in Western settings with a relatively more consistent match between cultures of the patient and therapist, and methods of investigation and treatment (such as psychotherapy) formulated in that culture, it is nearly impossible to mete out a single, pure kind of therapy to an individual patient over the course of therapy. Furthermore, in India it may be especially difficult to maintain "the correct" therapeutic stance, as it is formulated and taught from authoritative textbooks, for many patients the clinician encounters. The ambiguities arising in the course of adapting the standard theory to actual practice require the therapist to become an expert in the acrobatics of abstractions.

Rapport

At the outset, a therapist is responsible for creating a therapeutic environment in which a patient feels free to voice all doubts, disappointments, hopes, and fears. The patient's family may help in this task. The importance of a relatively intact family in Indian culture is compelling and cannot be overemphasized. In some cases, the family may even compete with the therapist to maintain the priority of their relationship, complicating the therapist's efforts to establish a therapeutic rapport, as indicated by the following case extract.

> A young adult professional was in therapy for anxiety and obsessive complaints with irritable bowel syndrome. He was the only son of a widowed mother who was a schoolteacher. She perceived the doctor's attempts to form a rapport with her son as intrusive and unwelcome, and she resisted them. She persistently questioned the formulation of a psychogenic origin of his emotional complaints. The referring physician internist remained firm in asserting that there was no biomedical basis for her son's suffering. When rapport was eventually established, she said to the therapist: "I told my son that the doctor has won. Doctor, you have really won over me!"

More often, however, effective rapport is welcomed, and a cultural perspective is invaluable in establishing and enhancing that rapport. It is an immense relief for patients to find a therapist who can understand and relate to them in the terms of their culture. Progress is quicker when both share the same first language. A tactful remark or question by the therapist lets the patient know that the therapist understands many of the cultural attitudes and beliefs about the patient's illness experience. This speeds up the process of building rapport.

Needs of Patient's Family

The needs of the patient's family more routinely require attention in psychiatric practice in India than in the West, where the clinical priority of the individual, rather than the family, has shaped the approach to therapy (Payson, Wheeler, & Wellington, 1998). Nuclear families placing more priority on individuals within the family are increasingly common these days in urban India. Nevertheless, in general terms Indian families are relatively more intact than in the West, and Indian patients are also more likely to be dependent on their families, both materially as well as emotionally. Attention to the Indian family, therefore, is an integral feature of therapy, and the significance of their role must be acknowledged—sometimes just through the patient individually, but often through interactions with the family directly that would not be considered appropriate in a Western practice. The unseen presence of the family is always there when seeing any patient in therapy. A question may also arise about whether the therapist should see the patient first or interview a relative first. As indicated in the previous section, some family members may resent the apparent intimacy that is a part of therapy that breaches family borders.

Transference and Countertransference

Because of the acknowledged importance of an effective rapport, and as a result of trying to establish it quickly (to limit the duration and cost of therapy), intense transference relationships may quickly emerge. The joint family paradigm in India entails a number of culturally defined family relationships that are widely understood and influential, even among people who live in nuclear families. The nature of these relationships is often a topic for theater, literature, and television. Based on the influence of such joint family paradigms, the nature of the transference may integrate the therapist into the social system as a family member with reference to a recognized relationship within the joint family. The style and process of therapy often needs to adjust to accommodate the intensity of the transference and the priority of social relationships. Interpretation of the transference need not be quick or complete so long as it does not affect the progress of the therapeutic work (Schaeffer, 1998). The nature of the patient's transference, however, may be highly informative about psychological experience and interpersonal relationships with reference to the cultural paradigms of experience, meaning, and joint family relations. Managing transference toward a therapeutic goal, rather than aiming to fully interpret or resolve it, is a culturally appropriate modification of the process of therapy (Goldstein, 2000).

The boundaries between real and transference relationships may also be shaped by these culturally defined relationships of the joint family. The following case extract illustrates the point and shows how the cultural context permits a wider range of options in their relationship for managing the interpersonal stressors that may affect both patients and therapists, but still within the context of an effective therapeutic relationship:

> A middle-aged housewife was being seen in therapy for dissociative and somatoform symptoms. The therapist himself was rather distraught in one session because his eldest daughter was unwell. When the patient walked into the clinic room, she was quick to notice and comment that something was wrong with the doctor. The therapist decided to acknowledge the validity of her assessment and disclosed to his patient what was bothering him. Then the patient asked him an unexpected and seemingly irrelevant question.
>
> "Is my condition serious, doctor?"
>
> The therapist replied, "No, but why do you ask?"
>
> The patient explained, "Only so that you can cancel my appointment for today and return to your sick daughter quickly."
>
> The doctor accepted her offer, and the patient prepared to leave. As she reached the door she commented, "Look, doctor, I tell you not to worry too much; your daughter will be fine. And I can tell you like an elder sister, that one does get worked up with such things when it is your first child!"

By invoking the paradigm of the relationship of elder sister in their interpersonal relationship, this patient gracefully reversed the roles of the helper and the person coming for help. The flexibility of the well-known culturally defined relational paradigms permitted that, and subsequently the therapy proceeded effectively.

Cultural Assessment of Selected Clinical Issues

Stress and Related Disorders

In the assessment of stress and related disorders it is necessary to consider the stressful life events or ordinary daily hassles experienced by the patient, his subjective appraisal of the stressful events, and his coping strategies and repertoire. An emic assessment framework focusing on experience, meaning, and behavior facilitates assessment of the patient's illness experience. Examining patterns of distress provides an elaboration of a patient's stressful experience with reference to psychological and cultural contexts. Attention to perceived causes may identify otherwise unspoken subjective explanations. Consideration of help seeking specifies actual and planned behavior, which may then be considered with reference to the practical issues of the case. An emic approach to the conceptualization, assessment, and management of these disorders facilitates the effectiveness of a supportive approach, and experience suggests this decreases reliance on tranquilizers and pharmacotherapy.

Psychosomatic Disorders

The causes of psychosomatic disorders are often poorly understood, especially by patients, but also by clinicians. The varieties of illness experience are especially diverse, and much time may pass before symptoms are configured as illness and a decision to seek help motivates this person to decide what kind of help may be appropriate. There are many branches of medicine and options for treatment that various doctors and healers may suggest. One may reasonably expect diverse formulations to emerge from a patient's EMIC account of such problems. Examples of common perceived causes for disorders commonly seen in practice include backaches resulting from menstruation or tubal ligation; disorders of fatigue and weakness owing to sexual experience, semen loss, a history of child abuse, abuse from in-laws, overwork and exertion, concerns (real and unreal) about having been infected with human immunodeficiency virus (HIV), and violating cultural ideas about what should and should not be eaten. Patients are assured by a therapist's appreciation of the role of various perceived causes, and attention to these ideas enhances the empathy required for effective therapy to proceed.

As in the West, but probably more so in urban India, patients are reluctant to consult a psychiatrist or counselor for their psychosomatic conditions. Stigmatizing misconceptions about psychiatry and psychology, which remain strong in India, contribute to this reluctance. It is also useful to understand and acknowledge a patient's ideas about "treatment received but not desired," and "treatment desired but not received" in developing and discussing a therapeutic plan. Such considerations, which are among the considerations in our emic assessment framework, lead to discussion in the clinical consultation of a patient's past experience with treatment. Stigma and the diminished self-esteem that follows initially from a psychiatric formulation of the problem is a concern for both patients and their families. These concerns may delay help seeking and/or lead to premature termination of treatment. Stigma entailing either or both the perceived social response (real or unreal) and the experience of social rejection contribute to the burden, and this may be an important factor leading to deliberate self-harm and suicide. A clear understanding of patients' experiences, their subjective explanations and anticipations, and what they consider the "most useful help" contributes to effective therapy for somatoform problems that frequently arise in clinical practice.

Sexual Abuse

Nearly everywhere it is hard to decide to disclose, and to actually disclose that one is a victim of sexual abuse. It is even more difficult in Indian settings because of either the real or anticipated tendency to blame victims, and because of broader cultural taboos that restrict frank discussion of sex-related topics. Both the fear of rejection and actual experience of rejection by those whose support is especially needed, contribute to suffering. Acknowledging this cultural context of sexual abuse may often enhance the value of assessment and therapy. Questions about sexual abuse in the routine course of clinical evaluation help patients appreciate the authenticity of the inquiry and the relevance of their experience. Some patients are more likely to disclose and value therapeutic attention to their prior experience of sexual abuse in the context of clinical consultations based on an emic assessment framework, as illustrated by the following case extract:

> A 23-year-old female student came for treatment of difficulty in concentration, lack of motivation, decreased socialization, mood swings, failing memory, and increased irritability approximately 2 to 3 months before her academic examinations. She was preoccupied with her sister's marital problems in the United Kingdom and could not focus on her studies. She could not interact with her friends freely. When her father working as a professional in the United Kingdom offered her to come to the United Kingdom for further education, she could not bring herself to decide whether she should go. She continued to be irritable with her mother with whom she was staying in Pune. She maintained that she forgets whatever she has read a few hours before and even routine daily events. A diagnosis of adjustment disorder was made and help was offered in study skills in view of her approaching examinations. She failed to respond to supportive psychotherapy and tranquilizers.

> She agreed to participate in a cultural study of psychiatric illness. In the course of an EMIC interview, she was asked to reflect on the cause of her problems. She discussed memories of childhood sexual abuse, which she

had not previously disclosed to anyone else, perpetrated by a servant in her childhood home. She discussed this in response to a probe question in the perceived cause section of the interview, explaining that she held herself responsible as she ruminated on traumatic memories.

She had lost trust in the goodness of life in general, and with the current stress of the upcoming examinations, she found herself irritable, moody, disinterested, and unable to concentrate and remember what she had just read. Successful treatment followed her disclosure of the traumatic events, enabling her to tap energy previously unavailable to her. After completing her examinations, she joined her sister and father in the United Kingdom.

The case history shows how many patients tend not to spontaneously report such traumatic events unless they are explicitly asked about them (or probed in the language of the emic interviews). This emic approach addresses recognized features of sexual abuse, such as difficulty with disclosure and the value of considering this aspect of current problems that may not otherwise be addressed in the course of therapy.

Conclusion

The therapist's scope of relevant interests and clinical effectiveness is enriched by attending to the influence of culture on mental health problems and their treatment. Clinical interests benefit from consideration not only of symptoms and psychopathology, but also from attention to the experience, meaning, and behavior that defines these problems with reference to their contexts. An emic assessment framework helps to identify and address clinically significant features of culture. In urbanizing societies influenced by a complex mix of local and outside traditions, this framework also helps to identify and examine competing cultural values that influence the character of mental health problems.

In the context of Indian culture the guru–chela (teacher–guide and student–follower) relationship is a powerful paradigm, with features that suggest a sacred and emancipating relationship. It is comparable in the strength of its bond to the relationship between parents and devoted children. Early consideration of culture and psychotherapy argued that the guru–chela relationship serves as a paradigm for psychotherapy in India (Neki, 1973). It is a cultural model and idealized standard for the expected roles of the guru as provider with specified obligations to those for whom he accepts responsible and their responsibilities to him.

Operationalized criteria and slick, precooked modules of therapy fall far short of the mark set by the cultural standard. By integrating clinical paradigms with a culturally sensitive emic approach, the therapist may more effectively gain access to the heart of the problem through the heart of the patient.

Discussion Questions

1. What is the necessity of understanding the local culture and its complexities to be able to practice psychiatry in an urban setting of a developing country?
2. What are the distinctive features and similarities between the form and content of therapy in Western culture and in an urban setting in India?
3. Would a focus on spirituality help the patient transcend general personal problems, or simply facilitate the patient's escape from the process of therapy and minimize an opportunity for individual growth?
4. Visualize a case of eating disorders from a Western cultural perspective. Prepare an EMIC interview schedule to facilitate the study of experience, meaning, and behavior related to this disorder to help a foreign psychiatric trainee in the assessment and therapy of such a case. In which other conditions could the EMIC interview possibly be used (e.g., acquired immunodeficiency syndrome [AIDS], psychiatric problems in the elderly)?
5. Discuss the value of the cultural epidemiological approach in making globally valid professional concepts applicable to local cultural contexts in training, research, and practice.
6. Discuss the special problems that you have encountered in obtaining the consent of a patient in practice and research. How could the culturally informed approach help the psychiatrist/therapist or researcher to resolve these problems?
7. What are some legal problems that might result from orienting practice to local cultural issues? What is the role of rapport and transference in the causation of such problems and/or their resolution?

Acknowledgment

We are grateful to our patients who taught us. Our special thanks are also due to Rajendra Kale, Vinod Chaugule, Meera Oke, Rohini Deshpande, Arvind Panchanadikar, and Hamid Dabholkar for their valuable help and comments.

References

Agashe, M. (1984, August). *The healing role of arts.* Paper presented at the International Conference on Art and Health. Bellagio, Italy.

American Psychiatric Association. (1994). *Diagnostic and statistical manual of mental disorders* (4th ed). Washington, DC: APA.

Angst, J. (1997). Recurrent brief psychiatric syndromes: Hypomania, depression, anxiety and neurasthenia. In L. L. Judd, B. Saletu, & V. Filip (Eds.), *Basic and clinical science of mental and addictive disorders,* Vol. 167. *Bibliotheca psychiatrica* (pp. 33–38). Basel: Karger.

Gabbard, G. O. (2000). A neurobiologically informed perspective on psychotherapy. *British Journal of Psychiatry, 177,* 117–122.

Goldstein, W. N. (2000). The transference in psychotherapy: The old vs. the new, analytic vs. dynamic. *American Journal of Psychotherapy, 54*(2), 167–171.

Group for the Advancement of Psychiatry (GAP). (2002). *Cultural Assessment in Clinical Psychiatry.* Washington, DC: American Psychiatric Press.

Guthrie, E. (2000). Psychotherapy for patients with complex disorders and chronic symptoms: The need for a new research paradigm. *British Journal of Psychiatry, 177,* 131–137.

Horacio, F. Jr. (2000). Culture, spirituality and psychiatry. *Current Opinion in Psychiatry, 13,* 525–530.

Kala, A. (2000, November 18–19). *Developments in private sector of psychiatry 1950–2000.* In Souvenir, 1st National Conference of Indian Association of Private Psychiatry (IAPP), New Delhi.

Kale, R. (2002, June). Neuroimaging: The internet makes a powerful case against those who believe the mind and brain are separate. [Electronic version]. *British Medical Journal, 324*(7352), 1529. Available: http://www.bmj.com

McGorry, P., & McConville, S. (1999). Insight in psychosis: An illusive target. *Comprehensive Psychiatry, 40*(2), 131–142.

Neki, J. S. (1973). Guru-Chela relationship: The possibility of a therapeutic paradigm. *American Journal of Orthopsychiatry, 43*(5), 755–765.

Payson, A., Wheeler, K., & Wellington, T. (1998). Health teaching needs of clients with serious and persistent mental illness: Client and provider perspectives. *Journal of Psychosocial Nursing and Mental Health Services, 36*(2), 32–35.

Pike, K. L. (1966). Etic and emic standpoints for the description of behavior. In K. L. Pike (Ed.), *Language in relation to a unified theory of the structure of human behavior* (pp. 152–163). The Hague: N. V. Uitgeverij Mouton.

Razali, S., Hasanah, C., Aminah, K., & Subramaniam, M. (1998). Religious-sociocultural psychotherapy in patients with anxiety and depression. *Australian and New Zealand Journal of Psychiatry, 32,* 867–872.

Registrar General & Census Commissioner, India. (n.d.) *Provisional data for 2001 census* [Online].Retrieved January, 2003 from http://www.censusindia.net/

Rouff, L. C. (2000). Clouds and silver linings: Training and experiences of psychodynamically oriented mental health trainees. *American Journal of Psychotherapy, 54*(4), 549–559.

Schaeffer, J. A. (1998). Transference and countertransference interpretations: Harmful or helpful in short-term dynamic therapy? *American Journal of Psychotherapy, 52*(1), 1–17.

Shamasundar, C. (1993). Therapeutic wisdom in Indian mythology. *American Journal of Psychotherapy, 47*(3), 443–450.

Sperber, D. (1996). *Explaining culture: A naturalistic approach.* Oxford, UK: Blackwell.

Surya, N. C., & Jayaram, S. S. (1996). Some basic considerations in the practice of psychotherapy in the Indian setting. *Indian Journal of Psychiatry, 38*(1), 10–12. (Reproduced from *Indian Journal of Psychiatry, 6*(3) (1964).

Weiner, S. (1997). The actor-director and patient-therapist relationships: A process comparison. *American Journal of Psychotherapy, 51*(1), 77–85.

Weiss, M. (2001). Cultural epidemiology: An introduction and overview. *Anthropology and Medicine, 8*(1), 5–29.

Weiss, M. G., Doongaji, D. R., Siddhartha, S., Wypij, D., Pathare, S., Bhatawdekar, M., et al. (1992). The explanatory model interview catalogue (EMIC): Contribution to cross-cultural research methods from a study of leprosy and mental health. *British Journal of Psychiatry, 160*(6), 819–830.

Weiss, M. G., Raguram, R., & Channabasavanna, S. M. (1995). Cultural dimensions of psychiatric diagnosis: Comparing DSM-III-R and illness explanatory models in South India. *British Journal of Psychiatry, 166*, 353–359.

Weiss, M. G., & Ramakrishna, J. R. (2001). *Stigma interventions and research for international health.* Background paper for Stigma and Global Health. Fogarty International Center, September 2001. (http://www.stigmaconference.nih.gov/FinalWeissPaper.htm)

Wig, N. N. (1996). The pioneers of Indian psychiatry, I: Dr. N. C. Surya: The lone rider. *Indian Journal of Psychiatry, 38*(1), 2–8.

Wig, N. N. (1983). DSM-III: A perspective from the Third World. In R. L. Spitzer, J. B. W. Williams, & A. E. Skodol (Eds.), *International Perspectives on DSM-III* (pp. 79–89). Washington, DC: American Psychiatric Press.

World Health Organization (WHO). (1995). *The ICD-10 Classification of Mental and Behavioural Disorders: Clinical Descriptions and Diagnostic Guidelines.* Geneva: WHO.

Chapter **6**————————————————————————

Empowering the Spousal Relationship in the Treatment of Japanese Families with School Refusal Children

Kenji Kameguchi

This chapter describes Family Activation Programs, a Japanese style empowerment approach to the prevention of school refusal based on L'Abate's Family Enrichment Programs. Rising school refusal in Japan is discussed within the context of enormous social changes including the emergence of the nuclear household, increased urbanization, and the increased participation of women in the workforce. Attention is paid to empowering the spousal relationship of parents of school refusal students that has been influenced by a tradition of three generational systems. Three case studies of Japanese families are presented.

Families with Children with School Refusal Behavior

The characteristics of families of children with school refusal behavior are almost as heterogeneous as those of the children themselves. Many psychodynamically oriented authors initially characterized these families as enmeshed or dominated by a problematic mother–child relationship. Common descriptors of the latter included dependent, hostile, vacillating, exploitative, and guilt inducing (W. B. Frick, 1964). In addition, fathers were often described as passive and unwilling to interfere in the lives of family members. In case studies, school refusal behavior was largely associated with a hostile or self-perceived incompetent mother who rejected her child or who facilitated overdependency and school absenteeism (Kearney, 2001).

Recent researchers have evaluated a wider spectrum of family dynamics in this population using more sophisticated instruments. Bernstein, Svingen, and Garfinkel (1990) examined 76 families of children with school phobia using the Family Assessment Measure (FAM; Skinner, Steinhauer, & Santa-Barbara, 1983). The authors attributed the lack of problems in one group to the children's "quiet, compliant, and eager to please" (p. 29) nature.

Kearney and Silverman (1995) provided a synopsis of the literature and contemporary research and contended that six patterns of family dynamics generally pervade families of youth who refuse school. The enmeshed family is characterized by parental overprotectiveness and overindulgence toward a child as well as dependency or less independence among family members. Another pattern is the conflictive family, which is characterized by hostility, violence, and coercive processes (Patterson, 1982). This pattern pervades many families of children with school refusal behavior. The detached family is characterized by poor involvement among family members in one another's lives. In many such cases, a child's misbehavior is not addressed until it is extreme. The isolated family is marked by little extrafamilial contact on the part of its members and may be less likely to seek treatment compared with other families. The healthy family is characterized by the cohesiveness, and appropriately expressive members who solve problems effectively. Finally, many families of this population show a mixed familial profile, or characteristics of two or more family patterns. Kearney and Silverman (1995) outlined how these familial patterns were related to different functions of school refusal behavior.

Culture and Context

The problem of school refusal in Japan dates from around 1964, with it first being reported in innercity children and later in rural areas and among adolescents (Kameguchi & Murphy-Shigematsu, 2001). School consultations gradually became centered on this problem. Most of the children involved were described as "good children" who wanted to go to school, but for some reason could not, to the great dismay of their parents and themselves.

The number of Japanese children who refuse to go to school in the absence of specific physical reasons, has been rapidly on the rise with more than 139,000 cases reported in 2001. This figure is more than 12 times the number just 20 years ago, and only includes children in elementary and junior high school, the 9 years of compulsory education. These children either overtly refuse to go to school, or claim that they cannot.

Awareness of this problem began at a time when the Japanese educational system was being widely praised for its success in producing a nearly universally literate population with high scores on standardized achievement tests. Nearly all youth attended high school, with almost half proceeding to universities, junior colleges, or specialty schools. Japanese political leaders boasted of Japan's "intelligent society," particularly in comparison with the United States.

However, the problems associated with this educational system have become increasingly apparent. Educational uniformity, extreme pressure, exclusively exam-oriented curriculum, and group bullying have surfaced as aspects of Japanese education negatively affecting children. Schools are increasingly criticized for their rigidity, excessive demand for conformity, and narrow focus on academic success.

Psychologists charge that the emphasis on producing standardized "good boys and girls," has been at the cost of a lack of attention to fostering the development of each person's uniqueness (Sato, 1997). Some school refusers, especially those who show signs of problems in learning or in human relations are disturbed by teacher's lack of personal involvement. Children are valued only if they are successful academically, leading to alienation and anomie in many. In extreme cases, youth who have committed sensational and seemingly senseless murders of school children in recent years have claimed that a grudge against the school system instigated their criminal behavior. Almost all Japanese children have very limited experiences in human relationships and mutual understanding because of their heavy study load in preparing for highly competitive entrance examinations, which typically includes many tutoring lessons.

Although not denying problems within the school system, the school refusal literature has long emphasized a family perspective (Kawai, 1994). Earlier reports on school refusal that focused on the desire to escape from a bad situation at school involving bullying and pressure, began to be replaced by those indicating more general problems of human relations (Ishida & Takei, 1987). A narrow focus on the schools has been discouraged, in favor of a wider social perspective that includes the family. Family therapy began to be used for the treatment of school refusal cases in the mid-1980s (Kameguchi, 1998; Okado, 1990; Suzuki, 1990).

Changing Families in Japan

Japan has experienced enormous social change in the past 40 years, including the near disappearance of the three-generation household and the emergence of the nuclear household, intensified urbanization, and an increase in the participation of women in the work force. These changes have been accompanied by erosion of the traditional Japanese family structure, a changing workplace, rising divorce rates, increased reports of child and spousal abuse, and the highest rate of youth crime and violence in Japanese history (Hayes, 2001). In response to these changes, there has been a growing interest in the provision of counseling and psychological services to individuals, families, and groups.

Today's Japan is characterized by nuclear families living apart from their families of origin in urban apartments or single-family suburban homes. Unlike the extended, multigenerational families of the past, today's families are organized around the married couple. Traditions and ceremonies have been secularized and are now performed by a new service industry that takes care of what had for centuries been the province of the family. Increasing longevity, the destigmatization of "singleness," especially for women, and greater individual freedom and autonomy are shaping today's young Japanese couple. Moreover, the expectation of a long and healthy life by Japanese, who now live on average past 80 years, has altered the attitudes and behavior of young men and women, in particular. Neither men nor women appear to be in a hurry to get married, postponing marriage into their late 20s while increasing the proportion of single women in their 20s to over 40%. In addition, it is projected that one in four of the 800,000 married couples in Japan will file for divorce this year. All of these changes have resulted in an enormous shift in the traditional family structure.

With Japanese anticipating the longest lifetime in the world, Japanese are also reproducing themselves at the lowest birth rate (1.41) of any other industrialized nation. The Japanese society of 50 years ago comprised primarily young and middle-aged Japanese and stands in stark contrast to the society being created today that will consist of middle-aged and senior Japanese who will be living with a growing population of non-Japanese (Hayes, 2001).

American observers recognize the success of the system in providing Japan with well-educated citizens who form an invaluable base for Japanese productivity and Japan's relatively low level of violence. At the same time, they are reluctant to adopt the Japanese system either because they doubt the uniformity and centralized control would be acceptable in America or because the long hours and regimentation required on the part of students goes against American concepts of individual freedom (Imamura, 1989).

Japanese, on the other hand, recognize the deficiencies of their system. However, because success in the system is so tied to employment opportunity, few individual Japanese are willing to chance their children's futures by either choosing an alternate form of education or not sending their children to prep school (juku). Moreover, the only other model of education with which most Japanese are familiar is its own rigid prewar system.

Family systems differ throughout the world on a number of dimensions. Comparing Japan to America, Kiefer (1974) points out three such differences as relates to the educational process: (a) the Japanese middle-class mother is more solely responsible for children's education, (b) the Japanese mother–child (especially mother–son) tie is more intense, and (c) Japanese individuals are bound to the family for life and learn to consider the effect of all their actions on their families. The American child makes more of a distinction between family controlled areas and those outside of the family.

In Japan, the mother is viewed as totally responsible for seeing that her children succeed in school (Imamura, 1989). The mother's involvement is structured by the high number of pupils per teacher (40/1) even at the elementary school level. Historically, the extreme loyalty and dedication to their companies removed men from the emotional and instrumental activities of their homes and families. Their absorption in work and absence from the home gave rise to what has been aptly described as "fatherless families" (Wagatsuma, 1977). Rigid role boundaries developed, with men devoted to work and women to the home. The resulting separation and imbalance in the family dynamics have been called a "pathology of the maternal society of Japan" (Kawai, 1994). This "mother-centered family" has long been blamed by some psychologists as the major factor in school refusal.

Fragile Aspects of the Spousal Relationship in Japanese Families

Relationships between men and women are being altered as members of both genders seek more satisfying ways of being together. Both the feminist movement and now the men's movement have provided broader definitions of male and female, masculine and feminine—as separate beings and in relationships. There are currently few meaningful models because stereotypical roles have been denigrated and sometimes discarded. Each couple has to evolve and agree upon an effective dyadic pattern for themselves as there is widespread confusion about the balance between the needs and desires of self and others, between one's rights and responsibilities, and between one's freedom and commitment (Kaslow, 1996).

In many Western countries, the search by many couples for egalitarian relationships based on respect, trust, sharing, and reciprocity has been intense. Nonetheless, in some Latin American, Arab, and other Third World countries, traditional male dominant/female submissive roles/relationship patterns are still in ascendance and permeate all of those societies' institution and relationships. Family psychologists can assist couples to find a dynamic relational mode that uniquely fits individual and joint needs and style (Philpot, 1990), and provides them with the time, energy and commitment that enables their parenting ability to flourish so that their children are amply loved and cared for (Kaslow, 1996).

In the present postindustrial society, the majority of women become full time child-rearers after working full-time, and then return to work in later years. But there is also a large group of full time child-rearers, mostly highly educated women who "marry up," and then engage in the task of encouraging their children to reach the same level of attainment as their fathers (Ueno, 1994). Expectations and pressure for academic achievement are extremely high, with a resulting high level of stress in childrearing.

Women in these middle- to upper-class highly educated families attempt to place children from an early age on the academic ladder leading to big name universities. To secure places in well-known private elementary schools, or even preschools, children must study for examinations, a task that places pressure on mothers hopeful that their children will secure a good academic record from an early age. These anxious mothers, eager to provide their children with the best educational opportunity, send them to special cram schools for supplementary training, or hire individual tutors (Simons, 1991).

Some women feel that a mother's identity can only be gained from the educational attainment of their children. In terms of family dynamics, these women derive much of their emotional closeness from their children to compensate for the lack of intimacy with husbands. The actions of mothers in "keeping children at home" may represent an attempt to separate and protect the self and child from the father to avoid conflict, or may be a way of attacking the fathers. Alternatively, mothers' overinvolvement in their children's lives may be a way of freeing the fathers to work. The lack of intimacy as a couple and the sense of responsibility as a wife are cogently stated in the phrase "genki de rusu ga ii," which expresses a wife's wish that her husband is healthy but away from the home.

Despite Japanese mothers' commitment, their degree of satisfaction with regard to child rearing is low compared with that of mothers in other countries, according to international surveys (Yamada, 1998). In addition, these surveys show that Japanese children are also comparatively less satisfied and less hopeful about their lives. Economic problems have increased academic competition, and it has become more difficult for parents to provide their children with a higher standard of education than they experienced.

Although these mothers are investing so much of themselves in their children's education, there are also indications that the mother–child relationship has changed in other ways as well. Some clinicians have observed that many mothers are not capable of providing for the security and dependency needs of their children (Doi, 1981, 1988). This may result from ambivalence concerning their roles as mothers, as the most susceptible women to child-rearing neurosis are full-time homemakers with high academic achievements themselves. They grudgingly accept their role and are uneasy about their ability to rear children to reach the same level as their husbands. This apparent loss of confidence in the singular identity of motherhood is occurring paradoxically at the same time that the mother–child relationship has potentially become more intense because of the smaller size of the family.

In some cases, the anxiety, depression, feelings of inadequacy, and lack of identity significantly impair the child-rearing abilities of some mothers of school refusal children. Clinical cases of children with such disorders as separation anxiety related to the ambivalence and vulnerability of their mothers have been reported (Imai, 1998; Kawanaka, 1998). Such children are trapped between their desire to separate and a need to remain with their mothers. Children are insecure with regard to the degree to which they are loved by parents/mom.

The mothers in such families are overprotective, overinvolved, and interfere in their children's lives. Therefore, the children do not progressively develop the ability to separate psychologically, and when they reach the age when they should be more autonomous, they are unable to engage in the age-appropriate tasks of identity. Feeling burdened by their mothers' obsessiveness and anxiety, the children's actions are a way of demonstrating and rebelling against the mothers' overinvolvement (Suzuki, 1988). However, these children also want their feelings to be indulged by the mother, a psychological concept referred to in Japanese as "amae" (Doi, 1981, 1988). They struggle with the desire to be indulged as well as to become an autonomous being. These conflicts accelerate and are exacerbated during puberty and adolescence.

Most school refusal kids are so-called good children who are obedient to parents and teachers and perform well in school until their change in behavior. By refusing to go to school, children use their strongest weapon against their all-powerful and controlling mothers. As the children grow up, their actions may escalate to more overt aggressive behavior (Kawai, 1986).

However, just as it is too simplistic to blame only the schools, it is also wrong to blame only the mothers without viewing the problem in a broader context. The struggle of children has been described as a fight against the "great mother" of the maternal, fatherless society (Kawai, 1994). The enemy is not their mother, but the "great mother" in their psyche. Of course, children also want a paternal figure, but the fathers are incapable of fulfilling these needs.

The resulting imbalance in what Fromm (1956) called "maternal love" and "paternal love" creates psychological conflict for the child. Western societies such as the United States are often described as paternal, whereas Eastern societies, such as Japan, are called maternal, but every society needs to maintain some level of balance between the two principles. The maternal principle that provides containing, unconditional love must be balanced by the paternal principle that disciplines or even cuts bonds when a child's behavior is unacceptable. An influential Japanese psychologist has argued that the balance in Japan has shifted dangerously to the maternal principle, resulting in artificially good children raised by overly protective mothers, some of whom rebel in forms such as school refusal (Kawai, 1986).

Although we have spoken mainly of the problem of nuclear families, multigenerational families still comprise a large minority of families, and in these families, school refusal has an additional dimension. The intergenerational conflict can be deep, with mothers feeling trapped in a situation in which they cannot assert themselves against mothers-in-law and in which husbands are not supportive. In any case, the growing numbers of school refusal children represent a crisis in the contemporary Japanese family. Family therapists may help resolve these fragile aspects of the spousal relationship in families with school refusal children.

Interventions

In the early 1980s, Kameguchi (the author) and collaborators began to introduce various therapeutic approaches to the treatment of families with a child refusing to go to school. These included strategic, structural, systemic, and experiential approaches. Kameguchi became very interested in the work of L'Abate and his collaborators who have discussed the prevention of school-related problems in American families. On the basis of their clinical experiences, L'Abate and his colleagues have found that many families need to complete some basic training to allow their members to communicate with each other more constructively and effectively. Their Family Enrichment Programs (FEP) used less experienced intermediaries than psychologists as indirect facilitators (L'Abate, 1990). This led Kameguchi and his collaborators to develop a Japanese version of FEP, named the "Family Activation Programs (FAP)." The basic ideas of FAP are derived from FEP, but Japanese team members have modified them for Japanese culture and families. Kameguchi (1987b) mainly selected nonverbal programs rather than verbal ones because of Japanese client's hesitancy to self-disclose in interviews. They have also reframed the refusal behavior of children as positive in order to facilitate empowerment of the fragile spousal relationship.

FAP consists of 15 lessons which are organized from nonverbal to verbal, from behavioral to cognitive, and from those based on individual experiences to those based on family experiences (Kameguchi, 1987b). It is now being applied to therapist training programs, clinical practice, and research activities focusing on family systems. We are hopeful that FAP also will prove to be beneficial in preventive efforts focusing on children in school systems.

Kameguchi (1992) introduced the idea of the fuzzy function to evaluate whether given generational boundaries are sufficiently distinct in clinical cases. The concept of family membrane, with its selective permeability, also helps us to operationalize the idea of generational boundaries. Kameguchi, Urabe, and Ikeda (1990) introduced a graphic method for describing the family membrane that together depicts a family system. It is similar to Lewin's graphic method for depicting conflict in marriage that is based on his famous Field Theory (Lewin, 1948). However, Kameguchi's method differs from Lewin's by depicting a family relationship as an organic and psychological whole. The psychological concept of family membrane describes the fuzzy and ambiguous boundaries of a system containing individual subsystems, such as the parental subsystem, sibling subsystems, and whole family system (Kameguchi, 1991, 1992). The family membrane is assumed to integrate the psychological entities represented by the family members. Ackerman (1958) focused on the processes of adjustment to a wide range of vicissitudes that affect relations among family members. The family membrane includes the dyadic membranes that interconnect two family members, function as "bonds," and exert their binding force in accordance with the characteristics of given dyads. A symbiotic dyad has an undifferentiated membrane that fuses the membranes of two individuals. A disengaged dyad has a vulnerable membrane that is easily interrupted by various factors. In the case of "a double-bound" dyad, there is a twisted membrane that is characterized by contradictory communication patterns.

Ideally, the spousal relationship (parental membrane) should assume a key role in organizing the family system. However, the symbiotic mother–child dyad in many Japanese families interferes with the empowerment of the spousal relationship and tends to weaken the father–child dyad. These contradicting movements of dyads lead to a malfunctioning family system by limiting interactions among dyads and preventing the family system from developing into a harmonious state. In particular, weakness of the spousal relationship leads to vague generational boundaries between a parental and child dyad. The unclear and fuzzy generation boundary interferes with the developmental tasks of adolescents by not allowing them to know and experience the critical differences between the parental generation and their own generation, as well as psychologically separate from the parents (Kameguchi, 1996). At the same time, it is very hard for parents to separate from their adolescent children in the absence of clear generational boundaries (Minuchin & Fishman, 1981). Kameguchi (2000) also paid special attention to the implicit bond between the Japanese husband and his mother that might discourage the empowerment of the spousal relationship. He assumed that the therapist must decrease the invisible but dominant relationship between the husband's mother and her son, and facilitate the empowerment of the spousal relationship in the therapeutic process. Such a therapeutic move would counter the child's school refusal.

Families of school refusal children come in for treatment every 4 weeks. Each session consists of three phases: (a) an interview between the family and two therapists, (b) therapeutic work chosen from the FAP, and (c) a concluding phase during which the principal therapist gives the family members instructions for the period until the next appointment. Basically, the author's approach to cases of school refusal is based on the Milan systemic approach (Selvini-Palazzoli, Boscolo, Cecchin, & Prata, 1978). However, FAP techniques are also utilized, such as the Family Image Test or Family Clay Sculpture (Kameguchi, 1987a; 1989). These techniques appear to fit Japanese spouses because of their characteristic communication style in which indirect or nonverbal ways are favored (Kameguchi & Murphy-Shigematsu, 2001).

Spouses thus can communicate with each other in a more relaxed manner rather than in the confrontational style characteristic of the Milan approach. Therapists also can assume a peripheral position as an audience for the spousal performance. It is assumed that such collaborative experiences in therapeutic sessions gradually empower the fragile aspects of the spousal relationship.

Case Studies

Case A

Mr. and Mrs. A, 40 and 39 years old, respectively, requested treatment for their son, Taro, 12. They also had a daughter, Hanako, 7. Taro had stopped going to

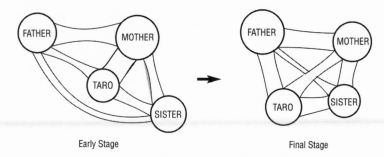

Early Stage   Final Stage

FIGURE 6.1. Changes in the family system of case A.

school, complaining of hypochondriac pains for 5 months. All family members attended the family therapy sessions every 4 weeks. Basically, school refusal was viewed as a signal that both the identified patient (IP) and his family members were having difficulties progressing through a particular stage in the natural, unfolding life cycle of the family, rather than as constituting a "disease" within the IP.

After three sessions, Taro started to attend school occasionally. The parents were partially relieved by this change, but still worried about his hypochondriac complaints and laziness. The therapeutic focus shifted to existing problems in the parents' families of origin and their spousal relationship. However, Taro's occasional school refusal and irresponsible behavior at home still persisted at the time of the seventh session.

The therapist redefined Taro's problems as supplying crucial cues for creating better bonds between the parents who had been extremely busy with their own preoccupations, and had no time to talk with each other about child rearing. Subsequently, the therapist gave Taro two paradoxical tasks, asking him to be absent from school on an infrequent basis and to do his house chores "capriciously." These tasks puzzled both parents, and also empowered their shared commitment to monitoring Taro's daily behavior in spite of their busyness. At the next session, Taro reported that he completed the tasks. His parents did not express any complaints about his behavior. Rather, they were astonished by the remarkable change in his improved school attendance, active participation in housekeeping tasks, and homework (Fig 6.1).

Case B

Mr. and Mrs. B, 35 and 33 years old, respectively, requested treatment for their son because of his school refusal. They had two children, Hiro (IP), 9, and his younger brother, 7. Hiro refused to go to school, complaining of a poor appetite at lunch time. At the beginning of his school refusal, the parents attempted to force him to go to school, but this endeavor was unsuccessful.

The therapist conducted circular interviews with the family and perceived a lack of core family imagery that would depict them as an integrated whole. The therapist introduced a body-oriented technique to empower the spousal relationship at the level of body experience or body image. At this initial stage of therapy, Hiro began to go to school at times and when accompanied by his mother. Subsequently, the therapist introduced the clay sculpture technique to enable the family to arrive at a family image at the more concrete level. After they had finished their clay work, the therapist resumed the circular interview procedure guided by clay work, which led to rapid changes in family imagery and to greater mutual understanding. Hiro began to go to school by himself and play with his friends. Based on the experiences of the therapeutic sessions, both parents took a more active role in the family, and the mother became more gentle toward Hiro.

The crucial change in the spousal relationship happened in the ninth session when Hiro remembered a fight between his mother and father's sister over their house sharing when he was 3 years old. Hiro indicated that he took the side of his mother against his aunt. The father began to understand the necessity of his own active involvement in demarcating a clear boundary between his nuclear family and family of origin. His wife had been suffering because of alienation from her husband's relatives.

The husband's younger sister had trouble with her husband, and quite often visited her parents' house accompanied by her four children. This house was located next to the B. family's house. The husband's sister and her children intruded into the B. family's house in a rude manner, which irritated Mrs. B. At the same time, Mrs. B. lost many friends, who moved to another town to accompany the big factory's relocation. She became depressed and was not gentle toward her son, Hiro.

The therapist supported the father's awareness of his need to take an active role in establishing boundaries between his nuclear family and family of origin. The therapeutic focus on the father resulted in the mother becoming more secure and joyful. Such changes in the spousal relationship positively influenced Hiro's self-esteem and activity in his peer group. Hiro began to visit his friends' homes and also invite them to visit his home. The therapist believed that these changes in the family relationships encouraged Hiro to re-attend school (Fig. 6.2).

Case C

Tomoko, a 13-year-old girl who lived with her parents, two younger sisters, paternal grandmother, and a dog, had refused to attend school for almost a year. Because she also refused to come to the initial family therapy session, the therapist asked the parents to come to the next session accompanied by the dog, which Tomoko liked very much. All family members including Tomoko and her dog, showed up at the third session. It was the first time Tomoko had visited a

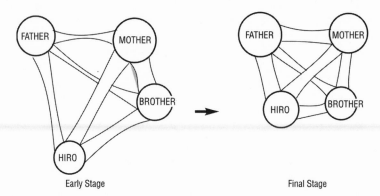

Early Stage   Final Stage

FIGURE 6.2. Changes in the family system of case B.

clinical family psychologist, and the dog played a critical role during the tense interview process. The therapist felt that the dog saved Tomoko in an emotionally delicate situation through his naïve reactions.

Tomoko drew a picture together with her two younger sisters at the fourth session. They drew their father as a person in woman's dress. The father was surprised at Tomoko's relaxed attitude during that session. The grandmother, who was taking charge of housekeeping as the acting mother, expressed her strong expectation of Tomoko's rapid recovery.

After four sessions, Tomoko returned to school, but only a few days later she again refused to go to school. The father was worried about her future because of uncertainties in her psychological development. In contrast, the mother displayed a rather stable and supportive attitude toward her. The parents became sensitized to the subtle differences in their child-rearing attitudes toward Tomoko. The therapist reframed their attitudinal differences as constituting a more differentiated spousal relationship. He aimed to support the father's active involvement in addressing the school refusal behaviors of his daughter. He also accepted the mother's supportive attitude to her daughter. The therapist tried to keep his active neutrality to empower the fragile spousal relationship that had been dependent on the dominant paternal grandmother.

At the sixth session, the father complained that he did not receive any clear messages from the therapist on Tomoko's prognosis. The therapist encouraged the father to disclose his worry about Tomoko's returning to school. The father began to express his own feelings and emotions toward his eldest daughter, Tomoko. The father said that Tomoko did not show any serious concerns with the implicit meaning of the task given in the former session. For the first time, she refuted the father's accusation of her relaxed attitude at home. The therapist understood that the separation process between the father and daughter had started. Then, the therapist restrained the parents not to push Tomoko to go back to school until the end of that year in order to avoid too many initial changes in their family system. The mother reacted to the prescription with an expression of great relief.

At the next session, the father expressed confusion about controlling his emotions in response to Tomoko's attitudes toward him. The mother reported a big fight between the father and Tomoko a few days previously related to treatment of the dog. The therapist thought that it was necessary to empower the executive function of the spousal relationship. The therapist viewed the active involvement of the father as necessary to deal with this family crisis. The father disclosed his worry about Tomoko's future. Furthermore, he discussed his father, who had been a strict soldier and also dominant at home, and the scarce communication between his father and children. The paternal grandmother agreed with him, and also expressed her wish to yield her parental role to her son and daughter-in-law. The mother smiled and disclosed her wish to protect Tomoko from any psychological pressure related to her school refusal behavior. The parents discussed their different parental roles without any intrusion by the paternal grandmother.

The therapist worked with the family to make the fragile spousal relationship a more active and differentiated one through the utilization of a pet as a transitional object and the arrangement of Tomoko's participation in a horse riding club. The dominant paternal grandmother gradually yielded her parental role to Tomoko's parents, who began to share their parental roles for Tomoko. Tomoko resumed her peer relationships as well as her academic work with the assistance of a private tutor at home.

The therapist multiply focused the counseling process on the two generational boundaries, namely, between the grandmother and parents and between the parents and Tomoko. The therapist intervened to empower the spousal relationship in order to deal with Tomoko's behavior as an executive unit. This

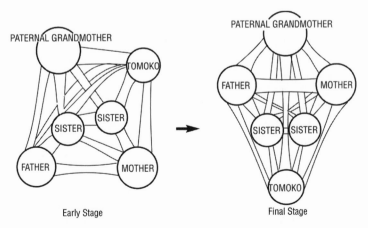

FIGURE 6.3. Changes in the family system of case C.

facilitated the grandmother's exit from her overprotection of Tomoko. Free from these boundaries, Tomoko began to assert her strong will to attend the horse riding club every Sunday. Following the changes in the spousal relationship, Tomoko started to go to school again. Then, the therapist suggested that the parents ask the classroom teacher to participate in the next family therapy session for the purpose of reinforcement. The teacher discussed Tomoko's classroom behavior, and supported the parents by providing positive remarks regarding Tomoko's peer relationships. At the same time, the paternal grandmother became more peripheral in the family system (Fig. 6.3).

Later, it was reported that Tomoko remained symptom-free during junior high school. She also passed the entrance examination to high school.

Conclusion

There are many challenges for the fields of counseling and clinical psychology that have traditionally been concerned with the individual as a focus of study. However, these case studies are best understood from a contextualist perspective (Liddle, 1987). Contextualism generally refers to the view that behavior cannot be understood outside of the cultural context in which it occurs. It is concerned with the interaction between the organism and its environment, and the changing individual in a changing world (Szapocznik & Kurtines, 1993).

The fuzzy state of generation boundaries in Japanese families with school refusal children becomes evident in family therapy. The problem of school refusal is emblematic of the large gap between school systems and family systems and between teachers and students. Japanese parents today have a general tendency not to draw clear boundaries between their children and themselves. Many children react to this situation and unfortunately fall into the gaps between contradicting principles of school and family systems.

Although predicting a higher incidence of school refusal in the near future, the author advocates early effective preventive programs both in families and schools. Special attention should be paid to empowering the spousal relationship of parents of children with school refusal behavior in Japan. The spousal relationships have been implicitly trapped in the web of three generational systems, including the paternal and maternal grandparents. This is best understood within the cultural context of Confucian societies, in such countries as China, Korea, and Japan.

The Confucian human perspective, which sets "filial piety" as a core concept, still has some relationship to each latent factor of recent educational problems such as overprotecting children, psychological independence of children from parents, and family relationships. Shimomi (1997) assumed that the individual power that had accelerated development and diversification of the new postwar society of Japan was in fact derived from the spirit of obedience and loyalty associated with filial piety and the maternity of Confucian society.

If we follow Shimomi's view and assume that the root of Confucian culture is supported by maternity, it can be understood that schools, as part of the cultural system are also supported by maternity. For instance, the term "a fanatic educator mom," although outdated, symbolizes the close connection between mothers and the educational system. In other words, in Confucian society, maternity actually overwhelmingly controls school as well as family systems.

The popularity of feminism has gradually changed the spousal relationship from traditional and unequal to more collaborative. However, it has been suggested that there is quite a difference between both sexes in the acceptance of feminism. Parents with school refusal children might benefit from professional support in dealing with the contradictory aspects of multigenerational relationships of Japanese families.

Discussion Questions

1. From a culturally sensitive perspective, what is the best way to treat school refusal children and their families?
2. What steps can practitioners in Japan take to prevent school refusal problems in community settings?
3. How can Japanese parents prevent school refusal problems in their homes?
4. How can Japanese parents collaborate with school teachers and administrators to help prevent or intervene in school refusal problems?
5. What are the societal and psychological implications of an increase in school refusal in Japan?

References

Ackerman, N. W. (1958). *The psychodynamics of family life.* New York: Basic Books.

Bernstein, G. A., Svingen, P. H., & Garfinkel, B. D. (1990). School phobia: Patterns of family functioning. *Journal of the American Academy of Child and Adolescent Psychiatry, 29,* 24–30.

Doi, T. (1981). *The anatomy of dependence: The key analysis of Japanese behaviors.* Tokyo: Kodansha.

Doi, T. (1988). *The anatomy of self: The individual vs. society.* Tokyo: Kodansha.

Frick, W. B. (1964). School phobia: A critical review of the literature. *Merrill-Palmer Quarterly, 10,* 361–373.

Fromm, E. (1956). *The art of loving.* New York: Bantam Books.

Hayes, R. L. (2001). Counseling in the 21st century: One American's view on the future for Japan. *Proceedings of Special Lectures for Japan Family Counseling Association, 4,* 17–30.

Imai, A. (1998). Sanninn no Tokokyohiji o Motsu Hahaoya e no Shinriteki Enjo. [Psychological support of a mother with three school refusal children]. *Sonoda Gakuen Joshi Daigaku Ronbunshu, 33*(II), 37–48. Hyogo, Japan: Sonoda Joshi Daigaku.

Imamura, A. E. (1989). Interdependence of family and education: Reactions of foreign wives of Japanese to the school system. In J. J. Shields, Jr. (Ed.), *Japanese schooling* (pp. 16–27). Pennsylvania State University Press.

Ishida, K., & Takei, M. (1987). *Ushinawareta Kodomo Kukan.* [The lost space for children]. Tokyo: Shinyosya.

Kameguchi, K. (1987a). "Circular core imagery" in family therapy. *Proceedings of the Third International Imagery Conference,* 344–45.

Kameguchi, K. (1987b). Kaokukinou Kasseika Puroguramu no Sakusei to Kentou. [Research and development of activation programs for family functions]. *Annual Progress of Family Psychology, 5,* 95–111.

Kameguchi, K. (1989). Tokoukyohi no Kazokuryouhou Jirei. [A case study in the family therapy of school-refusal]. *Japanese Journal of Family Psychology, 3,* 45–54.

Kameguchi, K. (1991). "Kazoku Kyoukaimaku" Gainen to sono Rinsyoteki Oyo. [The concept of "family membrane" and its clinical application]. *Japanese Journal of Family Therapy, 8,* 20–29.

Kameguchi, K. (1992). *Toward a theory of family membrane in describing family systems.* Paper presented at the Centennial Congress, American Psychological Association, Washington, DC.

Kameguchi, K. (1996). Chaotic states of generational boundaries in contemporary Japanese families. In M. Cusinato (Ed.), *Research on family resources and needs across the world* (pp. 235–242). Milano: Edizioni Universitarie di Lettere Economia Diritto.

Kameguchi, K. (1998). Family therapy with Japanese families. In U. Gielen (Ed.), *The family and family therapy in international perspective.* Trieste, Italy: Edizioni Lint Trieste.

Kameguchi, K. (2000). *Kazoku Rinsyo Shinrigaku.* [Clinical family psychology]. Tokyo: Tokyo University Press.

Kameguchi, K., & Murphy-Shigematsu, S. (2001). Family psychology and family therapy in Japan. *American Psychologist, 56*(1), 65–70.

Kameguchi, K., Urabe, M., & Ikeda J. (1990). Kazoku Sisutemu Zuhou niyoru Kazokuryohou no Kokasokutei. [Evaluating the effectiveness of family therapies by the family system graph method]. *Japanese Journal of Family Psychology, 4,* 25–36.

Kaslow, F. (1996). Families and family psychology in the 21st century: Recent trends and predictions for the future. In M. Cusinato (Ed.), *Research on family resources and needs across the world* (pp. 127–144). Milano: LED.

Kawai, H. (1986). Violence in the home: Conflict between two principles—maternal and paternal. In T. S. Lebra & W. P. Lebra (Eds.), *Japanese culture and behavior* (pp. 297–306). Honolulu: University of Hawaii Press.

Kawai, H. (1994). *Bosei Shakai Nihon no Byori.* [The pathology of the mother principled society of Japan]. Tokyo: Chuo Koronsha.

Kawanaka, J. (1998). Tokokyohiji no Sonogo to Hahaoya no Sinri Katei tono Kanren ni tuite. [The relation between the development of school refusal children and their mothers' state of mind]. *Japanese Journal of Family Psychology, 12*(2), 89–107.

Kearney, C. A. (2001). *School refusal behavior in youth: A functional approach to assessment and treatment.* Washington, DC: American Psychological Association.

Kearney, C. A., & Silverman, W. K. (1995). Family environment of youngsters with school refusal behavior: A synopsis with implications for assessment and treatment. *American Journal of Family Psychology, 23*, 59–72.

Kiefer, C. W. (1974). The psychological interdependence of family, school, and bureaucracy. In *Japanese culture and behavior: Selected readings* (p. 346). Honolulu: University of Hawaii Press.

L'Abate, L. (1990). *Building family competence: Primary and secondary prevention strategies.* Newbury Park, CA: Sage.

Lewin , K. (1948). *Resolving social conflicts.* New York: Harper.

Liddle, H. A. (1987). Family psychology: The journal, the field. *Journal of Family Psychology, 1*, 5–22.

Minuchin, S., & Fishman, H. C. (1981). *Family therapy techniques.* Cambridge, MA: Harvard University Press.

Okado, T. (1990). Perspectives on family psychology in Japan. [Special issue]. *Japanese Journal of Family Psychology, 4*, 39–53.

Patterson, G. R. (1982). *Coercive family process.* Eugene, OR: Castalia.

Philpot, C. L. (1990). Toward a systemic resolution of the battle of the sexes. In F. W. Kaslow (Ed.), *Voices in family psychology: Vol. 2.* (pp. 244–260). Newbury Park, CA: Sage.

Sato, K. (1997, August 7). Therapist advocates "eachness" in all. *The Japan Times.*

Selvini-Palazzoli, M., Boscolo, L., Cecchin, G., & Prata, G. (1978). *Paradox and Counterparadox.* New York: Jason Aronson.

Shimomi, T. (1997). *Ko to bosei no mechanism.* [Mechanism of filial piety and maternity: From perspective of Chinese women history.] Tokyo: Kenbun Publishers.

Simons, C. (1991). The education mother (*Kyoiku mama*). In B. Finkelstein, A. E. Imamura, & J. J. Tobin (Eds.), *Transcending stereotypes: Discovering Japanese culture and education.* Yarmouth, ME: Intercultural Press.

Skinner, H. A., Steinhauer, P. D., & Santa-Barbara, J. (1983). The family assessment measure. *Canadian Journal of Community Mental Health, 2*, 91–105.

Suzuki, K. (1988). *Tokokyohi.* [School refusal.] Tokyo: Kongo Shuppan.

Suzuki, K. (1990). School refusal viewed through family therapy. In C. Chiland, & J. G. Young (Eds.), *Why children reject school: Views from seven countries* (pp. 98–105). New Haven, CT: Yale University Press.

Szapocznik, J., & Kurtines, W. M. (1993). Family psychology and cultural diversity. *American Psychologist, 48*(4), 400–407.

Ueno, C. (1994). Women and the family in transition in postindustrial Japan. In J. Gelb & M. Palley (Eds.), *Women of Japan and Korea: Continuity and change* (pp. 23–42). Philadelphia: Temple University Press.

Wagatsuma, H. (1977). Some aspects of the changing family in contemporary Japan: Once Confucian, now fatherless. *Dawdles, 106*, 181–210.

Yamada, M. (1998). *The Japanese family in transition.* Tokyo: Foreign Press Center.

Chapter 7

Rewriting Stories of Distress

Culture-Sensitive Strategic Therapy
with Ultra-Orthodox Jews in Israel

Eliezer Witztum
Yehuda Goodman

Culture-Sensitive Strategic Therapy represents an integration of the narrative paradigm and the notion of idioms of distress. The influence of religious symbols on Ultra-Orthodox Jewish clients' narrative constructions of distress is reviewed. Therapy aims to integrate the patients' symbolic idioms into more personal and concrete forms and utilizes techniques specific to the client's culture and their role in it. Clients assume active roles in finding new solutions. Two case studies with Ultra-Orthodox Jewish men in Israel who experience distress connected to their past history, personal vulnerabilities, and external stresses, illustrate this approach.

Culture, Narrative, and Therapeutic Interventions

Our basic conceptualization of disorders and therapeutic interventions in cross-cultural settings combines the notion of "idioms of distress" with the narrative paradigm (see Witztum & Goodman 1999a, 1999b). The concept of "idioms of distress" was suggested by Nichter (1981), who made a distinction between psychosocial distress and its symptomatic manifestations in local social spheres. Idioms of distress describe disorders that are socially and culturally constructed, but are not necessarily institutionalized and recognized as a "culture-bound syndrome" (for a Jewish example, see Bilu, 1985). These idioms are weaved on the basis of collective cultural symbols, but the way they are used and experienced

Adapted from Witztum, E., & Goodman, Y. (1999). Narrative construction of distress and therapy: A model based on work with Ultra-Orthodox Jews. *Transcultural Psychiatry*, *36*(4), 403–436. Reprinted with permission from McGill University.

are not necessarily widespread, and they might even be specific to an individual. In any case, such idioms have not gained social recognition and canonization by the individuals' society and the mental health profession.[1]

The efforts to "read" idioms of distress in accordance with the patients' perspectives and the attempt to interpret the narratives within which these idioms are located are important from a research perspective and for understanding the relevant society (in our case the Jewish Ultra-Orthodox community in Israel) and for the construction of appropriate therapeutic interventions. Understanding the idioms through which distress and suffering are expressed is the basis for establishing an empathic attitude, creating a therapeutic alliance, and planning and executing culture-sensitive interventions. The proposed strategic therapeutic intervention aims at helping the patient to find an alternative narrative-plot that could be adapted to the Jewish Ultra-Orthodox culture. A carefully planned intervention is especially important in a cross-cultural setting in which the therapist and patient belong to differing sociocultural worlds. (In our case the primary therapist, Eliezer Witztum, was secular and the patients were religious.)

Our emphasis on the narrative construction of distress grew gradually. The central argument of the narrative paradigm in the social sciences in general (Polkinghorne, 1988) and psychology in particular (Sarbin, 1986) is that narratives are a "root metaphor" for constituting and expressing social life and individuals' experiences. Reconceptualizing the notion of "idioms of distress" according to the narrative perspective makes us more cautious not to organize personal distress as a cluster of "symptoms" or "idioms"—isolated from each other and lacking some interconnections. Idioms of distress can be better described and analyzed as narratives people tell.[2] It seems that the psychiatric diagnostic procedure and the DSM manual aim at organizing the clinical picture as a set of symptoms. Still, even the positivistic-oriented psychiatric procedure can include the narrative dimension as part of the overall picture of the distress (Verhulst & Tucker, 1995).

A life story, like any other story, includes a few components: space and time framework (setting), characters, scenes, plot, recurring themes, explanatory models, and a moral lesson. The life story serves an important intrapersonal aim of integrating various, sometimes conflicting, elements into a coherent whole that combines past, present, and anticipated future. Life stories give their protagonist a sense of continuity and serves as a basis for personal identity (McAdams, 1988).

Usually "life stories" do not cover the whole life of their teller. Rather, they are stories about certain meaningful periods or certain experiences. Such narratives shed new light on the teller's life (Garro, 1994). Illness narratives belong to this category. Narratives of prolonged suffering and chronic illness are a special genre. They relate to various contexts and disruptions in the protagonist's life, enabling him or her to express hurtful and dramatic experiences (Kleinman,

1988). By telling illness narratives, persons are trying to answer many questions: What happened to them and what actions did they take? Why did they carry out those actions? Who helped them and who did not? How did the illness influence their life? Beyond all these questions stands the existential question, Why did it happen to me? An illness can become a very meaningful experience. Like other crisis situations, it can create a new perspective on life, changing ways individuals think about themselves, their present situation, and their past and future. What was taken for granted in the personal, interpersonal, and social spheres is now challenged (Keyes, 1985).

Analyzing and mapping different types of illness narratives helps therapists in the employment of their interventions. From a literary point of view, illness narratives may include chaotic stories that lack direction; they may constitute closed stories that bring their protagonists to dead ends, or they might be stories that lack any meaning (Omer, 1994). Actually, the narrative metaphor, taken from literary studies, can impose much more coherence and meaningfulness than the actual "broken narratives" of the clients (Kirmayer, 2000).

The narrative perspective has another important dimension: It changes our understanding of the "truth" and "reality" of the distress. A personal life story in general, and an illness narrative in particular, not only mirror experiences, but can also change and create personal reality (Bruner, 1990; Gergen & Gergen, 1988; McAdams, 1988). This relationship between "life" and "story" can serve as the basis for a positive change of one's painful experiences. The idea is to find a way of changing the narratives that accompany and constitute them. Indeed, the narrative paradigm opens new avenues in psychotherapy—that in fact already include several schools with different foci (McLeod, 1997). The postmodern psychoanalytic tradition, for example, emphasizes the hermeneutic and narrative dimension in psychotherapy. It focuses on creating new meanings, or alternative stories in the "here and now" of the transferential relationship. It is quite different from the older tradition that aimed at interpreting—actually revealing and uncovering—what is historically true in the life of the patients (Aumada, 1994; Spence, 1982).

On both theoretical and practical levels, our approach can be placed along the spectrum of the cognitive and social constructivist positions within the narrative paradigm. The cognitive constructivist approach conceives of the patients' stories as a form of mental representation operating within individuals' minds. More specifically, it sees "narratives" as a set of schemas or scripts that reflect a dynamic sequence of possible actions. The social constructivist, by contrast, conceives narratives as existing not within people's minds but within a culture and between people. Accordingly, narratives are understood as collective and public meanings that can be played out by persons (McLeod, 1997).

Much thought is given in narrative therapy to frame the principles that guide the therapeutic intervention and create a desired change. According to a cognitive constructivist approach, the aim of a narrative intervention is to achieve the double processes of differentiation and integration: Patients who tell only one "problem story" or "distress story" are assisted in constructing and discovering alternative ways to frame distress (differentiation). During the process of integration, patients come to realize that the alternative construction is more compelling, coherent, and applicable to their lives (Russell & van den Broek, 1992). According to social constructivist approaches, therapeutic efforts are focused on externalizing and reflecting on the problem in the therapeutic setting. One way to conceptualize the "disorder" is to view it as the rigid roles played out by patients and their significant others (family). Patients identify with the roles assigned to them according to the accepted narratives, and cannot free themselves from the constant and unchangeable characteristics that stem from these roles (White & Epston, 1990). Hence, the aim of the intervention is first to reflect on this minidrama and then to play out a different plot. Accordingly, the narrative interventions as described later in this chapter are not based on the narrative contents alone, but may include the utility of rituals and mobilization and particularization of symbolic elements from the patient's world. In sum, the aim of narrative therapy is to change the problematical cognitive scheme that characterizes one's narrative (Russell & van den Broek, 1992), or to rebuild the story "lived" by the client in new directions (White & Epston, 1990). The sequence of events in the intervention itself is built on the narrative paradigm; it can be organized as a narrative sequence aimed at "rewriting" a new story (Mattingly, 1994; Sluzky, 1992).

Like the construction of life stories in general, the distress narrative is always narrated in a certain social context and with relation to cultural meaning systems. Stories are not only private, idiosyncratic, and personal. Persons create and (limit the scope of) their stories and experiences by relating to collective meaning systems and narrative genres common to their culture (Rosenwald & Ochberg, 1992). Thus, a narrative is a meeting point between the individual and her culture. The influence of the "culture" is expressed in many ways, among which are the inner structure and common themes of the narratives. The different elements of the narrative are constructed in such a way as to conform or challenge the basic moral and cosmological order and social norms accepted in the teller's culture. Sometimes, the other direction might. Cultures are reshaped, and common meanings are reexamined by the stories individuals tell (Sluzky, 1992). A therapeutic intervention that emphasizes the influence and constraints that local cultures put on the construction of the distress uses this understanding in the construction of a culture-sensitive intervention (Zimmerman & Dickerson, 1994). Moreover, the "same" distress is told in various social contexts with different participants. Thus, narratives relate and express the power relations of the social situations in which they are told (Good, 1992). Thus, the therapists should also take into account the social context of the distress narrative and their interventions.

In this chapter we propose a model that integrates the narrative paradigm with the notion of idioms of distress—accompanied by a specific strategic intervention. As illustrations, we present two selected cases taken from a pool of more than 20 similar patient narratives. The commonality of the narratives is related to the introduction of supernatural figures in the stories and other characteristics that we will discuss. This work represents the harvest of 15 years of clinical work and research in The Culture and Religion Treatment and Consultation Unit that serves the Ultra-Orthodox community of Jerusalem and that is part of the North Jerusalem Community Mental Health Center. The suggested model is a form of meta-analysis of some of the work conducted over the years.

Culture and Context

The Ultra-Orthodox Jews (The Haredim)

Before delving into the narratives let us sketch briefly the broader social context of these narratives, namely the world of the Ultra-Orthodox Jews (the *Haredim*) in Israel. The *Haredi* society in Israel is part of the fundamentalist movement that struggles with the processes of modernization and secularization (Heilman & Friedman, 1991; Marty & Appleby, 1993). *Haredi* Jews constitute about 250,000 to 350,000 of Israel's Jews and about 150,000 to 200,000 of American Jews—the two main centers of Orthodox Jewry. The Ultra-Orthodox Jews are characterized by their commitment to the study of the Torah (especially the Babylonian Talmud) in the *Yeshivot* (religious academies) and by their strict adherence to the Jewish law, the *Halachah* (literally: "the way"). The *Haredim* distinguish and distance themselves from secular society, in various ways. For example, their dress and appearance make them stand apart from their secular environments: For men this includes wearing caftans and black hats and growing a beard and long earlocks (these later traditional norms have a long history in Judaism, starting from the Bible as stated in Leviticus 19:27, "Ye shall not round the corners of your heads, neither shalt thou mar the corners of thy beard" and up to recent history in which these markers have become important embodiments of Jewish identity for the Haredim; for women it means modest clothing and for the married a head covering. (This may range from a kerchief over a shorn head for the most extreme to a wig for those less so.) Some *Haredim* distinguish themselves by speaking in Yiddish, a Jewish-German language, spoken in Israel only by Ultra-Orthodox Ashkenazic Jews, thus creating and emphasizing social and symbolic boundaries between themselves and others (Heilman, 1992). In addition, they have created environmental and residential barriers—especially segregated neighborhoods—behind which they build their relatively insular communities. They also send their children to their own schools in which only those who share their values and lifestyles are included. The *Haredim* are also overwhelmingly endogamous, arranging marriages rather than allowing individuals to find mates according to the demands of romantic love (Heilman & Witztum, 1997). The *Haredim* follow a puritan way of life, keeping strict separation between the sexes from an early age. Men are the carriers of the cultural traditions, whereas women are responsible for the household and in many instances become the breadwinners of the family. The boys are brought at the age of 3 to the *Heder* (kindergarten), where they are taught to read and study religious texts. Girls are trained to run the household.

Of course, the *Haredi* society is not homogeneous. It includes various social groups and ideological schools that differ in terms of worldviews, social organization, religious sensitivities, and moral values. Looking from the outside these differences might seem minor and meaningless, but for the Ultra-Orthodox they have great significance and involve ongoing power struggles. The social divisions among the *Haredim* include differences related to ethnic background (European, *Ashkenazic* versus Middle-Eastern and North African, *Sephardic*) and religious affiliations (Lithuanian, *Mitnagdim* versus Hasidim). There are also tensions between born *Haredim* and repentents who joined the *Haredi* world at a later age.

The general population in Israel tends to portray the Ultra-Orthodox society as a community that lives in a "Jewish Ghetto" in modern Israel (Heilman, 1992). According to this image, the Ultra-Orthodox are perceived as a community that strives to close itself off from the polluting influences of the secular modern world by building strong social and symbolic boundaries between themselves and it. Like any other popular image there is probably some truth in it: Most *Haredim* tend to live in separate Ultra-Orthodox neighborhoods where their lifestyle conforms to Ultra-Orthodox values, customs, and social norms. It is also probably true that in many areas of their lives the Ultra-Orthodox succeed in their efforts to use internal resources. Ultra-Orthodox values stress mutual help, which inspired the establishment of numerous funds and free services to the community. Paradoxically, closing itself off from the secular society is also made possible by the increasing political power of the Ultra-Orthodox and the growing involvement in the political Israeli scene that enables them to invest even more in their own institutions. The ability to keep members under their own wings is being strengthened by the process of "importing" knowledge from the outside: Many *Haredim* are new repentents. Some gained knowledge and various skills in their former life. Others came to Israel from other countries in the West, especially America; thus, introducing modern knowledge and sensitivities into the Ultra-Orthodox community (Bilu & Goodman, 1997). Hence, much interaction is taking place in actuality between the *Haredi* society and the secular society. Accordingly, another possible image of the relationship between the Ultra-Orthodox and secular society is the transaction. Although this image does not fit some of the *Haredi* explicit ideologies, the Ultra-Orthodox can be portrayed as constantly negotiating their social and symbolic boundaries. The new repentents and the drift of some *Haredim* back into secular society is one testimony to the complicated relationship between the two societies. Even the most extreme Ultra-Orthodox need to use secular services, and the emphasis on learning only *Torah* limited the Ultra-Orthodox capabilities in providing the entire social services necessary to maintain an autonomous society.

One area where the boundaries seem more permeated is mental health. In spite of the fact that the *Haredim* developed various institutions for treatment of the mentally disturbed (Goodman 1997), the Ultra-Orthodox need the help of professional psychiatrists, psychologists, and social workers. This need was met by an important process that took place on the secular and professional side. In the past 20 years there has been a development of communal psychiatry in Israel that brought with it the establishment of community mental-health centers in addition to the psychiatric hospitals. One of these clinics was the North Jerusalem Community Mental Health Center within which our team was operating. The cross-cultural encounters in the clinic between the secular psychiatrist and the Ultra-Orthodox patients are characterized by complicated transference and countertransference processes that are related to the contrasting cultural identities of the participants (Good, Hererra, Good, & Cooper, 1985). Only gradually did the therapists develop a culture-sensitive therapy suited to the *Haredim* (Bilu & Witztum, 1993; Greenberg & Witztum, 1991) and engage in researching the cultural characteristics of the expression of mental disorders among them (Greenberg & Witztum, 1994).

Case Studies

Joseph and the "Dead Girl Spirit"

Joseph is 26, married 1 year, and father of a 2-month-old baby. Joseph is Israeli born to a *Haredi* (Ultra-Orthodox) family, and he went through a typical Ultra-Orthodox educational track: *Heder* and *Yeshivot*. At the time of the referral to our clinic, he was studying in a *Kollel* (school for married pupils). His main complaint was that a woman revealed herself to him, especially at night, and complained that he did not help her in the aftermath of a serious accident and that this negligence caused her death. He added that he had lately found it difficult to concentrate on his studies and he had suffered from guilt feelings, anxiety, and depression. He frequently awakened at night and was afraid to fall asleep again. Joseph told us that a few months ago while he was visiting his parents, a serious road accident occurred near their house. He heard a terrible crash and screams and ran outside. He panicked at the terrifying scene: A young woman was lying in a pool of blood on the sidewalk. He wanted to help her and save her life, but because he was ignorant of first-aid, he did not know what to do and felt helpless and paralyzed. Soon an ambulance arrived. The woman was put on a stretcher, covered with a blanket, and taken away. Shortly after this incident, Joseph started dreaming about a girl standing before him, dressed in white, blaming him harshly, "Why didn't you rescue me and save my life?" Joseph also sensed the girl as an unseen shadow accompanying him during the day and repeating her severe accusations. Eventually, he consulted with his wife, who noticed his lack of concentration and his inability to sleep. At that stage he refused to consult with his Rabbi or any other person in order to avoid being labeled as "insane." His dysphoria and distress grew and, as he phrased it, "my life went off track." Finally, when the situation deteriorated even further, his wife persuaded him to approach our outpatient clinic.

Screened by a social worker and a clinical psychologist specializing in PTSD (posttraumatic stress disorder), he was found to be suffering from guilt feelings, confusion, and concentration difficulties. Thought disorder was suspected, especially when he told them that he felt the woman's presence throughout the entire day. They suspected that this feeling could be considered delusional. Still, they hesitated to diagnose the case as PTSD or psychosis. They decided to transfer the case to our therapeutic team, which included at that time a secular psychiatrist (E. W.), an Ultra-Orthodox clinical psychologist (T. Buchbinder), and a secular psychologist and anthropologist (Y. G.).

Our impression was that Joseph suffered from a kind of traumatic dissociative state. A therapeutic intervention was designed on two levels: First, according to the biomedical paradigm, Joseph received medication for symptoms of anxiety and depression (SSRI, Favoxil). Second, we constructed a therapeutic narrative plot that followed the cultural idioms in which Joseph expressed his distress. This therapeutic intervention included a few stages that unfolded an alternative narrative: On the cognitive level we tried to persuade Joseph that there is no proof that the girl died. Perhaps she was covered with the blanket to warm her up, said the psychiatrist. Second, we suggested that the next time the girl appears, he should explain to her that he is a *Yeshiva* student, not a physician, and that an authorized physician instructed him to tell her that he could not do anything to help her. We also urged Joseph to create a continued dialogue with the girl. We instructed him to do this in order to provide him with a more active and emotionally significant role in rescuing himself from the persecuting spirit. We instructed him to tell the girl that he will be doing a *Tikkun* ("fixing"—a phrase taken from the *Kabbalah*, Jewish mystical traditions) for her soul. We elaborated a little more on this cultural idiom, which was constructed as a counterpart to his idiom of distress. The *Tikkun* involved study of *Mishnayot* (comprehensive legal text completed 220 CE and served as the basis of the vast legal corpus of the *Talmud*) to help her soul rest in peace and ascend to heaven. This would be an act of kindness to her poor soul that "got stuck" and "was traveling between the worlds." This intervention in Joseph's narrative was constructed in his cultural terms and metaphors. The purpose of the intervention was to provide support and encourage Joseph to become more active. Thus, the therapists tried to join the patient's world, creatively and actively changing maladaptive patterns and feelings of powerlessness. The climax of the therapy was a letter Joseph wrote in which he described what he did as a result of this strategic therapeutic intervention.

> I saw the shadow of the figure, and asked her "What do you want from me?"
> She answered: "I told you many times in the past, I am here, because I want to know, why did you not save me?"
> And I answered: "Because I could not; I do not know first aid."
> "Then," she said, "you should have called somebody to save me."
> I told her that I went to Meiron to visit the grave of the holy Zaddik Rabbi Simon bar Yohai[3] and prayed for the *"Tikkun"* of her soul, and *I am demanding now that you give me rest and stop appearing to me."*
> Then I called my wife and the girl ran away.

A year after his first arrival at the clinic, Joseph is relatively free from the encounters with "the dead girl spirit." Overall, there was a significant improvement in his functioning, but he was still suffering from problems and doubts about his future as a student in a Yeshiva.

Summoning a Punishing Angel

Ezra, a newly orthodox young man, married and a father to a girl, was brought to the clinic by his older brother, himself a long-time penitent and Rabbi (Witztum, Buchbinder, & van der Hart, 1990). The primary complaint was "bizarre behavior." Ezra's thought processes were intact, but the content of his thinking indicated auditory and visual hallucinations of a persecutory nature. He appeared neglected, uncooperative, severely depressed, and only partially oriented to place and time. He was diagnosed as suffering from a major depressive episode with psychotic features.

Ezra's problems could be traced back to the traumatic death of his father, a chronic alcoholic, when Ezra was 15 years old. One night his father felt sick, but Ezra refused to stay by his side. That night his father died. Ezra felt deeply guilty about his neglect. Soon after this tragic event he became depressed and started using drugs. At 18, however, under the influence of his brother, he quit drugs and joined the military. Two years prior to admission, following his brother's footsteps, Ezra became religiously observant, married, and started praying for a son to name after his late father. When instead of the desired son his wife gave birth to a girl, his distress and shock were unbearable. He started hearing voices that he identified as coming from an angel who was sent to punish him for the neglect that had led to his father's death. To absolve himself, the angel ordered him to afflict himself by fasting frequently and otherwise eating minimally, by abstaining from sexual relations, and by wearing old and tattered clothes. Aside from these ascetic behaviors, Ezra immersed himself in various mystically based practices to obtain forgiveness: He frequented sanctuaries of popular saints all over the country and engaged in nightly rituals to mobilize their assistance.

Ezra's brother took it upon himself to bring him to the sessions and actively participated in all of them. Ezra was given medication—a small dose of antipsychotic to which an antidepressive was added later. The therapists started the strategic therapy by suggesting that Ezra should write his father a letter asking for his forgiveness. They thought that this might help relieve the guilt feelings that underlay his chronic mourning (for using letters and leave-taking ritual with the bereaved, see Witztum & Roman, 2000).

In the third session Ezra brought in an emotionally expressive letter he had written. The letter expressed his fears that the personal angel would turn him into a stone in his next incarnation. What follows is a verbatim translation (from Hebrew) of that letter:

> Father, I just want to ask for your forgiveness and pardon. I know that I am to blame for your death, but I ask for forgiveness. I did not know that this is how it would turn out. I want to see you alive. Just to hear you saying: "I forgive you." Until I see you alive I will not believe that you have forgiven me. I have an angel that helps me to afflict myself. Please appear to me. I do not want to be reincarnated as a stone, and therefore I cry the whole night. I wait for the angel to teach me mystical secrets of the upper spiritual worlds. Then I will know that you have forgiven me.

Ezra read the letter while crying and trembling. He mentioned that he felt a little better after writing the letter and that his sleep was improved; however, his self-affliction continued as before. Similarly, he maintained his visits to the gravesites and the ritual lighting of candles.

The therapists emphasized to Ezra that he was functioning as one suspended between death and life, and asserted that the personal angel must be protective, not punitive. They asked him to change his tattered, dirty jacket because such dress was not becoming to a religious student. The patient agreed to comply with this request. In addition, the therapists asked him to bring a picture of his late father to the next meeting. At the fourth meeting, the therapists found that Ezra had removed his worn, dirty jacket for 1 day, but then resumed wearing it, obeying his angel who had warned him that he would be reincarnated into inert matter. The therapists and brother bargained with Ezra until he agreed to have the coat dry cleaned. Afterward, Ezra took out his father's picture and stared at it with great emotion, breaking into sobs. The therapists asked Ezra to investigate the nature of the angel, particularly finding out its name and to ascertain if the angel was concerned with his benefit, or was just an evil spirit in disguise. The brother said he saw some overall improvement in Ezra's condition. At the fifth meeting the therapists noted some regression in Ezra's condition. He felt increased fear of the angel, and refused to change or clean his clothing. He did agree to remove his dirty coat after the upcoming "Ninth of Av" (a Jewish fast

day commemorating national tragedies that occurred on this day), and accordingly gave his wife a written promise to that effect. He could not ascertain the
name of the angel other than that it was related to the circle of the angel Raziel.
He revealed to the therapists that he summoned his angel by reading a text from
the mystical tract *The Book of Raziel* (a collection of Jewish mystical, cosmological, and magical materials, first printed in 1701, see Dan, 1972) after lighting
eight candles aligned in a specific geometric form. He demonstrated to the therapists how he read the text "swearing" the angel to appear. Modest improvements
appeared at the next two sessions. Ezra smiled and made eye contact on a few
occasions, but continued to speak minimally. The angel still dominated Ezra
and reacted to symptomatic improvement by ordering an intensification of ascetic practices, including eating even smaller amounts of food. In the month
proceeding Rosh Hashana—for the devout a period of reflection and purifica-
tion—Ezra made a pilgrimage to the Holy Ha'Ari's (principal Kabbalist, flour-
ished in late 16th century) gravesite in Safed (in northern Israel) and the graves
of other saints in Tiberias (also a town in northern Israel, next to the sea of
Galilee). At the gravesites, he recited special penitential prayers based on
Kabbalah. Afterward he commented that although he still felt the angel "deep
inside" he also felt less frightened of the angel and of his threats to turn him
into a stone in his next life. Nevertheless, Ezra continued to wear the dirty old
hat, complying with the angel's demands for ascetic practices. The angel led him
to believe that his father had not forgiven him, and therefore he had to continue
the afflictions and refrain from improving his emotional condition. Claiming
that the angel so ordered, Ezra even temporarily stopped taking his medication.
The therapists and brother strove to persuade Ezra to resume taking his medication. Within 2 weeks he went back to taking small doses of antidepressive medication (Anafranil). In the 10th session, Ezra arrived wearing a fancy new hat. He
reported that now the angel wanted him to mourn the destruction of the temple
in Jerusalem (70 ACE) and not the death of his father. The therapists confronted
this behavior, saying that such mourning is practiced in Av alone, not in the
following month of Elul, the month preceding Rosh Hashana, which is a reflective time of personal soul searching. Ezra thereupon erupted into tears. The
therapists made a positive interpretation of this behavior as reflecting "appropriate reality orientation" and "spiritual maturity." The brother reported that Ezra's
concentration had improved and he had resumed studying *Talmud* (a compendium of generally legalistic and nonmystical material redacted in 6th century
ACE). However, he studied alone. During the next 2 weeks Ezra's outward functioning improved, but there was increased evidence of self-affliction: He ate less
and stopped taking medication once again. At the 11th and 12th sessions, the
therapists arrived at the conclusion that they had to approach the angel more
directly. The therapists wished to summon the angel and order it to cease afflicting Ezra. The brother-Rabbi was greatly excited about this healing possibility,
adding that he and the two therapists could serve as a lay Jewish religious court

of three for purposes of summoning the angel. It was decided to enact this ritual procedure at the next session, 2 weeks later.

Although the patient and his brother arrived late for the next session (bringing candles and the necessary text), the therapists decided to proceed with the ceremony because of the great need and expectations aroused. The therapists locked the door, turned off the lights, and closed the window shutters. The room was then quiet and dark. The patient set up the candles to fix the form of an eight-stemmed candelabra, and lit them with trembling hands. The therapists then ceremonially stated that a Jewish court of three (the two therapists, Dr. Buchbinder and Prof. Witztum, and the brother) was formally constituted. The brother, leading the ritual, asked Dr. Buchbinder, to read the prayer. The text was cantillated in religious singsong fashion. Concomitantly, Ezra began swaying and moving his head in an increasingly rhythmic vigorous fashion, and seemed to be unself-conscious. He appeared to enter a trancelike state accompanied by his own ecstatic singsong of a two-syllable phrase repeated with increasing loudness and force. In fact, he was probably presenting to the therapists and his brother his technique of entering this altered state of consciousness. Ezra then informed the therapists that the angel was present. The atmosphere in the room was charged and thick. The therapists gave suggestions to the angel not to punish Ezra or persecute him because he had suffered enough. The brother hurriedly stated that on behalf of the court, he ordered the angel to cease afflicting Ezra and no longer return "for good or bad" (purposes). Ezra appeared to be stunned and confused. The therapist (Eliezer Witztum) explained to Ezra that from then on the angel had no right to disturb him, because the angel was from a different realm. The brother, quiet, tense, and emotional from the ceremony, told Ezra to blow out the candles in one breath, thus ending the ceremony. The court declared that Ezra was now a free man, under his own control. The brother hurried to open the shades and windows and turn on the lights. He then handed *The Book of Raziel* to the therapists, saying that Ezra no longer needed it. At the next session, the 14th, the patient entered the room with a grin and the brother reported several significant changes. First, Ezra now ate normally, and no longer weighed his food or gave himself small portions. Second, he had resumed relations with his wife. Finally, for the first time he began to interact and play with his infant daughter. The angel had appeared to Ezra several times without being summoned, but now acted in a much less invasive manner; he instructed Ezra to study Talmud (nonmystical texts) and read from the Kabbalistic work *Tikunei Zohar* (mystical texts). The antidepressive medication was increased.

At the 15th session, the patient stated that the angel did not appear, and the brother reported that Ezra was now more sociable; careful with dress and grooming; learned the Talmud and functioned more appropriately at home. At the next session it was reported that the angel appeared twice, but only to praise Torah study. The brother related that soon a memorial meeting would be convened in honor of their late father; the brothers were studying *Mishna* and chapters from the mystical *Zohar* to elevate the soul of their father. The therapists viewed this as a culturally normative practice and a clear sign of improvement. At this point, the patient and his brother moved from Jerusalem to Tiberias, where the latter was to become head of a Yeshiva. The therapists and brother agreed that Ezra had to attend a monthly follow-up session. The brother reported that Ezra had chosen life, and although he was saddened by the loss of his father, he did not blame himself heavily anymore. The father who used to appear as a threatening black apparition now appeared dressed in white and bathed in light.

Follow-up

Four months later Ezra came with his wife who had stopped his medication because of a misunderstanding while the brother had gone abroad. Ezra appeared kempt in dress and was oriented to place and time. His cooperation was good. Affect was sad, thought processes were intact, and there were no auditory hallucinations or visits of his personal angel. In spite of the premature stopping of the medication Ezra was not psychotic, and there were no visits from his personal angel. He remembered very well the ritual of the court and the incantation. The therapist suggested that he should take a maintenance dose of antidepressive medication for the next few months, and he agreed.

We now summarize the two narratives using two tables. Table 7.1 describes the narrative construction of the distress, whereas Table 7.2 summarizes the therapeutic intervention. These tables serve as a basis for our proposed model.

Interventions

The four columns in Table 7.1 contain the various aspects that constitute in our theoretical conceptualization the basic elements of distress. Indeed, these columns represent diverse constructions of distress based on different possible epistemological perspectives without any attempt to reduce one to the other. The task of the therapist is to integrate them on a practical level and to build a suitable and specific intervention for each patient. Although the columns of Table 7.1 allow us to clearly view the distinct perspectives used to understand the narratives, the rows allow us to compare between the cases and point out some of their similarities and differences.

The first column represents the supernatural entities and protagonists who participate in the narratives. In all these cases the narrator is represented as the protagonist whose distress is explained as caused by a difficult and complicated relationship with supernatural figures. These "significant others" (using a psychodynamic term) of the stories are entities borrowed from Jewish demonology. The stories include various figures that constitute the "other world" of Jewish

TABLE 7.1. Narrative Construction of Distress

Name of the Case	Narrative in Cultural Terms	Circumstances	Diagnosis in DSM-IV/ Phenomenological Terms	Possible Psychodynamic Understanding
1 Joseph and dead girl spirit	Protagonist is persecuted by a dead girl spirit that blames him for letting her die	Witnessed road accident where a young woman was injured	Posttraumatic stress disorder	Anxieties focused on blood and trauma. Background identity problems: masculinity, religious doubting, his status as a married man, and the separation from his parents' home
2 Summoning a punishing angel (Ezra)	An angel summoned by the protagonist prescribes him ascetic assignments	Peculiar behavior after the birth of his first daughter	Major depressive episode	Unresolved mourning, ambivalence, and guilt feelings over father's death expressed in depressive mood

mystical and magical traditions—such as angels, demons, and spirits (Trachtenberg, 1974). In the first story the spirit behaves like a ghost (a dead girl spirit). Each of these figures has specific symbolic and narrative characteristics in the Jewish mystical tradition that participates in the construction of the narratives (and of patients' experiences). The nature of the supernatural figure and the possible plots associated with it are used by therapists as a clue and a guide for possible directions of intervention.

The second column represents the theoretical assumption that distress is connected not only to the personal past history and vulnerabilities of the person (biology, family history, traumatic childhood, etc.), but also to the external, present stressful circumstances (serving as "a stimulus"). The kinds of stresses the patients encountered were: road accident and personal loss and its past sediments (loss of father by Ezra). Sometimes these traumatic circumstances are not revealed immediately in the patient narrative or are camouflaged. Exploring and exposing the specific circumstances and their meaning to the patients requires sociocultural and psychocultural sensitivities by therapists.

The third column represents the normative medical–psychiatric "idiom of distress." We are careful not to consider these terms (or clusters of symptoms organized in various categories) as a full translation of the distress. The cases we are dealing with do not constitute only one type of mental disorder. Rather, they represent a wide spectra of mental disorders such as dissociative reaction (traumatic circumstances), and major depression (sometimes with psychotic features).

The fourth column represents possible psychodynamic formulations. From such a perspective one can argue that the two demonstrative cases were characterized by common features. These male patients suffer from a variety of identity problems and pathological personality traits, aggravated by trauma and external stresses. In these cases there are one or more basic conflicts concerning masculinity–femininity, activity–passivity, high–low self-esteem, and loss and separation (see also Mann's 1973 formulations). Another possibility is to consider the possible developmental model: a traumatic, unresolved, ambivalent, or problematic relationship with "a significant other" (usually the father or father figure) from the past interacts with a recent traumatic event (terrorist attack, road accident) or loss (death of a father). Another variation occurs in cases of transitional periods (marriage, fatherhood, etc.), which are related to certain aspects of the person's identity. These processes are—in diverse measures—unacknowledged by the narrators/sufferers and one can argue that they were expressed in various phenomenological levels: somatic symptoms, emotions, cognitive schemas, patterns of behavior, and interpersonal relationships. All these personal expressions of distress are organized in narrative schemes and constructed by a web of collective cultural meanings and symbols, which take place in a specific social context.

Table 7.2 describes some important aspects of the interventions. These were strategic and multilevel—pharmacological, behavioral–cognitive, and metaphoric–symbolic. A culturally sensitive approach—in these cases, especially symbolic and metaphoric—needs special elaboration. The intervention itself was related to the emic terms that the patient brings to the therapy (first column in Table 7.1). However, underlying the strategic intervention, the therapists strive to integrate

Table 7.2. Strategic Narrative Intervention and Techniques

Name of the Case	Techniques	Strategic Narrative Intervention
1 Joseph and dead girl spirit	The therapist created an alternative scene in which patient acts as an active hero enabling him to change his fate and resolve the distress. Narrative constructed in transitional metaphorical domain	Patient is instructed to open a dialog with the dead girl spirit in which he will help her to redeem her soul
2 Summoning a punishing angel (Ezra)	During the ritual, patient entered a state of nonpossession trance. Narrative constructed in transitional metaphorical domain	Using symbolic ritualistic trial, angel is summoned by the protagonist and then persuaded to change from an enemy to an ally

various aspects of the distress they can conceive of: the cultural world, the circumstances, the diagnosis in medical terms, and the possible psychodynamic understandings (all four columns of Table 7.1). Note that these are just possible avenues and they do not exhaust the cases at hand. Other possible interpretations may include the relationships of patients with their significant others, possible family dynamics and possible community-related issues (sociodynamics). Admittedly, at times, the micropolitics in the clinic, its limited resources, or the noncooperation of the patients' family or community, prevented the therapists from exploring and trying out other possible interpretations and interventions. These perspectives contain dialectical tensions, especially between secular, Westernized understanding on the one hand, and the patients' explanatory formulations and their religious beliefs on the other. The therapists' professional and ethical role is to navigate carefully between these poles. The biomedical and the possible psychodynamic understandings (etic) could not be applied and transmitted directly to the patients, except if "translated" back to their cultural (in our cases: Jewish religious) world. Knowledge of the specific cultural meanings is a prerequisite, and of course of immense importance, but it is not enough. Cultures possess rich textures with diverse narratives and plots that could be interpreted and suggested to the patients. How do the therapists choose the "right" one? Much work has been carried out by trial and error. Analyzing the more successful interventions carried out by the team revealed that the intervention processes were tailored by combining the patients' clues and the therapist's understandings and conjectures. It is impossible to utilize general instrumental solutions—even those that follow cultural guidelines—without relating to the specific circumstances of the individual patient.

An example that demonstrates the importance of understanding the phenomenological and possible psychodynamic aspects of the individual patient is taken from the case "summoning a punishing angel." The therapeutic intervention employed by the therapist can be considered as a kind of ego-state therapy (Watkins & Watkins, 1997). The intervention treated the "angel" as an analog to a malevolent alternate personality and strove to integrate this part of the patient's personality (as in therapy of dissociative identity disorder). The therapists planned to create a dialog with the angel, to negotiate with him, and to try to convert him from an antagonist to an ally. In contrast, the patient's brother-rabbi tried to exorcise the angel according to the Jewish cultural code of treating possession. Although the brother's intervention implemented a known Jewish cultural plot, it was inappropriate, according to the therapists' view, in this specific case. It could even be dangerous, because from a phenomenological vantage point, that move could strengthen the patient's guilt, depression, and sadness. From a psychodynamic perspective, one could argue that the patient's angel represented an alter ego, and as such, a significant part of the patient's reality. It was connected to the conflict with his father and the remorse, guilt and unresolved grief after the father's sudden death. Thus, the aim of the therapeutic intervention was to integrate this component and not to expel it (that was what the brother tried to do). Through the symbolic strategic maneuver the therapists tried to help fix what might be conceived as the ambivalent relationship with the internalized father figure. Thus, recognizing a cultural plot that relates to the narrative of the patient is not enough for constructing an appropriate and successful intervention.

The last column of Table 7.2 illustrates a range of techniques used to implement the various intervention principles. These included over the years the usage of narrative reconstruction, hypnosis, guided imagery, persuasion and authoritative suggestion, cognitive restructuring and empowerment, and applying and customizing mystical rituals. Again, the necessary precondition of using any specific technique is the understanding of the cultural and symbolic language of the patients, which is particularized to each patient by applying strategic and possible psychodynamic understandings. The next step is the integration of these understandings and their translation to therapeutic maneuvers (Bilu & Witztum, 1994; Daie & Witztum, 1991; Kirmayer, 1993).

These techniques should be examined from a dual point of view: the first is the strategic assumptions, and the second is the cultural perspective that relates to the idioms (or metaphors) and the narratives that organize them.

The strategic point of view means that the interventions were aimed at changing and reconstructing cognitive, behavioral, and emotional dimensions of the patient's life, especially with regard to interpersonal relationships. These interventions are not aimed directly at interpreting possible intrapsychic conflicts, although we believe that the narrative–symbolic strategic approach may indirectly influence intrapsychic processes (without insight-oriented interpretations and "working through").[4]

The cultural perspective implies that although the guiding principle of the intervention is strategic, the "language" of the intervention is the patient's. Therapists join patients' narratives and utilize their cultural (or in our case, religious) metaphors and idioms of distress and even introduce features that complicate the culturally expressed structures. The two cases illustrate diverse examples; that is, summoning a punishing angel and encouraging an empowering dialog with a supernatural entity (spirit) while suggesting to the patient to carry out specific, appropriate traditional ceremonies.

Discussion

We now analyze three main aspects of the case examples. The first refers to the supernatural type of idioms of distress, the other two refer to the narrative construction of idioms of distress that include both the narrative created by patients and the narrative created by its reframing and rewriting by the culture-sensitive therapist.

Supernatural Figures

Like any other culture, Jewish Ultra-Orthodoxy offers a rich matrix of stories and myths that are organized in specific genres. In expressing their distress clients are inspired by the cultural material in which they are embedded. Unacknowledged choices between various possible narratives and explanations offered by their culture might be related to physical, physiological, personal, interpersonal, and social factors that are only hinted at in the clients' stories (Young, 1976). It is not always easy to reveal or to reconstruct such hidden meanings created in the complicated fabric of interactions between the collective narratives and the personal distress.

Some Ultra-Orthodox Jews perceive and experience religious symbols as full of vitality and integrate them into their lives, including their stressful personal situation. Thus, the narratives constructed or adapted by *Haredi* clients who belong to Hassidic or Sephardic groups (especially the newly repentant) include figures that belong to metaphysical and supernatural realities. In the process of relating to (and projecting on) these supernatural "significant others" of these *Haredim*, clients may identify with them or perceive themselves as having a problematic relationship with them. According to such psychoanalytic interpretations, one can assume that behind the narrative scenes that are constructed and presented by the client there are personal distresses hidden and camouflaged not only from the therapist, but also from the patient himself. Thus, these narratives might be conceived as part of the "work of culture" and are similar to other "symptoms." Their function is to solve (although partially and problematically) intrapsychic, interpersonal, and social conflicts. The narratives organize subjects' experiences and defend them from stressful meanings that are too hard to deal with and if expressed directly would cause more anxiety, shame, and guilt (Obeyesekere, 1990). Following these interpretations one could conjecture various unacknowledged developmental issues: identity conflicts in general and gender identity in particular, and problems related to significant life transitions (leaving home, marriage, newborn child, divorce, loss, and bereavement). The conflicts might be expressed by individuals but relate to "family triangulation," which includes religious conflicts (Butler & Harper, 1994) and to the community's general concerns (Littlewood, 1983). Thus, we can also note problems around cultural values and ideological conflicts (such as spending one's whole life studying *Torah* versus working, a conflict especially salient among Jewish repentents).

The expression of personal distress using narratives that include supernatural figures enables clients not only to reveal their distress, but also to channel and restrain other expressions thereof. Using this collective cultural narrative enables clients to express and at times conceal their specific problems. This form of construction of the distress moves it at times from the sphere of mental illness to the sphere of spirituality and to moral categories of sin, holiness, and impurity.

This coping strategy (in psychodynamic jargon, "defense mechanism") provides clients with a way to express their distress without being labeled as "mentally ill" (such a label would hurt, for example, one's chances of finding a proper marital match).

Although this coping strategy can work at least partially for many patients, it is important to note that the clients' social network and significant others usually interpret extreme behavioral disturbances involving supernatural idioms of distress as a sign of "mental problems." However, usually no effort is made by the community or its leaders (the Rabbis) to interpret the specific meaning and possible significance of the distress narratives. People simply stigmatize the person, expressing such narratives as "problematic" and even "crazy." This is true not only for patients' family members and friends, but also for most spiritual leaders of the community. Moreover, in contrast to the efforts of culture-sensitive therapists, traditional healers, and *Kabbalists* usually offer stereotypic remedies that do not enter into the symbolic sphere and to the possible personal, interpersonal, or social meaning of these narratives.

Narrative Construction

The impact of culture on the construction of various possible narrative plots for the expression of distress is clearly visible through the gender category. The Jewish Ultra-Orthodox tradition enables men (but not women) to accomplish and actively participate in "cultural" life. Thus, storytellers of these dramas are usually men. In their narratives one can easily identify many characteristic masculine themes as noted in parallel research on male narratives in Western societies. Those male narratives are about a lonely hero who is busy performing various transactions and manipulations aimed at achieving a single, desired goal (Gergen, 1992). In our case, the stories are about a hero, or rather an antihero, who is desperately trying to save himself from various difficulties and agonies. In the underlying structure of the story, the distress is explained as a consequence of deviance from the moral order dictated by cultural values (Sluzky, 1992). The protagonist believes that because of his violation of accepted moral and religious norms he is being punished in line with the mythical–cosmic–moral order. According to some explanatory models of the Jewish tradition, this might mean encountering various demanding and frightening figures (spirits, demons, angels) that belong to different domains usually not accessible to ordinary human beings. These Jewish patients' dramas stand in sharp contrast to the stories arising from the genre of moral stories. In the ideal stories, the hero succeeds in fighting and overcoming his fleshly passions and drives. From an external point of view (especially a secular one), passive study of Torah in the *Yeshivot* might seem "feminine." However, paradoxically enough, Ultra-Orthodox men consider themselves as warriors fighting in the scholarly spheres of Torah study, for which they gain rewards in this world and furthermore in the world to come. Thus, the clients' (male) stories are also an effort to explain how and why they fail to fulfill social values and religious ideals (e.g., why they find it hard to concentrate while studying the Torah).

The figures and plots are constructed in specific social contexts and represent a meeting point between the individual experiences and the various narratives' schemas offered by the specific culture. By schemas we mean mythical–cosmic moral order implicit in the narrative, plots (e.g., various events are organized as battles against the forces of evil, or as a cycle of mending bad past experiences), protagonist's role and characteristics (e.g., a victim of circumstance by outside forces), coping strategies (studying mystical text, using ceremonies and rituals to be released of distress, recruiting the power of saints, *Zaddikim*), emotional expression and their management (e.g., what emotions are culturally and socially appropriate to express and how to control them in various situations), and ideal patterns of relationship (e.g., the obligation to obey authority figures: angels–Rabbis–fathers).

The analysis of the various narratives along these schemas points to the existence of a genre of distress stories in the context of Jewish tradition whose plots are shared by Jews who suffer from distress. Many of these stories belong to "closed plot type" (Omer, 1994). The efforts to be rescued from the difficulties are temporary alternatives to the "closed loop" situation. These fruitless attempts only aggravate and worsen the distress and lead to a deeper abyss. The metaphors that the protagonist uses to describe the situation are of losing his way, lacking direction, and being stuck in the same place. The clients' stories are focalized and describe a repetitious rendezvous with the supernatural figures whose specific form is characteristic to each specific individual. The protagonist describes long intervals of time, but the events are described as brief and episodic, and the dialogs are typically intermittent and broken. The stories are not like a complex and a coherent life story that contain a full and detailed biography and relate to various figures from the teller's life. The plot is simple and includes two stages. The first belongs to the past, in which a meaningful incident happened to the protagonist. The second begins in the past and continues into the present. The protagonist fails to release himself from the burden and the implications of the past event. He cannot continue his routine life as usual, but instead becomes preoccupied with the past event. These stories usually contain a pattern of a "frozen or arrested" relationship as their most salient aspect. These stories revolve around two central figures: the self and the other (Zimmerman & Dickerson, 1994). The first is the storyteller protagonist who represents the patient, and the other is attached to him in conflictual relationships saturated with tension. In the stories, the protagonist identifies with the oppressed figure. The protagonist's role in the drama is usually passive and childish, and his coping strategies are stereotypic and limited. Thus, the role of the therapist is to intervene actively and creatively to broaden the scope of the alternatives and supply possible solutions and closure.

Narrative Intervention

Strategic therapeutic intervention is direct and focalized (Rabkin, 1977). When it is integrated within the appropriate cultural framework its format may be termed culturally sensitive therapy. It does not relate to exotic healing—based on simple knowledge regarding the patients' culture. Rather, it aims at taking into account and incorporating:

1. Meaningful intracultural variation (e.g., noting the variety of Hassidic sects, or the different sensitivities regarding the place of rationality in religious life)
2. The individual patient with biography, intersubjective style, and social network, including significant others
3. Specific techniques appropriate to the patients' culture and their place in it (e.g., their explanatory model, value system, and norms of behavior (Heilman & Witztum, 1997), customs and life habits

The general goal of this kind of therapy is to integrate the patients' symbolic idioms presented at an abstract cosmological level into a more particular personal and concrete form (Dow, 1986). The therapist relates to the symbolic idioms and to the narrative as "transitional phenomena" (Winnicott, 1958)—as powerful experiences that mediate between "reality" (outer, shared, and objective) and "imagination" (inner, personal, creative, and subjective). This is an intermediate domain that is quite similar to the playful world of children. It is a "potential space" within which the therapist does not challenge the patient's story and experience, where the elements are located and where they belong (avoiding the choice between dichotomies such as "reality" versus "imagination"). For the purpose of therapy, the therapist joins the symbolic world of the patient trying to create a positive change by utilizing appropriate interventions (Bilu & Witztum, 1993). The therapist respects the "world" in which the patient dwells without undermining his cultural beliefs. As a general philosophy of this kind of strategic therapeutic approach, the secular therapist is ready to adapt a position similar to that expressed by Coleridge (1817/1983) in relation to the poetic "truth"—a temporary suspension of disbelief. A narrative intervention usually takes place in several stages. Patients arrive with short, fragmentary, and sometimes incoherent stories. They find it difficult to explore and explain the meanings of the patterns of relationships embedded in their stories. The stories include discordant and unreasonable elements without patients' awareness of such salient, incongruent aspects.

The cognitive and social constructivist approaches mentioned in the introduction emphasize alternative formulations of problems (narratives). In order to be effective these should be close enough to the patients' original narrative. The intervention is carried out by constructing an alternative script, representing—and changing—the patient's reality. Our approach emphasizes consideration of the collective cultural (symbolic) meaning systems and the specific social context (McLeod, 1997; Zimmerman & Dickerson, 1994) and utilizes the strategic therapy tradition (Haley, 1963). More specifically, we work within the symbolic transitional domains of the patient's narrative and do not try to impose a radically different way of representing the patients' reality. We try to add, develop, or edit alternative courses of events that can lead to positive closures (Hertzfeld, 1986). Our alternative plot[5] is subordinate to the inner logic of the patients' culture and the moral order that is assumed in the narratives (Sluzky, 1992).

One of the specific implementations of the culturally sensitive strategic approach is utilizing appropriate rituals (van der Hart, 1983). These are used even in cases when the patients themselves did not conceive of the ritual as a solution to their distress and may even doubt at first their ability to be helped through them. The use of rituals is deeply anchored in the cultural world of traditional and religious societies that believe that significant changes (even miracles) can occur rapidly and dramatically through rituals (Turner, 1964). The ritual is not conducted solely within the transferential relationship between therapists and patients, but can be carried out in a different domain (e.g., visiting saints' sanctuaries). Specific rituals can be repeated many times without losing their healing power. The ritual is aimed at creating a dynamic of change by resolving the symbolic conflict included in the relationship embodied in the patients' narratives. The ritual mends the inner and interpersonal damaged world of the patient. It also relates to the cosmic moral order that was disrupted as a consequence of what the patients conceived of as transgressions, misdeeds, or sins. Successful interventions cannot be achieved if the rituals will be carried out solely by the therapist. The ritual is not mechanistic and automatic. The intervention can only succeed if the patient is convinced that change is possible via the proposed ritual. Successes are based on the patient's direct experience (cognitively and emotionally) of the healing power of the ritual (Csordas, 1983). In addition, this strategic intervention is aimed at relating to unacknowledged conflicts in an indirect and nonthreatening mode in order to cope with them (e.g., unresolved mourning over father's death).

Therapeutic Techniques

The general intervention principles must be translated into a sequence of therapeutic stages. The cognitive school in narrative therapy suggests that the first stage of therapy is to facilitate patients' capacity to tell their story. In the second stage, the therapist helps patients normalize their reaction to stressful events and build healing stories that explain what happened and why. Close attention is paid to metaphors used by patients as indicators of emotional meanings of the narrative (Meichenbaum, 1995). Another formulation suggests five stages: (a) recalling, (b) objectifying, (c) subjectifying, (d) metaphorizing, and (e) projecting

(Gonçalves, 1995). In accordance with a strategic and culturally sensitive approach and based on our clinical experience, we propose a similar sequence.

The first stage involves joining and listening to patients' stories, helping them to clarify and express themselves openly, bridging gaps, and assisting them in focusing on main themes. A useful approach to establish confidence and gain credibility is to use language and metaphors that are borrowed from the patients' cultural world. This is especially true for those patients whose narrative includes relationships with supernatural figures that may sound bizarre even to their social network, not to mention skeptical, secular Western therapists often trained in the psychodynamic or biomedical (e.g., biological psychiatry) traditions. This stage enables the culturally sensitive therapist who is empathic and noncritical to foster a therapeutic alliance.

The second stage consists mainly of cognitive restructuring. The therapist tries to rebuild the story with the patient, reiterating it in a more reasonable, coherent discourse. By this reframing, the story gains logical sequence. It also strengthens its explanatory force, helping to reduce patients' confusion and anxiety. For example, in the first story the therapist helped Joseph to elaborate the connection between the idiom of the disturbing shadow and the trauma of the road accident.

The third stage reflects the turning point in changing the maladaptive behavior embodied in the narrative. The therapist concentrates on developing alternative plots in which patients will accept a more active role in their lives and the supernatural metaphorical domain. By doing this patients are transformed from suffering passive antiheroes to active protagonists who struggle with their fate. One technique to assist patients in actively elaborating their stories is to ask them to describe the identity of the supernatural figure featured in their stories. Next, therapists try to add new dimensions to the relationships with the figure, usually by encouraging the patient to talk back to the figure as opposed to passively listening to it, and by actively initiating new actions, thus taking more responsibility. For example in the first story the therapist suggests to Joseph that he should explain to the figure that he is not guilty and then to offer an alternative solution to her misery. An effort is made to break the vicious circle, adding coping strategies including recruiting new allies within the patient's social and cultural world. This could include utilizing and broadening the patient's social network, including chaperons, family members, friends, and peers from the *Yeshiva* (Heilman & Witztum, 1994). One can use the patient's belief in the power of the supernatural in order to establish alliances with positive supernatural figures. For example, patients may call on saints (Zaddikim) to help them (first story). One can utilize religious customs and the power of holy days (second story) and suggest that the patient should engage in Jewish rituals with a healing aim (in the two preceding examples).

In the fourth stage, the therapist aims at constructing a final scene in the narrative's sequence of events in which the patient will be able to depart and separate from his distress as expressed, especially in the form of a stagnant relationship with significant figures. This includes separation from the supernatural figure and the distress related to it. By means of this symbolic act, not only is the patient released from his symptoms, but harmony and cosmic order are restored. This therapeutic maneuver could be achieved by utilizing a healing ritual, which includes the dramatic principle of "rite of passage" from illness to functioning (van der Hart, 1983). Designing symbolic rites of separation that are congruent with the patient's narratives is the climax of the treatment.

Various metaphors are used for understanding the role of the therapist in these interventions, including coauthor, coplaywright, and director of the patient script. The therapeutic intervention aims at improving the patient's fragmented, closed script. In this revised "play" that culminates in the final stage, the now-active protagonist plays a new role according to the script written together with the therapist.

Strategic Interventions versus Psychodynamic Therapy

Let us return to the overall therapeutic picture. Our approach dialectically combines various considerations that operate behind the therapeutic "stage" and that are implemented on the "stage" itself using the cultural language of the patient. Central to these considerations are possible psychodynamic and sociodynamic understandings. However, we believe that a direct psychodynamic approach in such situations would likely be ineffective and possibly harmful. There are a few reasons for this strategy:

1. We are skeptical about the possibility of a full translation and transformation of the local symbolic world (e.g., the supernatural domain) to intrapsychic Western or Westernized terminology and world view.
2. Psychodynamic interventions, like any other intervention, assume a shared social and cultural world between therapist and patient (Dow, 1986), a situation that usually does not exist in these cases.
3. According to psychodynamic principles, the therapist is not supposed to suggest directly to the patient to behave in contrast to patient's values or norms; nevertheless, the psychodynamic approach does encourage introspection and invites the patient to gain more insight into himself and his social world. The patient is encouraged, then, to judge for himself various aspects of his experience, to develop an independent position and even to reform and radically change his present position. The Ultra-Orthodox patients, for example, are educated on obedience to religious norms and authority figures (Rabbis and fathers). Psychodynamic approaches assume opposite values and world view. Such an approach, even if applied subtly and with good intention, may un-

dermine patients' value systems and increase their conflicts (cf., Bergin, 1980; Ellis, 1980).

4. Beyond the previous ethical considerations, we found that when encouraged to gain insight into possible (unconscious or unacknowledged) conflicts, the Ultra-Orthodox patients usually react with mistrust, devaluation, and resistance, far beyond "expected" levels of "resistance" (Greenberg & Witztum, 1991).

5. Such patients (who arrive with a focalized narrative) expect and demand fast, efficient, and direct remedies that are more consistent with cognitive behavioral modifications (Buchbinder, 1994). Using the culturally sensitive model does not threaten patients' personal and "collective cultural defense mechanisms" (Spiro, 1987).

Conclusion

The general lesson from this chapter is that the relationship between the "universal" (or "Western") and the particular should be reciprocal. It is not only a one-way process of translation and adaptation of the local to the universal. The local clinical experience should reshape our thinking about what is a good intervention, and how best to work with patients. We argued that clinical work in cross-cultural settings—Jewish secular therapists and religious clients in Israel in our case—should be carried out by combining a strategic approach together with patients' cultural world. We also suggested that narrative-therapy approaches (especially the cognitive and social constructivist trends) developed in the West help to organize and shape such treatments. These approaches should be locally adapted by using strategic considerations coupled with the cultural and contextual factors in each case. For example, given the importance of ritual and religious symbols in the patients' world, the culture-sensitive strategic interventions should not be based on the narratives' contents alone, but should include the utility of rituals and mobilization and particularization of symbolic elements from the patients' sociocultural world.

Based on work in a psychiatric clinic in Israel that specializes in the Jewish Ultra-Orthodox community, we outlined various types of distress stories the Haredim have told, and analyzed the interventions that have succeeded in helping them cope with their distress. For example, during the many years of experience in the clinic it turned out that many Haredi individuals have been constructing and enacting a dramatic story inspired by shared cultural narratives. Here we concentrated on those saturated with mystical and magical themes. The patients arrived at the secular psychiatric clinic quite hesitantly. Our proposed model for intervention related to mental illness narratives told by antiheroes, the patients, mostly men, trapped in unresolved relationships with nonhuman figures—without enough personal or community resources to cope with their distress.

Culturally sensitive "reading" of such narratives combined with strategic considerations is important, we argue, for creating an empathic attitude and a therapeutic alliance in cross-cultural settings. The process of reading the distress is the first step of any treatment. This reading combines eliciting the narrative in its local cultural terms together with the interpersonal, family, and social circumstances of each case. The therapists also try to "translate" or relate the story to known psychiatric categories (DSM-IV phenomenological terms, especially for the pharmacological intervention), and to some possible psychodynamic and sociodynamic formulations and interpretations. This multiple-reading process evolves and develops during the entire treatment process.

The therapeutic interventions combine the usage of pharmacological means and a culturally sensitive strategic intervention. The intervention aims at helping patients to find and exercise alternative plots in which they become active, and that adhere to some common cultural themes in their society. Note that these common cultural themes were selected and highlighted by the therapists, who evaluate carefully which interventions could work out best given the various factors involved in the individual case. The factors for consideration are the complicated process of reading of the disorder (as described in the preceding); the success of the medicines to reduce troubling symptoms; possible techniques tailored around cultural characteristics (e.g., outlining a metaphorical transitional domain in which an alternative scene is suggested); specific strategic interventions (e.g., creating healing rituals and instructing the patient to become an active hero and open a dialog with the nonhuman figure); past experience of successful interventions; and practical concerns (e.g., the possibility of help from other social actors in the community).

Most important, the therapists help the patients to reconstruct the narrative in a way that harmonizes the patients' plots—giving new meaning to the patients' suffering and agony. The therapists strive to achieve a narrative closure in line with culturally accepted solutions that will relieve the patients from their distress. Specifically, the therapists assign the patients active roles in finding new solutions—through locally and newly adapted rituals.

Discussion Questions

1. What is the importance of "a therapeutic model"? Why not work just from a framework of "intuition," "experience," or "common therapeutic knowledge"?
2. What is "diagnosis" and "treatment" according to the authors? What is the proper relationship between "diagnosis" and "treatment" according to the authors?
3. In your opinion, how is the model suggested here relevant to other cross-

cultural therapies you know of? In what ways is it unique to the Haredi and Israeli local context?

4. What problems or questions are raised by the suggested combination of a strategic model together with psychological considerations—in the specific local context of tense power relationships between secular therapists and religious-Haredi clients in Israel? Relate also to other such contexts elsewhere (say in the contexts of ethnic, gender, or socioeconomic differences and asymmetric relationships between therapists and patients).

5. In your opinion, what other courses of actions or interventions were possible in the two specific cases described in this chapter?

6. How is the culturally sensitive therapy suggested here different from more conventional psychodynamic treatments?

7. How is the narrative model suggested here different from other narrative therapies?

Endnotes

1. The concept of idioms of distress resembles the term "illness" as distinct from "disease" (Kleinman, 1980). Both serve the effort to criticize the positivistic understanding of the biomedical model and to argue for a more relativistic approach. A critical discussion of anthropologies of disease, illness, and sickness is offered by Young (1982).

2. Our assumption is that the organization of idioms of distress in a narrative form is universal. This assumption should be examined across different cultures in an empirical manner.

3. According to Jewish mystical sources, Rabbi Shimon Bar Yohai is the author of the Zohar, the most sacred book in Jewish mysticism. The book had enormous influence on various Jewish communities (e.g., Goldberg, 1990). Rabbi Shimon bar Yohai is believed to be buried in north Israel, and his grave is probably the most important pilgrimage site in Israel.

4. Working through is the process in which the patient comes to terms with what has emerged as a meaningful insight in therapy. It is the transformation taking place from the moment of an initial awareness (in relation to an intellectual formulation) to a lived experience (Bateman & Holmes, 1995).

5. We make the distinction between a therapeutic effort to suggest an alternative narrative and an effort to suggest an alternative plot. Our emphasis is not on changing the whole framing of the narratives, but on editing the narratives as told by patients. In other words, the emphasis is put on moving patients' original plots to new directions.

References

Aumada, J. (1994). Interpretation and creationism. *International Journal of Psychoanalysis,* 75(4), 695–707.

Bateman, A., & Holmes, J. (1995). *Introduction to psychoanalysis*. London: Routledge.

Bergin, A. (1980). Psychotherapy and religious values. *Journal of Consulting and Clinical Psychology, 48*(1), 95–105.

Bilu, Y. (1985). The taming of the deviant and beyond: An analysis of Dybbuk possession and exorcism in Judaism. *The Psychoanalytic Study of Society, 11*, 1–32.

Bilu, Y., & Goodman, Y. (1997). What does the soul say? Metaphysical uses of facilitated communication in the Jewish ultraorthodox community. *Ethos, 25*(4), 375–407.

Bilu, Y., & Witztum, E. (1993). Working with Jewish Ultra-Orthodox patients: Guidelines for a culturally sensitive therapy. *Culture, Medicine and Psychiatry, 17*, 197–233.

Bilu, Y., & Witztum, E. (1994). Culture sensitive therapy with Ultra-Orthodox patients: The strategic employment of religious idioms of distress. *Israel Journal of Psychiatry, 31*(3), 170–182.

Bruner, J. (1990). *Acts of meaning*. Cambridge, MA: Harvard University Press.

Buchbinder, J. T. (1994). The professional credo of an Ultra-Orthodox psychotherapist. *Israel Journal of Psychiatry, 31*(3), 183–188.

Butler, M. H., & Harper, J. M. (1994). The divine triangle: God in the marital system of religious couples. *Family Process, 33*(3), 277–286.

Coleridge, S. T. (1983). Biographia Literaria, II. In J. Engell & J. W. Bate (Eds.). *The collected works of Samuel Taylor Coleridge*, No. 7. Princeton, NJ: Routledge and Kegan Paul and Princeton University Press. (Original work published in 1817).

Csordas, T. J. (1983). The rhetoric of transformation in ritual healing. *Culture, Medicine and Psychiatry, 7*, 333–375.

Daie, N., & Witztum, E. (1991). Short-term strategic treatment in traumatic conversion reactions. *American Journal of Psychotherapy, 45*(3), 335–347.

Dan, J. (1972). The Book of Raziel. In *Encyclopedia Judaica*, Vol. 13 (Cols 1592–1593). Jerusalem: Encyclopedia Judaica.

Dow, J. (1986). Universal aspects of symbolic healing: A theoretical synthesis. *American Anthropologist, 88*(1), 56–69.

Ellis, A. (1980). Psychotherapy and atheistic values: A response to A. E. Bergin's "Psychotherapy and religious values." *Journal of Consulting and Clinical Psychology, 48*(5), 635–639.

Garro, L. C. (1994). Narrative representation of chronic illness experience: Cultural models of illness, mind, and body in stories concerning the temporomandibular joint (TMJ). *Social Science and Medicine, 38*(6), 775–788.

Gergen, M. M. (1992). Life stories: Pieces of a dream. In G. C. Rosenwald & R. L. Ochberg (Eds.), *Storied lives: The cultural politics of self-understanding* (pp. 127–144). New Haven, CT: Yale University Press.

Gergen, K. J., & Gergen, M. M. (1988). Narrative and the self as relationship. In L. Berkowits (Ed.), *Advances in experimental social psychology* (pp. 17–56). San Diego: Academic Press.

Goldberg, H. (1990). The Zohar in Southern Morocco: A study in the ethnography of texts. *History of Religions, 29*, 233–258.

Gonçalves, O. F. (1995). Cognitive narrative psychotherapy: The hermeneutic construction of alternative meanings. In M. J. Mahoney (Ed.), *Cognitive and constructive psychotherapies: Theory, research and practice* (pp. 139–162). New York: Springer.

Good, B. J. (1992). Culture and psychopathology: Directions for psychiatric anthropology. In T. Schwartz, G. M. White, & C. A. Lutz (Eds.), *New directions in psychological anthropology* (pp. 181–205). Cambridge, MA: Cambridge University Press.

Good, B., Hererra, H., Good, H., & Cooper, J. (1985). Reflexivity, counter-transference and clinical ethnography: A case from psychiatric cultural consultation clinic. In R. Hahn & A. Gaines (Eds.), *Physicians of western medicine* (pp. 193–221). Dordrecht: Reidle.

Goodman, Y. (1997). The exile of the broken vessels: Reality construction and therapeutic discourse at Jewish ultraorthodox settings for the treatment of the mentally disturbed in Israel. Unpublished doctoral dissertation, The Hebrew University of Jerusalem, Jerusalem.

Greenberg, D., & Witztum, E. (1991). Problems in the treatment of religious patients. *American Journal of Psychotherapy, 45*(4), 554–565.

Greenberg, D., & Witztum, E. (1994). The influence of cultural factors on obsessive-compulsive disorder: Religious symptoms in a religious society. *Israel Journal of Psychiatry, 31*(3), 211–220.

Haley, J. (1963). *Strategies of psychotherapy.* New York: Grune & Stratton.

Heilman, S. C. (1992). *Defenders of the faith: Inside Ultra-Orthodox Jewry.* New York: Schocken.

Heilman, S. C., & Friedman, M. (1991). Religious fundamentalism and religious Jews. In M. E. Marty & R. S. Appleby (Eds.), *Fundamentalisms observed,* Vol. 1. The Fundamentalism Project (pp. 197–264). Chicago: University of Chicago Press.

Heilman, S. C., & Witztum, E. (1994). Patients, chaperons and healers: Enlarging the therapeutic encounter. *Social, Science and Medicine, 39*(1), 133–143.

Heilman S. C., & Witztum, E. (1997). Value-sensitive therapy: Learning from religious patients. *American Journal of Psychotherapy, 51,* 522–541.

Hertzfeld, M. (1986). Closure as cure: Tropes in the exploration of bodily and social disorder. *Current Anthropology, 27*(2), 107–120.

Keyes, C. (1985). The interpretive basis of depression. In A. Kleinman & B. Good (Eds.), *Culture and depression* (pp. 153–174). Berkeley, CA: University of California Press.

Kirmayer, L. J. (1993). Healing and the invention of metaphor: The effectiveness of symbols revisited. *Culture, Medicine and Psychiatry, 17,* 161–195.

Kirmayer, L. J. (2000). Broken narratives: Clinical encounters and the poetics of illness experience. In C. Mattingly & L. Garro (Eds.), *Narratives and the cultural construction of illness and healing* (pp. 153–180). Berkeley, CA: University of Berkeley Press.

Kleinman, A. (1980). *Patients and healers in the context of culture: An exploration of the borderland between anthropology medicine and psychiatry.* Berkeley, CA: University of California Press.

Kleinman, A. (1988). *The illness narratives: Suffering, healing and the human condition.* New York: Basic Books.

Littlewood, R. (1983). The antinomian Hasid. *British Journal of Medical Psychology, 56,* 67–78.

Mann, J. (1973). *Time-limited psychotherapy.* Cambridge, MA: Harvard University Press.

Marty, M. E., & Appleby, S. R. (1993). Introduction: A sacred cosmos, scandalous code, defiant society. In M. E. Marty & S. R. Appleby (Eds.), *Fundamentalisms and society: Reclaiming the sciences, the family and education,* Vol. 2. The Fundamentalism Project (pp. 1–22). Chicago: University of Chicago Press.

Mattingly, C. (1994). The concept of therapeutic 'emplotment.' *Social Science and Medicine, 38*(6), 811–822.

McAdams, D. P. (1988). *Power, intimacy and the life story–personological inquiries into identity.* New York: Guilford Press.

McLeod, J. (1997). *Narrative and psychotherapy.* London: Sage.

Meichenbaum, D. (1995). Changing conceptions of cognitive behavior modification. In M. J. Mahoney (Ed.), *Retrospect and prospect in cognitive and constructive psychotherapies: Theory, research and practice* (pp. 20–26). New York: Springer.

Nichter, M. (1981). Idioms of distress: Alternatives in the expression of psychosocial distress: A case study from south India. *Culture, Medicine and Psychiatry, 5,* 379–408.

Obeyesekere, G. (1990). *The work of culture: Symbolic transformations in psychoanalysis and anthropology.* Chicago: University of Chicago Press.

Omer, H. (1994). Narrative reconstruction. *Critical interventions in psychotherapy: From impasse to turning point* (pp. 44–67). New York: W. W. Norton.

Polkinghorne, D. E. (1988). *Narrative knowing and the human sciences.* New York: State University of New York Press.

Rabkin, R. (1977). *Strategic psychotherapy.* New York: Basic Books.

Rosenwald, G. C., & Ochberg, R. L. (1992). Introduction: Life stories, cultural politics, and self-understanding. In G. C. Rosenwald & R. L. Ochberg (Eds.), *Storied lives: The cultural politics of self-understanding* (pp. 1–18). New Haven, CT: Yale University Press.

Russell, R. L., & Van den Broek, P. (1992). Changing narrative schemas in psychotherapy. *Psychotherapy: Theory, Research, Practice, Training, 29*(3), 344–354.

Sarbin, T. (1986). Narrative as a root metaphor for psychology. In T. Sarbin (Ed.), *Narrative psychology: The storied nature of human understanding* (pp. 3–21). New York: Praeger.

Sluzky, C. (1992). Transformations: A blueprint for narrative changes in therapy. *Family Process, 31*(3), 217–230.

Spence, D. P. (1982). *Narrative truth and historical truth: Meaning and interpretation in psychoanalysis.* New York: W. W. Norton.

Spiro, M. E. (1987). Religious systems as culturally constituted defense mechanism. In B. Kilborne & L. L. Langness (Eds.), *Culture and human nature* (pp. 145–160). Chicago: University of Chicago Press.

Trachtenberg, J. (1974). *Jewish magic and superstition: A study in folk religion.* New York: Atheneum.

Turner, V. (1964). An Ndembu doctor in practice. In A. Kiev (Ed.), *Magic, faith and healing* (pp. 230–263). New York: Free Press.

van der Hart, O. (1983). *Rituals in psychotherapy.* New York: Irvington.

Verhulst, J., & Tucker, G. (1995). Medical and narrative approaches in psychiatry. *Psychiatric Services, 46*(5), 513–514.

Watkins, J. G., & Watkins, H. H. (1997). *Ego-states: Theory and therapy.* New York: W. W. Norton.

White, M., & Epston, D. (1990). *Narrative means to therapeutic ends.* New York: W. W. Norton.

Winnicott, D. W. (1982). *Through paediatrics to psycho-analysis.* London: Hogarth Press. (Original work published 1958).

Witztum, E., Buchbinder, J., & van der Hart, O. (1990). Summoning a punishing angel:

Treatment of a depressed patient with dissociative features. *Bulletin of the Menninger Clinic, 54,* 524–537.

Witztum, E. & Goodman Y. (1999a). Narrative construction of distress and therapy: A mode based on work with Ultra-Orthodox Jews. *Transcultural Psychiatry, 36,* 403–436.

Witztum, E., & Goodman Y. (1999b). Further reflections on therapy, psychology, anthropology and Haredim. *Transcultural Psychiatry, 36,* 465–475.

Witztum, E., & Roman I. (2000). Psychotherapeutic intervention in complicated grief: Metaphor and leave-taking ritual with the bereaved. In R. Malkinson, S. Rubin, & E. Witztum (Eds.), *Traumatic and nontraumatic loss and bereavement: Clinical theory and practice* (pp. 143–171). Madison, CT: Psychosocial Press.

Witztum, E., van der Hart, O., & Friedman, B. (1988). The use of metaphors in psychotherapy. *Journal of Contemporary Psychotherapy, 18*(4), 270–290.

Young, A. (1976). Internalizing and externalizing medical belief system: An Ethiopian example. *Social Science and Medicine, 10,* 147–156.

Young, A. (1982). The anthropologies of illness and sickness. *Annual Review of Anthropology, 11,* 257–285.

Zimmerman, J., & Dickerson, V. C. (1994). Using a narrative metaphor: Implications for theory and clinical practice. *Family Process, 33*(3), 233–245.

Chapter 8

The Killing and Burning of Witches in South Africa

A Model of Community Rebuilding and Reconciliation

Michele B. Hill
Greg Brack

A model of community rebuilding and reconciliation in South Africa based on a group counseling approach and applied to witchcraft persecution and trauma is described. The relationship between witchcraft persecution and South Africa's history of social upheaval is reviewed. The chapter presents a case study of a Pilot Reconciliation Group Counseling Session aimed at the reconciliation of conflicting groups, including perpetrators and survivors. Cultural considerations for counselors working within a particular South African subculture are outlined.

Witchcraft Persecution in South Africa

In South Africa, since 1994, hundreds of suspected witches have been burned to death and thousands of older women and men suspected of witchcraft have fled to one of seven refugee camps established by the Ministry of Safety and Security in the rural Northern Province (Chandler, 1997; Ntsewa, 1998). Most of the psychological, sociological, historical, or anthropological literature relates to the process of persecution, and the psychosocial influences at work in the cycle of violence. When the killing stops, these same factors continue to stress the system, and have a role in the profound aftermath of the violence. In order for counselors to successfully intervene in South Africa, it is important that such professionals understand the complex multidimensional factors embedded in an historical network of relationships. The goal of the present chapter is to review the literature on this phenomenon and then to discuss a specific intervention used to address first the violence and then the reconciliation process.

Psychological and Social Causes of Witchcraft Persecution

Witchcraft and witchcraft persecution are not new phenomena. Anthropologists and social scientists have been studying witch killings all over the world for many decades. In the 1920s and 1930s, Evans-Pritchard (1950) conducted the first ethnography of witchcraft in a tribal community with the A-Zande people of Africa. Evans-Pritchard (1950) lived among the group as an observer, and his study is the foundation upon which all subsequent research in witchcraft violence has been built.

A belief in witchcraft was a foundational position that supported much of what occurred in the A-Zande life (Evans-Pritchard, 1950). For the A-Zande, witchcraft was used to describe many of life's problems. When individuals encountered tragedy, they attributed the event to witchcraft. They did not use witchcraft as a way of excusing work responsibility or fate. Witchcraft was used to explain the reason people may have acted irresponsibly or encountered misfortune. For instance, a person might plant a crop in a bad plot of ground, and it would not grow. Although everyone recognized that planting in the bad plot resulted in the failure, witchcraft was used to explain why the farmer would have made such a catastrophic error in planting. In many ways, it would appear that witchcraft was a way of saving face when one encountered adversity. It is important to note that few witch accusations among the A-Zande ended in death (Evans-Pritchard, 1950).

The accused witch was someone who had a negative encounter with the accuser (Evans-Pritchard, 1950). Typically, the accused person represented someone of lower social status or was atypical in some manner (e.g., had no children). Although anyone was a potential target, the recognized witch generally represented the most troublesome, difficult, and eccentric individual in the community. Evans-Pritchard (1950) hypothesized that the belief in witchcraft and the accusation against witches provided a highly efficient method for dealing with the emotional turbulence among the group. Basically, it served as a social regulator (Evans-Pritchard, 1950).

Between 1957 and 1958, Reynolds (1963) studied the witch trial phenomenon in former Rhodesia, now Zimbabwe. He used administrative records and participant interviews. The study illustrated that the intervention of the colonial administration and missionaries interfered with the traditional procedures for handling such problems. What resulted was a legalistic nightmare where over 100 people became caught up in the hysteria. Reynolds (1963) concluded that culture is dynamic, and witchcraft beliefs and practices are subject to change with the pressures of new conditions. Reynolds (1963) concluded that the greatest pressure facing the African culture has been the presence of the European. The tensions and problems created by European influence and values on traditional cultural practices resulted in a breakdown of the old culture.

Reynold's conclusions are supported by Credo Mutwa (1996), a noted historian, traditionalist and *sangoma* (traditional healer) in South Africa. Mutwa has stated that colonialization actually served to increase witchcraft killings throughout Africa. The influence of Western Europe upon the witchcraft problem in Africa was to alter the traditional means for punishing a witch from banishment to death. In the traditional South African practice, witch killing was a last resort, and death by burning was forbidden, because burning was equated with the perpetrators' loss of soul (Mutwa, 1996). Unfortunately, few researchers have investigated how witch persecution cycles begin as opposed to why burnings occur. In the 1970s, explanations for witch killing ranged from revenge . . . to drug use. Macfarlane (1970) and Briggs (1996) hypothesized that scapegoating was the critical element. That is, scapegoating was a means of handling grievances between community or family members. Throughout the 1970s, others focused on a variety of reasons, including: (a) interpersonal conflict between community members (Midelfort, 1972), (b) an attempt to suppress medical practice by midwives (Ehrenreich & English, 1973), (c) decline of magic and the rise of formalized religion (Thomas, 1971), and (d) the use of drugs that add to suggestibility (or create zombielike states) (Carporael, 1976).

Demos (1982) sought a more comprehensive explanation. He integrated psychology, sociology, and history in his study of the Salem witch persecution in North America in the 17th century. Despite the historical, cultural, and psychological differences between Demos' work and Evans-Pritchard's (1950) work, there are some striking parallels. First, both cultures totally accepted a belief in witchcraft. Second, both cultures accepted and observed the harmful affects of witchcraft. Third, both cultures had formal social procedures for dealing with harmful witches. Finally, both cultures accepted the death of the witch as a last resort. From his analysis, Demos constructed a rough composite that the stereotypical accused witch was female and middle aged (40 to 60 years). She had few to no children and was frequently involved in trouble and conflict with other family members. She openly professed to practicing a medical vocation on an informal basis. Typically, she was of relatively low social position and was caustic in her personality style.

In addition to these individual factors, there also were community factors. Demos (1982) stated that the entire New England community was undergoing dramatic shifts in child-rearing practices and individual professional development. The communal group structure of Europe was metamorphosizing into the individualistic ideals of frontier America. New England was in the grip of Indian attacks, disease, and political instability. Demos cited that New Englanders lived under a context of anxiety but were taught to ignore or repress it with individualistic aggression and assertiveness. The pressure of trying to blend old communal values with this new individualistic system seemed to erupt periodically into witch allegations. Such events allowed people to focus their repressed anxieties and provided a place to put the blame for the latest misfortune. Demos is clear that many of these accusational periods did not lead to cohesion but rather to the disintegration of the community. This is in opposition to notions surrounding the A-Zande where the witch accusation seemed to serve the purpose of community cohesion.

Ben-Yehuda (1981) reviewed the research literature in pursuit of a more comprehensive perspective to understanding this phenomenon—one based on a social psychological frame. Ben-Yehuda combined the many ideas from the vast literature to formulate specific hypotheses for researchers to focus on regarding the underlying causes of witch persecution. One of these hypotheses was the "minority group persecution model" that states witch trials are just one of many forms of community scapegoating of minorities. Other researchers have agreed with this hypothesis, going one step further to suggest that misogyny and gender are the root causes of the persecution (Barston, 1994; Klaits, 1985; Lederer, 1969). Another of Ben-Yehuda's hypotheses was the "educational model," which states that preenlightenment education, especially prescience education, predisposes cultures to witch belief systems and the trials that may accompany them. Current research in South Africa suggests that even in villages with ample postenlightenment education and scientific training, witch persecution continues unabated (Commission on Gender Equality, 1998). Thus, education, even scientific, does not quell belief that witches exist as evildoers.

The Process Model may provide the most useful explanation of witchcraft accusations and violence. Shermer (1997) ascertains that there are both *internal* and *external* components to the witch persecution phenomenon. For Shermer, an internal component can be defined as a "prevalent feeling of loss of personal control and responsibility, and the need to place blame of misfortune elsewhere" (p. 101). External components involve those stresses outside of the individual, such as "socioeconomic stress, cultural and political crises, religious strife, and moral upheavals" (p. 101). For example, extreme changes or ongoing stresses in the environment, such as unemployment, would provoke the individuals within the community to feel increasingly fearful or out of control of their lives. Shermer believed that the combined forces of internal and external components self-organize into what he has called the "Witch Craze Feedback Loop" (p. 101).

In this feedback loop, it is critical to understand the internal forces or emotions (i.e., fear and anger) that lead to its creation. The individual feels fearful and angry at the personal situation that drives forward accusations of witchcraft. This is consistent with the theory of Demos (1982). When accusations are made and there is a "lack of fear" in surrounding community members, the witch craze never grows in intensity and eventually accusations are ignored. Thus, Shermers' model shows that witch violence occurs at the nexus of internal and external vectors. Shermer illustrates that it is not social change alone that causes the witch craze, but rather the feelings being experienced by the individuals in relationship to the social change. The potential for violence increases when the entire social fabric is awash in fear and anger from stress and change in the complex mixture of internal and external domains.

Culture and Context

South Africa's witch craze can be directly linked to its history of immense social upheaval. The Northern Province's history in the last hundred years is filled with war, apartheid, corruption, migrant labor forces, and problematic education that, in all, have led to the destruction of the family unit, lack of chiefly rule in the communities, the rise of the rebellious youth movement, and the pervasion of unbearable poverty (Delius, 1996). The African National Congress (ANC) began its struggle against an apartheid system in the 1960s. In 1985, the youth of the Northern Province became involved in the ANC and formed their own distinct subgrouping called the Congress of South African Students (COSAS) and took over most local control. It was at this point that the youth turned to witchcraft killing in the villages (Delius, 1996). Witchcraft in the Northern Province is considered a great threat to the welfare of the community (Delius, 1996). *Witches* (baloi) are defined as those individuals who use magic and spells to render harm and destruction to community members and their property (Mutwa, 1996). Therefore, it has historically been perceived by communities that ridding the village of a witch is a positive event ("Neverdie," 1998), yet in the 1990s many communities erupted into profound violence and murder.

The National Crime Information Management Centre of South Africa statistics showed that in the Northern Province between April 1994 and April 1995, 228 murders of suspected witches were reported (Ntsewa, 1998). South Africa's Northern Province Ministry of Safety and Security reported that between 1995 and 1996 more than 300 people had been killed by adolescent mobs, and thousands had lost their property to burnings (Ralushai, 1998). From January to June of 1997, there were 700 legal cases in the court system involving witchcraft violence (Sullivan, 1998). Thus, by 1998, South Africa had been forced to create "witch sanctuaries" for survivors (i.e., those individuals suspected of witchcraft that lived through the witch persecution) fleeing their communities and possible execution (Ntsewa, 1998). The average murder victims were females, between 40 and 70 years of age, suspected of witchcraft, who met the "stereotypic profile" identified by Demos (1982).

The average murder suspects (perpetrators), though, are males between 14 and 26 years of age. These perpetrators are described as militant youth revolting against a society that could not support them (Shapshak, 1996). These youth had been educated in the changing South African school system and many had several years of formal education at universities. Most were unemployed with little hope of finding jobs after completing college (Ntombele-Nzimande, 1998). An unemployment rate of 32% prevailed throughout South Africa at the time of the greatest violence, and was far higher in some regions, with women and youth the hardest hit (Reddy, 1996). Thus by 1998, the extent of the violence against suspected witches had reached crisis proportions.

Interventions

In September of 1996, the Northern Province began its largest crackdown of witch killers. A crowd of 52 youth were brought before the magistrate and charged in connection with the murder of 33 suspected witches in 1994 (Shapshak, 1996). Since then, hundreds of teenagers and young adult men have been arrested and sentenced for ritual murders and witch burnings (Shapshak, 1996). Sadly, the crisis escalated, and in 1998 the Commission on Gender Equality held the First National Conference on Witchcraft Violence in Thohoyhandou, South Africa. The Commissions involvement is owed to the fact that more than 80% of the accused are females and their families (Commission on Gender Equality, 1998). Discrimination against women being labeled as witches is historically similar across cultures (Demos, 1982). However, the conference brought together all relevant individuals to discuss the problem of witchcraft violence. The conference lasted for five intensive days. The three general themes of the conference involved: (a) *stopping the violence* in the communities, (b) *healing the traumas* of the communities, and (c) *reconciliation* of the communities. During the conference, the Minister of Safety and Security, government officials, community and religious leaders, traditional healers and leaders, academicians, victims, perpetrators, and international delegates adopted the Thohoyandou Declaration on Ending Witchcraft Violence (Commission on Gender Equality, 1998). The conference and resulting declaration focused on treating the internal and external causes of the violence.

The declaration offered a plan of action toward not just ending the violence, but dealing with the aftermath. The following recommendations from the declaration directly involve the counselor: (a) economic empowerment of women (i.e., career counseling and consultation), (b) victim support (i.e., trauma counseling and grief work), (c) reintegration and reconciliation of communities (i.e., communication skills, family counseling, conflict management), (d) public education (i.e., life skills building, resources management), and (e) research and evaluation (i.e., needs assessment, program efficiency, policy reformation) (Commission on Gender Equality, 1998).

Case Study of a Pilot Reconciliation Group Counseling Session

During the conference, members of the Commission on Gender Equality recognized that there was a unique opportunity to try to reconcile the conflicting groups. Because of the presence of both survivors of the violence and convicted perpetrators, creating a space for healing and reconciliation was attempted. Why try to reconcile survivors of violence with perpetrators? Interviews with violence survivors illustrated that a key problem was that survivors deeply wanted to return to their homes, but this is a deadly prospect (Commission on Gender Equality, 1998). The attachment of the survivors to their villages cannot be underestimated, and is rooted in a long association of the land with family, ancestors, and history. Second, most survivors felt "unheard," misunderstood, and alienated. They and the conference organizers believed that offering them the chance to speak in a structured group setting could be therapeutic. Thus, the purpose of the Reconciliation Group Counseling Session (RGCS) was to implement a group counseling approach that could promote "sustainable reconciliation" with traumatized individuals in communities divided by violence caused by witchcraft persecution with the opportunity for all parties to be heard.

Participants for the group were convicted youth perpetrators, survivors of the violence who had fled their villages, and identified relevant stakeholders to the reconciliation process. It is important to note that this was the first known meeting between relevant stakeholders held outside of a courtroom or a violent mob scene. There were 15 group members, including the present authors. Thirteen members were South African. The authors were invited to the conference because of their experience with trauma counseling, conflict resolution, and knowledge of South African culture. The leader of the group asked the counselors to assist the group process and be available for any mental health concerns and associated problems that might arise from the potentially volatile encounter. The leader of the group was a known proponent of human rights and reconciliation in the community and member of the Commission who had the prestige and respect of all the group members, and the conference participants at large. All stakeholders at the conference recognized that she had both the reputation and personality to set up and conduct such a group.

Prior to the RGCS, the conference organizers asked for 10 individuals from several neighboring villages to attend the conference as representatives for the "perpetrators." Only five males voluntarily agreed to come to the conference and to then subsequently participate in the RGCS. Four of the survivors at the conference, three females and one male, voluntarily agreed to be in the group. A specific translator was selected because of her ability to translate the Tsonga language. All other group members, including the female group leader, a male religious leader, and a female traditional healer, were asked if they would participate, because of their well-known status at the conference.

Because of their training in counseling and psychology with South Africans, the authors served as the group counselors/facilitators. The RGCS took place in a tiny room, adjacent to the conference proceedings. The group met for a little more than 2 hours. The group leader called the meeting a "Reconciliation Group Counseling Session" from the beginning. Group participation was defined first by the fact that all members agreed to be there voluntarily. Second, members were asked to participate because of their role within the community. Their role in the community then became their label in the group and subsequently their role in the group. For example, a minister was asked to participate as a representative for religious leaders (his label). His role in the group was to ensure that members were being treated fairly, and that the church was recognized as helping in the process. Besides the role of religious leader, the other role labels were group leader, translator, survivor, perpetrator (youth), traditional healer, group counselor/facilitator (second author), and researcher (first author). The researcher in this group was asked to participate because of her international visitor status and background knowledge. The role of the researcher was to report the findings from the group to governing organizations that could aid in establishing laws and problem solving. Additionally, the function of the researcher was to write and talk about the cycle of persecution and possibilities for reconciliation recognized by the participants for the purposes of educating others through avenues of communication.

Participation was further defined by one's leadership status. The leaders tended to speak more often and tended to speak for others in the group. For example, there was a leader among the perpetrators and he tended to speak for the youth group.

Time and leadership were the early focus of the group process. Time was discussed in a pragmatic fashion throughout the session because of the 2-hour limit. For example, the group leader stated, "so, let us hear from [all of the group members] so that we can finish at 11 o'clock. [But don't rush because] we can just take our time." However, with regard to time, the authors noted that the group appeared to have three stages. The three stages were labeled: beginning, working, and final reconciliation stage. Three core issues defined group stages: (a) rule setting, (b) storytelling, and (c) critical moments. Leadership style permeated all stages and interactions.

The beginning stage was recognized as a time for rule setting. Establishing rules was seen as critical to the perception of safety of participants. For example, the leader of the group delineated that everyone would get a chance to speak voluntarily, and that it was not expected for anyone to admit guilt. For example, she said, "When I say you [the youth perpetrators], I don't mean the five of you I mean all of the youth that have been involved." This indicated that the leader and group agreed that these five perpetrators were to speak for the greater community. This allowed them to feel safe in speaking, because they did not have to admit personal guilt. This was further supported by comments such as "we don't want you to confess." Another part of rule setting was stating the purpose of the group many times to the members, which further assisted in establishing safety. The primary purpose of the group was "establishing peace and reconciliation." Counseling was defined for members, as "we just want to talk and come up with ideas on how we can bring all of you together."

The group moved into the working stage as group members told their stories. Survivors each took a turn in telling their personal story, and the entire group offered empathy and suggestions to their problems. For example, one survivor was having difficulty with her grandson because of the trauma to the family (his mother was killed). The group processed this issue for a lengthy time and suggested several ways to help, one of which was personal counseling for the grandson. There was a transition moment between the survivors and perpetrators talking in the working phase. A male survivor (referred to in the group as the "old man") became very agitated after the survivors' stories had been told. The anger appeared to result from the fact that a woman was running the group and that he felt he had to assert himself as an elder. He refused to hear from the perpetrator until the leader acknowledged his place in the group as an elder. She spoke with him swiftly and directly. The words she used assisted him to feel honored. She then shifted the focus to the perpetrators and he agreed to hear from them. The perpetrators' sharing was different than the survivors'. Although they spoke from personal experience, they did less storytelling. They used their personal stories only if it assisted to illustrate their ideas about stopping the violence and reconciling the communities. A transition out of the working phase into the final reconciliation phase seemed to transpire when survivors and perpetrators had finished telling their personal stories.

A critical moment seemed to begin the final reconciliation phase of the session. At the end of the perpetrators' time, one of the group counselors asked how everyone felt about the group session. To everyone's surprise, the perpetrators admitted that killing suspected witches was wrong, because it was against "human rights." Culturally, this is a shocking admittance. According to the South Africans we spoke to from differing communities, to say such a thing is considered to be "condoning" or "collaborating" with witchcraft—a very negative and deadly admittance even in the context of the public conference. The perpetrators also admitted that the youth should respect their elders. This admittance moved the group into its final stage—the "moment of reconciliation." The survivors stated that they were "very grateful, they were very happy that their children [the youth] will be able to do something instead of lying around, then turning to killing." One of the perpetrators spoke for all of them saying, "it feels good to face a survivor, we never thought we could be in the same room." The leader wrapped up the session by thanking everyone for participating. She emphasized, "that everyone of you are important, and you have opened our eyes. To the youth I am saying that I like you all, and I respect you. I would like to get your names because you will become our closest contacts."

With regard to the leader's style for running the group, it was noted that she was subtle in the way she set the rules and moved the group through stages. She did this with her tone of voice and choice of wording. She tended to soften her voice when she wanted to make an important point about what she wanted from group members or in directing the group's focus. She attended to both survivors and perpetrators simultaneously with her choice of words. For example, "we care very much for those people that have been afraid, and we care for the youth that has gone rampant, because some of them just went as a mob." The leadership style she used is similar to the authoritarian style in Western group literature outlined by Lewin (1944). Most members spoke to her rather than to each other, and she stated in her follow-up interview with the researcher that she wanted to control the group so "it was productive." She stated that she did not allow members to engage in "outright conflict with each other because it would have defeated our purpose." According to her, allowing outright conflict is something they have done in the courts, and it has not proven productive.

Conflict certainly was a concern considering the violent nature of certain participants. Of course, the most obvious tension was between perpetrators and survivors. This was most noticeable in the beginning of the group when they physically separated themselves and engaged in no conversation or eye contact. Other tensions included the verbal exchange between the "old man" and the leader, as stated. There was also tension between the "old man" and the perpetrators. The "old man" wanted the youth to recognize him as an elder. Group members interpreted both of these points of contention as the "old man" wanting respect. Additionally, there was tension between the religious leader and one of the group counselors stemming from the religious leader's need to understand the counselor's motivation toward group members, especially because the counselor was an international visitor. For example, the Lutheran minister stated that "the church and commission office are near to the villages in trouble and that they could provide services." There was also tension between the counselors and the leader that seemed to result from the counselors wanting to take care of the feelings of the survivors and perpetrators when the leader was not attending to their feelings. In fact, the counselors were in tension with most members of the group at some point during the session, and this was viewed as important because it allowed the other members to stay out of the tension or focus on group process. In approaching each tense interaction, the counselors sought to convey four critical concerns.

1. The counselors were there at the invitation of the group leader and the Commission.
2. There was no hidden agenda as to the progress or result of the group.
3. Everyone was to be listened to and respected.
4. Tension and conflict could and would be handled in a positive and appropriate manner.

By engaging in various tense interactions, the counselors could model and teach conflict management skills and show participants that within the structure of the group that they were safe and secure. Further, at times by "siphoning" the tension from the other participants to the counselors, hostility and rage could be compartmentalized and dealt with.

Importantly, all the tensions mentioned in the preceding were resolved within the group. In the final phase, as mentioned, the survivors and perpetrators engaged each other in a positive way. The resolution came about when the perpetrators acknowledged that all youth should recognize that killing is wrong and that the elders should be respected. For example, the leader of the youth stated, "I feel so bad for what has happened, but from henceforth I will respect another's right to life. I also feel so good, because I never thought I could face a survivor, and now I will be able to face the victims and from now henceforth I will respect their life." This brought an outcry of "joy" by the survivors. They stated being "very grateful and happy that at last their children will be able to do something else." This resulted in hugging between the survivors and perpetrators. This was the final moment of the group, the time that group members and researcher labeled as the "moment of reconciliation." The tension between the leader and the old man was handled in that transitional moment when he felt heard and respected in the group. The tension between the counselor and religious leader was resolved when they problem-solved together the issue of counseling in the community. Both agreed, "there should be a safeguard . . . that you must get down to the roots of the problem . . . and that a counselor could help [them] find other mechanisms for accessing sources." The counselor recognized the religious leader's importance in the process of providing counseling. The tension between the group leader and the counselor was diminished when the counselor sought permission from the group leader, as a sign of respect, to ask the survivors and perpetrators how they felt. The group leader agreed and admitted that the feelings were important. This request then resulted in the final reconciliation moment between the two groups mentioned. In general, the group leader directed the tension with all members toward her, thereby deflecting direct conflict between members and leading to greater cohesion between them. In the follow-up interview with the group leader, she confirmed this when she stated "that it was important for her to move the group." As mentioned, she believed that she should be the focus for the conflict.

Counseling Considerations

Considering the human cost of witch persecution, counseling efforts toward sustainable peace in these communities are crucial. South African participants of this group and people from various villages strongly believed that sustainable reconciliation is possible but warned of potential dangers in holding such groups without the proper training, understanding of the context, and inclusion of all involved parties.

To begin, a group counseling approach with this subculture of South Africa must include all members of each Kraal (clan/tribe). If any member is left out of the process, it could result in continued conflict and the RGCS would be considered a failure and never trusted again. Lederach (1997) refers to individuals often left out of the reconciliation and/or negotiation process as "rogue factions." As a reaction to being left out, these "rogue factions" perpetuate violence and undermine the reconciliation process and established negotiations. Literature from the field of conflict management with groups may help in understanding some of the unique dynamics of the RGCS that are similar to approaches outlined by Smith and Berg (1997). First, the group maintained a focus group approach where future goals of participants were discussed, such as living arrangements and employment. Second, the group members problem-solved the issues related to the community's current state of affairs (e.g., high rate of unemployment and disease) and how to build better relationships (e.g., resolve family and neighborhood jealousies). Third, the members were given a chance to tell their stories and a short amount of grieving did take place. In the problem-solving workshops for sustaining resolved conflict (Mitchell and Banks, 1996), group members are invited to participate because of their status in the community and their subsequent potential for maintaining order.

During the RGCS and in subsequent follow-up discussions with various group members several trends were identified that may guide similar future work. First, the leader of such groups must be accustomed to South African culture along with the cultural subtleties of verbal and nonverbal communication. Such is especially true because a leader may have to focus conflict in his or her direction in an effort to foster communication between members. The leader of the RGCS in this study facilitated the direction of conflict toward her rather than between the members. She managed this effectively through her authoritarian style of verbal and nonverbal communication. Group members, the researcher, and subsequent qualitative raters of the taped session stated that they were irritated with the fact that she often did not attend to feelings. Yet in retrospect, her style served to circumvent much of the hostility that could have occurred between survivors and perpetrators. In focus groups, the leader often remains the center of interaction (Morgan, 1997). This group leader intermittently adopted a focus group manner when she believed the group was getting off task. Therefore, only those trained and skillful in South African communication should attempt to lead such groups. South African communication is described as highly nonverbal, including subtle clues that most non-South Africans typically do not understand easily. Personal communication between individuals also changes from context to context and is therefore very fluid.

Second, the leader must be aware of the strong emotions that arise during such groups and how to handle them. Yalom (1995) describes a self-reflective loop that consists of plunging into the here and now, and plunging into feelings with an examination afterward of the plunge. Although this approach has proven important to the success of groups, it may not be appropriate at the initial stages of a RGCS such as this for several reasons. Although focusing on the here and now was done, the expression of emotions, especially strong emotions, is culturally inappropriate in this subculture of South Africa. Therefore, the leader may find it prudent to have a group counselor attend to any emotions displayed by group members while the group continues, almost as an adjacent session. The group counselor's primary role is to gauge and support the mental health of the group members. Further, the process of individual self-reflection is not only culturally inappropriate, but also not the intended purpose of a RGCS. A "community self-reflection" is a more appropriate term. The process of sustainable reconciliation following protracted conflict in South African communities is dependent on a change in mindset and agreement by a community rather than just the individuals. Because the process of counseling in South Africa is different than in Western culture, it may seem a "stretch" to Western-trained group counselors to call this a "group counseling session," but such work fits well with group processes in rural South Africa. In fact, we contend a group experience such as the one discussed in this chapter is one of the best means of conducting a "group counseling session." Western-trained group counselors may need to reframe the group counseling paradigm in order to become effective social service providers in many areas of South Africa.

It appeared that rule setting was the central issue for building safety in the group. When group members understood the rules of group and what was expected of them, they tended to be more responsive and less fearful of the process. Rule setting also included explaining what counseling is and how it can be of benefit. This is consistent with the literature related to group process (e.g., Tuckman & Jensen, 1977; Yalom, 1995) and to sustainable peace building (Lederach, 1997) where clarity of goals and member expectations are critical to early success.

After establishing safety, it was clear that the community must deal with public admittance and retribution in the group format. People need to tell their story to the entire community. The collective lifestyle in South Africa allows for the telling of one's trauma to the community (Sofola, 1983; cited in Makhale-Mahlangu, 1996). Here, the counselor could provide support and offer empathy when each member tells his or her story. The leader may need to refrain from attending to the emotional outburst of members to maintain the group process. Clearly, successive groups are necessary before sustainable peace is possible.

The RGCS discussed in this chapter appears to be the first recorded session in which members of witchcraft violence sat down together to discuss what happened to them and what they wish could be done about it. All group members said it was the first time they had been given the chance to discuss the trauma of what they experienced in any detail with someone listening. The survivors stated that for them, it was a cathartic experience to tell their story, to hear others' stories, and to hear the perpetrators state that it is wrong to kill witches or attempt to kill them. The perpetrators stated that it was cathartic to face the survivors and come to the realization that killing witches (those who are considered evildoers) was against human rights. Thus, training South African counselors in coleading such groups is advisable.

This group reflected the stages of group process, such as beginning, working, and ending. However, these stages will probably occur over many group sessions rather than only one session. Because this is consistent with Western group stage literature (e.g., Tuckman & Jensen, 1977), South African group leaders' further understanding of these stages and when the group is truly working may prove helpful to community attempts at an overall peace process. Nevertheless, if the community continues to face hardships, preventive measures and peace agreements may not be enough to stave off future violence.

Unfortunately, such work is still limited by the paucity of theoretical, clinical, and research literature about what happens to individuals, families, and communities during a violent outbreak and in the aftermath of a witch killing epidemic. What is clear from the literature is that individuals and communities are traumatized when an epidemic has occurred. Therefore, research on the effects of trauma and recovery from the field of traumatology could provide a helpful treatment paradigm (Herman, 1997). However, because of the complexity of psychosocial causes and effects of witchcraft violence, interventions developed for specific phases in the process may be more effective. In a simplified version of Shermer's (1997) witch craze feedback loop, there are three phases to the violence: (a) the accusation phase, (b) the persecution phase, and (c) the cessation phase. The accusation phase is defined as the time when an alleged victim of witchcraft begins accusing someone of being a witch. The persecution phase is when the accusations turn to convictions and the accused witch is in danger of being executed. The final phase or cessation phase occurs after the witch killing has occurred or when the suspected witch has escaped death and is now in refuge (Levack, 1992). Although the focus of the present chapter is the interventions in the third phase of the cycle, counselors must also seek to design interventions for the earlier stages as well.

Prevention

The crisis literature on primary, secondary, and tertiary prevention can be useful to clinicians when dealing with such violence (France, 1996). Primary prevention can avert crises before they produce harmful effects. Secondary prevention focuses on the early stages of current problems, in an attempt to decrease severity. Tertiary prevention assists individuals to regain higher functioning after experiencing a crisis (France, 1996). Efforts intended to reduce problems can and must occur at any of the three levels. Because primary prevention is concerned with halting accusations before they begin, the mental health counselor must be aware of the roots of witchcraft violence and address those areas before accusations arise. Here counseling activities can focus on the development of community infrastructures that treat the psychosocial needs of community members. According to Shermer (1997), the individuals are experiencing fear and anger toward the hardships in their lives and social change. It is this fear that leads to scapegoating (Briggs, 1996; Macfarlane, 1970) and interpersonal conflict (Midelfort, 1972). However, all counseling interventions should be culturally sensitive to the traditional beliefs in witchcraft and counselors should consider the impact that such beliefs will have on their interventions, either prevention or remediation. The goal of the counselor is not to eradicate or alter the belief system but rather provide alternatives to violence.

Counselors may seek to provide community members with alternative explanations for life's difficulties rather than malicious witchcraft. Essentially, the role of education is to teach people that other explanations for life's travails are available and that blaming others for witchcraft may not be necessary. Although research has demonstrated that scientific education alone cannot prevent a witch craze (Ben-Yehuda, 1985; Hoffer, 1997), counselors who work at the level of primary prevention educate to prevent the witchcraft accusations from beginning.

Delius (1996) described the Northern Province in South Africa as being fraught with poverty, illness, and family disintegration. Primary prevention activities also need to address these psychosocial problems. Interventions include career counseling, economic empowerment projects for women and youth, life skills education, acquired immunodeficiency syndrome (AIDS) awareness, drug/alcohol treatment, and family counseling. Here also gender equity workshops and treatment for spouse abuse may prove crucial. The participants in the group reconciliation intervention described in this chapter were adamant that primary prevention was desperately needed to prevent another epidemic of violence.

Once the accusation and persecution phases begin, counselors must work to limit the violence and assist those who are now traumatized. At a level of secondary prevention, counseling interventions include (a) victim support, (b) further education, and (c) community stabilization. As outlined in the Thohoyandou Declaration (Commission on Gender Equality, 1998), counseling should include victim support. That is, counselors need to deal with the current basic needs of the individual, such as housing, food, and safety. It is critical for the multicultural counselor to be aware of the effects of stigma associated with being accused (Delius, 1996), the emotions of anger and fear that result from living through such trauma, and the accused's concerns about what the future may bring (Shermer, 1997). The central experience of most trauma survivors is disempowerment and disconnection from others (Herman, 1997). Clearly, if the person survives, he or she is stigmatized and ostracized from his or her community and family (Demos, 1982). Recovery can take place only if the counselor can build a relationship that offers safety and connection (Herman, 1997). This relationship can provide the basis for dealing with the victim's emotions. As a practical matter, many survivors live in rural areas, and mobile counseling units may need to be considered in order to reach these individuals.

For the counselor, secondary prevention with education seeks to severely limit future accusations. Once the accusations begin, educational vectors must begin to target the specific accusations and illustrate that alternative scientific explanations may exist. For example, many accusations in South Africa begin after a death that was caused by AIDS. Because most death certificates do not relate the death directly to AIDS, awareness education about the causes of such deaths could reduce witchcraft violence.

Community stabilization is another important intervention. An outbreak of witch killings demonstrates that there has been a breakdown of stability. This breakdown typically involves external pressures that feed on individual internal pressures (Shermer, 1997). In the Northern Province, for example, the lack of employment and high level of poverty or the death of many community members to AIDS (external) have led to fears of success and survival (internal). Economic development initiatives, community bonding activities, and health promotion outreach all can help to develop a community that has a sense of stability and well-being. It becomes imperative that the counselor educate the community about the negative results of accusations on the stability and welfare of the community.

After the cessation of witch killings, counselors must work to ameliorate the residual effects of crises (France, 1996). Here, tertiary prevention can address community leaders and role models toward the reintegration of perpetrator and survivor into the community and assist community rebonding (Boon, 1997). When the community redresses the injustices of the accusations, then forgiveness can occur. By responding proactively and fairly to witchcraft accusations, the community illustrates clearly that accusations are against the overall well-being of community members.

Along with continued community stabilization and education, tertiary preventions must involve a crisis intervention program. The availability of immediate assistance (France, 1996) and trauma treatment for accused individuals are fundamental aspects of crisis intervention. Therefore, in instituting a crisis intervention program, counselors should immediately triage the situation into workable solutions, such as the creation of safe houses and sanctuaries. Counselors could design widespread Crisis Incident Stress Debriefing (CISD) groups to help the accused heal from their ordeals. In addition, accusers must be helped to find alternative actions.

Many authors agree that traditional African means for handling witchcraft violence have been disrupted (e.g., Evans-Pritchard, 1950; Mutwa, 1996; Reynolds, 1963). Credo Mutwa (1996) has suggested that a return to traditional South African ways is the only means for stopping such violence—not more laws. He stated that counselors could provide a bridge for discussion between divided community members. Mutwa (personal communication, September 8, 1998) believes that all relevant stakeholders must be involved in these discussions and persons must be held accountable for their actions.

Conclusion

As discussed, the postapartheid South African government faces many psychosocial challenges. The most exciting aspect of this chapter, though, is the report of South Africa's approach to such challenges in innovative and novel ways. It is an unfortunate aspect of human existence that witch accusations and violence against accused witches is pancultural and panhistoric even in the 21st century. Sadly, the vast majority of such accused are women, often already having difficulty functioning in the changing community. Yet, although witch accusation and burning may be panhistorical and pancultural, the South African solution is a bold new step to resolving such crises. The South African NGOs and governmental structures have reached far beyond the stereotypical response of ignoring the violence or suppressing its existence. The present chapter illustrates that modern South Africa seeks a comprehensive solution that is embedded in cultural traditions and community needs. Western mental health workers would be wise to study how South Africa has tried to synthesize modern helping techniques with historical cultural beliefs providing a powerful model for those involved.

We believe that the pilot group described in this chapter exemplifies that such carefully planned tertiary prevention can address and begin to heal the extensive trauma occurring to participants of such violence. Counseling toward reintegration and reconciliation of affected communities after violence cessation should consider several important elements.

1. Witchcraft violence is deadly and any reconciliation of community members must be sustainable.
2. A group counseling approach could prove most successful, because it includes all "stakeholders"; i.e., traditional leaders, traditional healers, religious leaders, community members, survivors, and perpetrators, while utilizing a comfortable format for South African nationals.
3. Counselors may want to hold consecutive group sessions focused on the cessation of violence and reaching realistic agreements between all "stakeholders."
4. Counselors may need to work with an insider from the community for a greater chance of success. This may mean training "lay counselors" who are familiar with the history of the community involved and have the trust of the majority of the people affected. In African peace keeping efforts, the clarity

of goals, the inclusion of all relevant persons including those considered on the fringe of society, and public agreements to conditions have enhanced successes for sustainable peace in places such as Rwanda (Lederach, 1997).

Western multicultural counselors will need to rely on solid research and honest feedback from their South African partners to understand how to implement interventions in a cultural context that is very alien to them. In addition, counselors can benefit from such approaches in applying interventions in the United States with diverse populations. Clearly, more research and scholarship are needed to better understand and prevent such human suffering, particularly scholarly studies at each level of witchcraft persecution. Possible research questions include:

1. What types of programs, at the level of primary prevention, will most effectively curtail accusations (employment opportunities, programs geared at community development, alcohol and drug counseling)?
2. How can secondary prevention efforts, such as victim support counseling, be designed to effectively meet the needs of individuals (storytelling, reconnection, facing stigma)?
3. How can tertiary prevention efforts that incorporate crisis debriefing and trauma counseling assist reconciliation efforts (defusing, safety assurance, negotiation of terms for reconciliation)?

There is no simple explanation for the occurrence of witch accusations. The causes seem multifaceted and multidimensional. Therefore, counseling interventions also need to be multifaceted and multidimensional. Fortunately as the 20th century ended one of the bloodiest periods in human history, alternative mental health interventions for South Africa are offering professionals hope that the tragedies may eventually be replaced by healing.

Discussion Questions

1. How do you think the apartheid government's racist polices influenced the development of witch burning in South Africa?
2. What Western examples of scapegoating are similar to witch burning?
3. Why do you think many of the accused witches are elderly women and what does this reveal about gender dynamics in South Africa?
4. What other psychosocial interventions might stop the witchcraft craze/accusation and killings?
5. What are some risks of including witch burners in such restorative justice interventions as discussed in the chapter and how might such risks be minimized?

6. What would Western mental health workers need to know in order to assist the accused witches in recovering from their trauma?
7. How could similar violent outbreaks appear in communities in such countries as the United States, Britain, France, or Germany?

References

Barston, A. (1994). *Witch craze: A new history of European witch hunts*. New York: Pandora/ HarperCollins.

Ben-Yehuda, N. (1981). Problems inherent in socio-historical approaches to the European witchcraze. *Journal for the Scientific Study of Religion, 20*(4), 326–338.

Ben-Yehuda, N. (1985). *Deviance and moral boundaries: Witchcraft, the occult, science fiction, deviant sciences and scientists*. Chicago: University of Chicago Press.

Boon, M. (1997). *The African way: The power of interactive leadership*. Johannesburg: Zebra Press.

Briggs, R. (1996). *Witches and witchcraft: The social and cultural context of European witchcraft*. New York: Viking.

Carporael, L. (1976). Ergotism: Satan loosed in Salem. *Science, 192*, 21–26.

Chandler, N. (1997, April 28). Killing of 'witches' increases in N Province. *The Star*, p. 6.

Commission on Gender Equality. (1998, September). *The Thohoyandou declaration on ending witch craft violence*. Paper presented at the First National Conference on Witchcraft Violence, Thohoyandou, Venda, Republic of South Africa.

Delius, P. (1996). *A Lion amongst the cattle: Reconstruction and resistance in the northern Transvaal*. Randburg, Republic of South Africa: Ravan Press.

Demos, J. P. (1982). *Entertaining satan: Witchcraft and the culture of early New England*. New York: Oxford Press.

Ehrenreich, B., & English, D. (1973). *Witches, midwives and nurses: A history of women healers*. New York: Feminist Press.

Evans-Pritchard, E. E. (1950). *Witchcraft, oracles, and magic among the A-Zande*, 2nd ed. New York: Oxford University Press.

France, K. (1996). *Crisis intervention: A handbook of immediate person-to-person help*. Springfield, IL: Charles C. Thomas.

Herman, J. (1997). *Trauma and recovery: The aftermath of violence from domestic abuse to political terror*. New York: Basic Books.

Hoffer, P. C. (1997). *The Salem witchcraft trials: A legal history*. Lawrence, KS: University Press of Kansas.

Klaits, J. (1985). *Servants of satan: The age of the witch hunts*. Bloomington, IN: University Press.

Lederach, J. P. (1997). *Building peace: Sustainable reconciliation in divided societies*. Washington, DC: United States Institute of Peace Press.

Lederer, W. (1969). *The fear of women*. New York: Harcourt.

Levack, B. P. (Ed.). (1992). *Articles on witchcraft, magic, and demonology: A twelve volume anthology of scholarly articles*, vol. 4. New York: Garland.

Lewin, K. (1944). The group dynamics in action. *Educational Leadership, 1*, 195–200.

Macfarlane, A. J. D. (1970). *Witchcraft in Tudor and Stuart England*. New York: Harper.

Makhale-Mahlangu, P. (1996). *Reflections on trauma counselling methods* (Short article on mental health and reconciliation). Pretoria, Republic of South Africa: University of Witwatersand, Centre for the Study of Violence and Reconciliation.

Midelfort, H. E. C. (1972). *Witch-hunting in southwestern Germany.* Palo Alto, CA: Stanford University Press.

Mitchell, C., & Banks, M. A. (1996). *Handbook of conflict resolution: The analytical problem-solving approach.* London: Pinter.

Morgan, D. L. (1997). *Focus groups as qualitative research* (2nd ed.). Qualitative Research Methods Series, Vol. 16. Thousand Oaks, CA: Sage.

Mutwa, V. C. (1996). *Song of the stars: The lore of a Zulu shaman.* Barrytown, NY: Barrytown, Ltd.

Neverdie is the province's top Inyanga. (1998, May 26). *The Star,* p. 8.

Ntombele-Nzimande, P. (1998, September). *National Conference on Witchcraft Violence.* Paper presented at the First National Conference on Witchcraft Violence, Thohoyandou, Venda, Republic of South Africa.

Ntsewa, K. T. (1998, September). "*Witchcraft in the Northern Province 1990–1995*": *National Crime Information Management Centre.* Paper presented at the First National Conference on Witchcraft Violence, Thohoyandou, Venda, Republic of South Africa.

Ralushai, N.V. (1998, September). *Excerpts from the Report of the Commission of Inquiry into Witchcraft Violence and Ritual Murders in the Northern Province* (1995). Paper presented at the First National Conference on Witchcraft Violence, Thohoyandou, Venda, Republic of South Africa.

Reddy, J. (1996, April). *Economic Reconstruction [3.1].* National Commission for Higher Education: System, governance, funding [Online]. Discussion document of the framework for transformation. Available at http://star.hsrc.ac.za/nche/discuss/sgf_toc.html

Reynolds, B. (1963). *Magic, divination and witchcraft among the Barotse of northern Rhodesia.* London: Chatto and Windus.

Shapshak, D. (1996, September 27). "Northern Province targets 'witch' killers." *The Guardian,* pp. 1, 4.

Shermer, M. (1997). *Why people believe weird things: Psuedoscience, superstition, and other confusions of our time.* New York: W. H. Freeman.

Smith, K. K., & Berg, D. N. (1997). *Paradoxes of group life: Understanding conflict, paralysis, and movement in group dynamics.* San Francisco: New Lexington Press Organization Sciences Series.

Sullivan, T. (1998, March 27). "Witch hunts haunt Northern Province." *Imbhokodo,* pp. 1, 4.

Thomas, K. (1971). *Religion and the decline of magic.* New York: Scribner's.

Tuckman, B. W., & Jensen, M. A. C. (1977). Stages of small-group development. *Group and Organizational Studies, 2,* 419–427.

Yalom, I. (1995). *The theory and practice of group psychotherapy* (4th ed.). New York: Basic Books.

Diagnosis
and
Practice

Chapter 9

Diagnostic Challenges and the So-Called Culture-Bound Syndromes

Julie R. Ancis
Yuehong Chen
Doreen Schultz

This chapter focuses on the notion of culture-bound syndromes (CBS) and related diagnostic challenges. The treatment of culture and the inclusion of CBS in diagnostic classification systems, such as the DSM, are reviewed. The authors discuss the limitations of diagnostic classification systems, including their use cross-culturally, and directions for future classification and research of CBS.

Classification of Culture-Bound Syndromes

Culture-bound syndromes (CBS), or culture-related psychiatric disorders, have been discussed in the literature for decades (e.g., Lewis, 1975; Lin, 1983). These "syndromes" or "disorders" have been referred to in a variety of ways. Devereux (1956) described "ethnic psychoses" and "ethnic neurosis," Arieti and Meth (1959) discussed "rare, unclassifiable, collective, and exotic syndromes," which included but were not limited to "culture-bound syndromes," and Yap (as cited in Hughes, 1985) described "atypical culture bound reactive syndromes." CBS has been more recently and typically defined as the development of a unique psychopathology, or a collection of signs and symptoms, observed only in a certain cultural environment (Prince & Tcheng-LaRoche, 1987; Tseng, 1997). Commonly written about culture-bound syndromes include latah, amok, and koro.

The case of culture-bound syndromes represents a challenge to clinicians, particularly in the area of diagnosis. There has been a long debate in the literature regarding the role of biology and culture in the development of culture-bound syndromes; whether such behavior is universal or locally unique, and whether episodes are culturally based and "normal" behavior or examples of "authentic" disease and disorder (Hughes, 1996; Karp, 1985). Similar questions include whether culture-bound syndromes are stable over time, are truly distinct entities with commonalties to certain cultures, and whether there are common denominators among the CBSs (Aderibigbe & Pandurangi, 1995). Other questions concern whether culture-bound syndromes should be viewed as part of all diagnostic categories of psychiatric illness, or as static, bound entities (Hughes, 1998). These debates are important to consider in light of the prevalent use of diagnostic systems to classify psychiatric illness.

Historically, diagnostic classification systems, such as the *International Statistical Classification of Mental Disorders* developed by the World Health Organization, have paid limited attention to culture (Mezzich, Berganza, & Ruiperez, 2001). In the last few decades, there has been an increased interest in culture-bound syndromes. However, their treatment in diagnostic classification systems has gained attention only in the last several years. A list of culture-specific disorders are included in the "Diagnostic Criteria for Research" version of the *ICD-10 Classification of Mental and Behavioral Disorders* (WHO, 1992). Adaptations of the ICD-10 include the *Chinese Classification of Mental Disorders* (CCMD-3) (Chinese Society of Psychiatry, 2001), the *Cuban Glossary of Psychiatry* (GC-3) (Otero-Ojeda, 2000), and the *Latin American Guide for Psychiatric Diagnosis* (see Berganza et al., 2001). Although these systems are generally congruent with the ICD-10, they do represent attempts to allow for the inclusion of culturally distinctive diagnostic categories, such as qigong in the Chinese classification.

Mezzich, Berganza, and Ruiperez (2001) describe the *International Guidelines for Diagnostic Assessment* (IGDA) project started in 1994 as a move toward looking at the interface between culture and illness in psychiatric diagnosis. This project led to a more comprehensive diagnostic approach using the ICD-10 to include the assessment of the psychiatric patient as a whole person, not just a person with illness.

One of the most widely employed diagnostic tools in the mental health profession is the *Diagnostic and Statistical Manual of Mental Disorders* (DSM), published by the American Psychiatric Association (APA). The DSM is based on substantial empirical research, and provides standardized descriptive accounts of disorders based on symptoms and signs (Kleinman, 1987). This manual has been translated into 22 languages and is used by clinicians from a variety of training backgrounds, including psychiatrists, psychologists, counselors, and social workers. Despite the history of culture-bound syndromes in the literature, CBSs were not included in the psychiatric diagnostic system of the DSM until the fourth revision in 1994.

Several conditions led to the increased interest in cultural aspects of illness and subsequent attempts to incorporate culture into the DSM-IV. An increased awareness in cultural diversity, changes in related disciplines such as anthropology and sociology, the changing patient populations seeking psychiatric treatment, and the fact that the DSM is used internationally all influenced the focus on culture that was occurring at the time of the DSM-IV revision (Kirmayer, 1998; Mezzich et al., 1996).

The process of including culture-bound syndromes in the DSM-IV began in 1990 when the APA began preparing the fourth edition of the DSM. A conference on Culture and Diagnosis was held in 1991, jointly sponsored by the National Institute of Mental Health and APA. The purpose of the conference was to bring together a multidisciplinary group of experts in cultural psychiatry to begin generating ideas for the inclusion of culture in the DSM-IV.

The 1991 conference led to a NIMH-funded Work Group on Culture and Diagnosis. This group was formed to work in collaboration with the DSM-IV Task Force and Workgroups in order to enhance the cultural validity of the DSM-IV. Comprehensive literature reviews for each major group of disorders with specific cultural proposals were circulated and revised. The final versions of these review papers, completed in 1994, yielded the changes that were later included in the DSM-IV, although with several omissions that seem to have had a significant impact on the end result (Mezzich et al., 1999). The present chapter focuses on the glossary of culture-bound syndromes included in the DSM-IV.

The DSM- IV includes a list of 25 "culture-bound syndromes" in Appendix I of the text. The DSM-IV defines culture-bound syndrome as "recurrent, locality-specific patterns of aberrant behavior and troubling experience that may or may not be linked to a particular DSM-IV diagnostic category" (p. 844). The inclusion of culture-bound syndromes in the DSM-IV was an important and progressive step toward incorporating culture into diagnostic classification systems.

Limitations of Diagnostic Classification Systems

The criticisms of the treatment of culture, and more specifically, culture-bound syndromes in the DSM-IV illustrate some of the general limitations of diagnostic classification systems in describing the relationship between culture and psychiatric illness. Although the inclusion of culture in the DSM-IV was a progressive step, several authors (Hughes, 1998; Levine & Gaw, 1995; Mezzich et al., 1999) have criticized what was omitted in the DSM-IV revision and noted conceptual chasms between the intended treatment of culture-bound syndromes, or proposals by the initial work group, and the final DSM-IV version. For example, proposals that challenged universal nosologic assumptions were apparently left out of the revision process (Mezzich et al., 1999). Several key recommendations made by the Culture and Diagnosis Work Group that were considered crucial to an understanding of culture in the DSM-IV were either shortened or omitted entirely from the final version. This included a shortened version of a statement alerting the clinician to the challenges of using the DSM-IV in a multicultural society, which was reduced from 11 pages to two. Additionally, several simplified versions of proposed cultural considerations for specific disorders were included but apparently did not reflect the extensive effort of the group in providing advice related to diagnostic criteria and cultural considerations (Mezzich et al., 1999). As a result, there is a lack of operational suggestions on how to take cultural factors into account in diagnosis (Hughes, 1998). Finally, some CBSs appear to have been "grandfathered" into the text with no apparent system detailing why some were included and others excluded (Hughes, 1998).

Also, largely absent from the final DSM-IV revision was the proposed text explaining needed considerations when applying culture to the multiaxial schema (Mezzich et al., 1999). Similarly, a proposed cultural formulation outline that was intended to follow the section on multiaxial assessment was placed in the ninth appendix and several illustrative cases were left out completely (Mezzich et al., 1999). Finally, the title "Glossary of Culture-Bound Syndromes and Idioms of Distress" was shortened to "Glossary of Culture-Bound Syndromes" and omitted references to culture-specific terms within the text. A section on Western culture-bound syndromes was omitted entirely (Mezzich et al., 1999).

Ontological, phenomenological, and categorical problems with the inclusion of CBSs in the DSM-IV have been raised. As currently described in the DSM-IV, it is not clear whether CBSs are distinctly different from conventional syndromes, or just semantically and categorically different (Hughes, 1998). Their placement in a DSM-IV appendix implies that they are dissimilar from other diagnoses, yet there appear to be similarities between some conventional diagnoses and the culture-bound syndromes (Guarnaccia & Rogler, 1999; Hughes, 1998). For example, research with Latino patients has identified the comorbidity of ataques de nervios with a range of anxiety and affective disorders (Liebowitz et al., 1994). Similarly, some argue that CBSs are not restricted to specific cultures, but are widely distributed. Many syndromes that have been described as culture-bound include combinations of symptoms that have been observed universally, such as anxiety, social withdrawal, and somatic symptoms (Westermeyer, 1987).

By placing all of the culture-bound syndromes in an appendix, the DSM-IV fails to recognize that the term "culture-bound" refers to a heterogeneous group of phenomena. Levine and Gaw (1995) noted that all they seem to have in common is that they have folk diagnostic labels with culture-specific meanings. In fact, CBSs are essentially folk categories for certain conditions or behaviors. Interestingly, Many CBSs have not been developed as diagnostic entities based on criteria such as mental status, psychological or neurological examination, or response to treatment. As such, a variety of psychiatric conditions are demonstrated among persons described as having a folk syndrome (Westermeyer, 1973, 1987). Additionally, because culture-bound syndromes lack diagnostic uniformity and validity, it is difficult to attain universal descriptive criteria for describing illness caused by problems in language translation (Aderibigbe & Pandurangi, 1995).

One of the most important considerations in terms of CBS classification and diagnosis concerns the fact that the DSM of the American Psychiatric Association was developed and researched using a Western population and frame of reference (Lewis-Fernández & Kleinman, 1994). This system is a great advance for American psychiatry because it offers a standardized descriptive reference to determine appropriate diagnosis and treatment methods. However, generalizing its use to non-Western cultures, particularly in the treatment of CBSs is problematic, and further illustrates how diagnostic classification systems are limited when referring to the relationship between culture and illness. Applying Western diagnostic categories to the description of CBSs is problematic because DSM-IV inclusion implies that CBSs are afterthoughts rather than the product of a "culturally-informed approach" (Hughes & Wintrob, 1995).

Additionally, referring to illnesses which do not fall into DSM categories as "culture-bound syndromes" reflects ethnocentrism in the professions (Shimoji & Miyakawa, 2000; Simons, 1985). In attempting to classify all clinical cases with a "universal" nosological system, "atypical" DSM categories are considered to be culture-bound, whereas "typical" categories are considered "universal." Diagnostic categories in the main text are presumed to be culture-free (Hughes, 1996; Mezzich, Kleinman, Fabrega, & Parron, 1996). In essence, all illnesses, both physical and psychological, may be considered culture-bound. Disorders such as anorexia nervosa and multiple personality disorder may in fact be considered Western culture-bound syndromes (Kleinman & Cohen, 1997). Other Western culture-bound syndromes, such as obesity, could easily be suggested (Simons, 1985). Moreover, the issue of whether a particular trait or behavior is maladaptive is related to the cultural context and societal values. A behavior considered adaptive in one context may be maladaptive in another (Alarcón & Foulks, 1995; Karp, 1985). Relatedly, complaint patterns of disorders are influenced by idioms of distress. For example, the complaint pattern of depressed Puerto Rican women often suggests differences from standard psychiatric formulations of depression. The interaction between cultural norms and emotional expressions and culturally patterned situations that shape emotional distress must be considered (Koss-Chioino, 1999).

The Western frame of the DSM is further revealed in its perpetuation of the philosophy of dualism between mind and body, and between thoughts and emotions (Atkinson, Bui, & Mori, 2001; Lewis-Fernández & Kleinman, 1994). Several authors (e.g., Karp, 1985; Kleinman, 1987) believe that certain symptoms in non-Western societies can only be understood in their specific cultural context and may not be translatable into American languages. Misdiagnosis may result when the client and therapist do not share cultural meanings (Flaskerud, 2000) as cultural forces often shape symptom formation, modes of distress, psychiatric diagnosis, and treatment (Alarcón, Foulks, & Vakkur, 1998; Flaskerud, 2000; Tseng & Streltzer, 1997). Intervening variables such as socioeconomic status, education, gender, age, therapist ethnicity, and primary language of the patient and therapist can all affect diagnosis and ethnic comparisons. For example, according to the DSM-IV, dysphoria is the primary symptom of depression. However, research has demonstrated somatic idioms of distress in some cultures (e.g., pressure on chest and head among Chinese men, gastrointestinal complaints among Southeast Asian refugees in the United States). The diagnosis of a treatable disorder may be impeded if clinicians do not understand those local cultural idioms of complaint (Kleinman, 1988).

Kleinman (1979) described the application of a diagnostic system from one culture to another as if the category were culture-free as an example of a "category fallacy." Problems are created by transforming syndromes and symptoms prevalent in non-Western cultures to fit Western categorization. A specific example of a difficulty encountered by clinicians using a Western frame of reference to conceptualize a non-Western disorder can be illustrated in the case of huo qi da, a prevalent condition among Chinese that is characterized as a feeling of hot energy rising from the abdomen. Huo qi da cannot be conceptualized solely by physical signs and symptoms. For example, many Chinese believe that physical health is directly linked to the balance between yin (quiet/feminine energy) and yang (moving/masculine energy), and the internal harmony between three integrated vital elements of life: jing, qi, and shen. Jing refers to the channels that carry qi (vital energy of the physical body) and xue (blood) through the body. Shen is mental vitality and spiritual energy that determines the capacity of the mind in terms of thinking and the desire to live. When the vital energy becomes too strong, the body becomes internally hot, which causes physical discomfort. This further affects jing (the flow), and shen (the function of mind in thinking). The imbalanced flow of jing, qi, and shen leads to huo qi. Persons are described as having "huo qi" when they experience the discomfort of hot energy rising from the abdomen accompanied by symptoms of foul breath, acne, fatigue, slow movements, and slow speech. When the symptoms are severe, the person is described as "huo qi da." This feeling of discomfort is believed to be a sign of imbalanced energies and disrupted energy flow of the body. This imbalance is the cause of physical illness and a target to be treated in order that both energies can return to a smooth and balanced flow, and return the person to normal functioning.

Thus, unlike Western views of illness, the diagnosis of huo qi da requires the clinician to consider concepts of spiritual energy, harmony, balance, and mental vitality along with physical symptoms. A dualistic and largely Western framework denies the interconnectedness of mind, body, and spirit by placing an illness into an individualized category. The English language does not even have a word to match this Chinese condition. Moreover, huo qi da is a common illness that most people in China experience from time to time in daily life. Therefore, although a clinician unfamiliar with this condition may view it as a disorder, it is doubtful if most Chinese would agree.

Relatedly, interpretation of symptoms is typically affected by the observer's theoretical model and understanding of the sufferer's words and actions (Low, 1985). Most research has relied on classification of CBSs by highlighting prominent symptoms and placing disorders into an existing DSM category (Guarnaccia & Rogler, 1999). However, there are multiple views on which symptoms are predominant in which sociocultural context. Differences in research methods employed, theoretical models, and researcher's understanding of specific cultures have resulted in great variation in the analysis of the meaning of symptoms. For example, Low compared her research on nerves in Costa Rica and Guatemala with research conducted by others in Puerto Rico, Eastern Kentucky, and Outport, Newfoundland. She found common symptomology in different cultural contexts with varying cross-cultural meanings. Specifically, she found a marked similarity in the symptoms associated with nerves. However, cultural interpretation of the meaning of nerves varied. That is, attributions regarding the cause of nerves tended to reflect cultural explanations of etiology. Finally, the greatest amount of variation was found at the level of meaning, which reflects differences in cultural context and in each researcher's degree of understanding. Low concluded that strict comparison of cases is meaningless because of differences in participants, research sites, methodologies, and each researcher's cultural context and degree of understanding of the cultures. As such, Low proposed the use of the term "culturally interpreted symptoms" versus culture-bound syndromes.

The inclusion of culture-bound syndromes in DSM-IV has provided an opportunity to look at the role that culture plays in the diagnosis of psychological disorders. Although the DSM-IV's treatment of culture-bound syndromes has been met with some criticism, it has also raised questions to guide future development of classification systems of psychological disorders, as well as future research.

Directions for Future Classification and Research of Culture-Bound Syndromes

One major challenge to classification systems concerns the fact that at a sociocultural level the same distress reactions may be expressed differently because of cultural cues, language differences, and experience variations. Additionally, some have noted that all classifications, including Western classification systems (such as the DSM) are examples of a cultural structuring of human behavior and knowledge regarding illness (Hughes & Wintrob, 1995). Thus, the attempt to classify culture-bound syndromes, whether as distinct syndromes or part of already classified illnesses, is an activity to which culture seems inextricably tied. Additionally, several authors have specified the ways in which culture and social processes limit the development of an internationally valid system of diagnosis (Fabrega,

1994). In fact, regional classifications often serve a valuable purpose in the context in which they are devised (Sartorius, 1988; Stengel, 1959).

It has been suggested also that examining the context and symbolic structure of a cultural reaction may yield an alternative, and better, classification of CBSs than merely recording symptoms (Karp, 1985; Littlewood, 1983). The full symptom profile of the disorder is necessary to understand CBSs, rather than relying on a few predominant symptoms (Guarnaccia & Rogler, 1999). In addition, more attention to social factors, intracultural heterogeneity, and to how culture and other socioidentities such as gender interact can provide even better explanations of how culture-bound syndromes fit into diagnostic systems (Mezzich et al., 1999). As such, the CBSs in DSM-IV may be viewed as illustrations of a generic way to think about the relationships between psychiatric illnesses and cultural contexts instead of separate, bounded entities (Hughes, 1998).

Kapur (1987) proposed the development of a flexible and modifiable classification scheme to examine mental disorders at different levels; such as sociocultural, biological, and psychological. He suggested a relativistic and flexible classification strategy that is multilevel as opposed to multiaxial. The practitioner could then decide how many levels of discourses to operate on. This system would allow practitioners to keep improving descriptions in terms of new knowledge gained so that gradually one moves closer to a greater degree of concurrence at different levels. The classification would also be open to alternative expressions and meanings of disorders, acknowledging that there is no absolute truth.

Another necessary direction for future research involves improving the methodology by which culture-bound syndromes are studied (Alarcón, personal communication, November 5, 2002; Mezzich et al., 1999). One problem with CBS research methodology is the use of instruments to assess psychopathology in a certain population without considering how Western paradigms about distress may affect their validity (Bhui & Bhugra, 2001; Rogler, 1999). Researchers can improve methodology by attending to the limitations of using instruments in cross-cultural research into their research designs, particularly when these instruments are being used in a different cultural context from where they were developed (Bhui & Bhugra, 2001). Using indigenous concepts and languages to develop assessment instruments may also reveal a more accurate picture of a particular population (Rogler, 1999; Yang & Bond, 1990). Relatedly, immediate families, kinship networks, friends, and associates may be used to gather and interpret culturally influenced information about an individual (Ridley, Li, & Hill, 1998).

Using qualitative analyses, such as interviewing field researchers studying culture-bound syndromes, can also aid in the understanding of practical and clinical limitations of using instruments cross-culturally (Bhui & Bhugra, 2001). The integration of quantitative and qualitative approaches may provide a broader framework for cultural research (Lopez & Guarnaccia, 2000). In addition, integrating ethnographic, observational, clinical, and epidemiological research (Lopez & Guarnaccia, 2000) will yield more information about the so-called culture-bound syndromes and thus, better inform practice. Similarly, many fields, such as medicine, cultural studies, anthropology, sociology, and psychology have begun to study the impact of culture on illness. Such an integration of fields with multiple perspectives, in both methodology and research teams, will help further advance research on idioms of distress and CBSs (Lopez & Guarnaccia, 2000).

Examination of the salience of a CBS and subsequently, the individual's subjective experiences associated with the syndrome through a phenomenological approach may help to uncover which CBSs seem to be "true" syndromes associated with existing diagnostic categories versus illnesses of attribution or idioms of distress (Guarnaccia & Rogler, 1999; Levine & Gaw, 1995). More epidemiological studies, as well as in-depth, detailed case studies of CBSs will help to better understand CBSs from both the community and individual perspective (Guarnaccia & Rogler, 1999; Hughes & Wintrob, 1995). Examining other national classification systems in regions where the CBSs are locally classified for information may also help guide future CBS research (Aderibigbe & Pandurangi, 1995).

Conclusion

The inclusion of culture-bound syndromes in the DSM-IV was a monumental step toward beginning to address the relationship between culture and the etiology, symptoms, and course of psychiatric illnesses. Moreover, the Outline for Cultural Formulation that reviews factors one should consider for a culturally informed assessment, such as the individual's cultural identity, cultural explanations of illness, cultural aspects of one's psychosocial environment, and cultural elements of the relationship between the individual and the clinician, is clinically useful despite its placement toward the end of the text. Because all attempts to incorporate culture into a classification system will originate from some cultural context, it is important that future research directions consider the possibilities and limitations of this, including the need for a common language for psychological problems (Hughes, 1998). Future directions that include looking more broadly at the role culture plays in diagnosis, as well as examining methodological issues related to the study of culture and illness, should provide a clearer understanding of how to classify culture-bound syndromes in a way that promotes accurate, informed, and useful clinical practice.

At the time of this writing, the next version of the DSM, the DSM-V, is in revision and expected for publication around 2010. Discussions at the present time concern what sort of research would put the DSM on a firmer conceptual footing (R. D. Alarcón, personal communication, Nov. 5, 2002; L. J. Kirmayer, personal communication, Oct. 31, 2002). Kirmayer (1991) argues that no single classificatory system will suffice for all purposes. Rather, diagnostic categories should guide, but not direct, the observation and interpretation of natural events (Millon, 1991). At this time, the DSM may best be considered as an "evolving document that reflects science at the time of each edition" (Carnes, 2000, p. 159).

Discussion Questions

1. Given cultural differences in illness expression and modes of coping, what factors should be considered in diagnosing distress?
2. What source of information would you rely on to assess and diagnose CBSs or idioms of distress—the DSM-IV, research literature, or the client's sharing of information? What are the resultant clinical implications?
3. Should different cultures have different diagnostic systems and criteria? Why or why not?
4. What is your understanding of the relationship among mind, body, and disorders and how do you apply this understanding in clinical work?
5. How might disciplines outside of psychology inform our understanding of culture-bound syndromes?
6. Should DSM-IV categories be considered "Western culture bound syndromes"? Why or why not?
7. How might behaviors that are considered maladaptive in one culture be seen as adaptive in another?

References

Aderibigbe, Y. A., & Pandurangi, A. K. (1995). Comment: The neglect of culture in psychiatric nosology: The case of culture bound syndromes. *International Journal of Social Psychiatry, 41*(4), 235–241.

Alarcón, R. D., & Foulks, E. F. (1995). Personality disorders and culture: Contemporary clinical views (Part A). *Cultural Diversity and Mental Health, 1,* 3–17.

Alarcón, R. D., Foulks, E. F., & Vakkur, M. (1998). *Personality disorders and culture: Clinical and conceptual interactions.* New York: Wiley.

American Psychiatric Association. (1994). *Diagnostic and statistical manual of mental disorders* (4th ed). Washington, DC: Author.

Arieti, S., & Meth, J. M. (1959). Rare, unclassifiable, collective, and exotic psychotic syndromes. In S. Arieti (Ed.), *American handbook of psychiatry, Vol. I* (pp. 546–563). New York: Basic Books.

Atkinson, D. R., Bui, U., & Mori, S. (2001). Multiculturally sensitive empirically supported treatments—An oxymoron? In J. G. Ponterotto, J. M. Casas, L. A. Suzuki, & C. M. Alexander (Eds.), *Handbook of multicultural counseling* (2nd ed., pp. 542–574). Thousand Oaks, CA: Sage.

Berganza, C. E., Mezzich, J. E., Otero-Ojeda, J., Jorge, M. R., Villaseñor-Bayardo S. J., &

Rojas-Malpica, C. (2001). The Latin American guide for psychiatric diagnosis: A cultural overview. *The Psychiatric Clinics of North America, 24,* 433–446.

Bhui, K., & Bhugra, D. (2001). Transcultural psychiatry: Some social and epidemiological research issues. *International Journal of Social Psychiatry, 47*(3), 1–9.

Carnes, P. J. (2000). Toward the DSM-V: How science and personal reality meet. *Sexual Addiction & Compulsivity, 7,* 157–160.

Chinese Society of Psychiatry. (2001). *The Chinese classification and diagnostic criteria of mental disorders version 3 (CCMD-3).* Jinan: Chinese Society of Psychiatry.

Devereux, G. (1956). Normal and abnormal: The key problem of psychiatric anthropology. In J. B. Casagrande & T. Gladwin (Eds.), *Some uses of anthropology: Theoretical and applied* (pp. 3–48). Washington, DC: Anthropological Society of Washington.

Fabrega, H. (1994). International systems of diagnosis in psychiatry. *Journal of Nervous & Mental Disease, 182*(5), 256–263.

Flaskerud, J. H. (2000). Ethnicity, culture, and neuropsychiatry. *Issues in Mental Health Nursing, 21,* 5–29.

Guarnaccia, P., & Rogler, L. (1999). Research on culture-bound syndromes: New directions. *The American Journal of Psychiatry, 156*(9), 1322–1327.

Hughes, C. G. (1985). Culture-bound or construct-bound? The syndromes and DSM-III. In R. C. Simons & C. C. Hughes (Eds.), *The culture-bound syndromes: Folk illnesses of psychiatric and anthropological interest* (pp. 3–24). Dordrecht: Reidel.

Hughes, C. C. (1996). The culture-bound syndromes and psychiatric disorder. In J. E. Mezzich, A. Kleinman, H. Fabrega, & D. L. Parron (Eds.), *Culture and psychiatric diagnosis: A DSM-IV perspective* (pp. 289–307). Washington, DC: American Psychiatric Press.

Hughes, C. C. (1998). The glossary of 'culture-bound syndromes' in DSM-IV: A critique. *Transcultural Psychiatry, 35*(3), 413–421.

Hughes, C. C., & Wintrob, R. M. (1995). Culture-bound syndromes and the cultural context of clinical psychiatry. *American Psychiatric Press Review of Psychiatry, 14,* 565–597.

Kapur, R. L. (1987). Commentary on culture-bound syndromes and international disease classification. *Culture, Medicine, and Psychiatry, 11,* 43–48.

Karp, I. (1985). Deconstructing culture-bound syndromes. *Social Science Medicine, 21*(2), 221–228.

Kirmayer, L. J. (1998). The fate of culture in DSM-IV. *Transcultural Psychiatry, 35,* 339–342.

Kleinman, A. (1979). *Patients and healers in the context of culture.* Berkeley: University of California Press.

Kleinman, A. (1987). Culture and clinical reality: Commentary on culture-bound syndromes and international disease classifications. *Culture, Medicine, and Psychiatry, 11,* 49–52.

Kleinman, A. (1988). *Rethinking psychiatry: From cultural category to personal experience.* New York: Free Press.

Kleinman, A., & Cohen, A. (1997). Psychiatry's global challenge. *Scientific American, 276*(3), 86–89.

Koss-Chioino, J. D. (1999). Depression among Puerto-Rican women: Culture, etiology and diagnosis. *Hispanic Journal of Behavioral Sciences, 21,* 330–350.

Lee, S. (2001). From diversity to unity: The classification of mental disorders in 21st-century China. *The Psychiatric Clinics of North America, 24*, 421–431.

Levine, R. E., & Gaw, A. C. (1995). Culture-bound syndromes. *Cultural Psychiatry, 18*(3), 523-536.

Lewis, T. H. (1975). A syndrome of depression and mutism in the Oglala Sioux. *American Journal of Psychiatry, 132*, 753–755.

Lewis-Fernández, R., & Kleinman, A. (1994). Culture, personality, and psychopathology. *Journal of Abnormal Psychology, 103*, 67–71.

Liebowitz, M. R., Salmán, E., Jusino, C. M., Garfinkel, R., Street, L., Cárdenas, D. L., et al. (1994). Ataques de nervios and panic disorder. *American Journal of Psychiatry, 151*, 871–875.

Lin, K-M. (1983). Hwa-byung: A Korean Culture-Bound Syndrome? *American Journal of Psychiatry, 140*(1), 105–107.

Littlewood, R. (1983). The migration of culture-bound syndromes. Paper presented at the seventh meeting of the World Congress of Psychiatry, Vienna, Austria.

Lopez, S. R., & Guarnaccia, P. J. J. (2000). Cultural psychopathology: Uncovering the social world of mental illness. *Annual Review of Psychology, 51*, 571–598.

Low, S. M. (1985). Culturally interpreted symptoms or culture-bound syndromes: A cross-cultural review of nerves. *Social Science Medicine, 21*, 187–196.

Mezzich, J. E., Berganza, C. E., & Ruiperez, M. A. (2001). Culture in DSM-IV, ICD-10, and evolving diagnostic systems. Cultural psychiatry: International perspectives. *The Psychiatric Clinics of North America, 24*, 407–419.

Mezzich, J. E., Kleinman, A., Fabrega, H., Jr., & Parron, D. L. (Eds.). (1996). *Culture and psychiatric diagnosis: A DSM-IV perspective.* Washington, DC: American Psychiatric Press.

Millon, T. (1991). Classification in psychopathology: Rationale, alternatives, and standards. *Journal of Abnormal Psychology, 100*(3), Special Issue: Diagnoses, dimensions, and DSM-IV: The science of classification, 245–261.

Otero-Ojeda, A. (2000). *Third Cuban glossary of psychiatry.* Havana: Hospital of Psychiatry.

Prince, R., & Tcheng-Laroche, F. (1987). Culture-bound syndromes and international disease classifications. *Culture, Medicine and Psychiatry, 11*, 3–19.

Ridley, C. R., Li, L. C., & Hill, C. L. (1998). Multicultural assessment: Reexamination, reconceptualization, and practical application. *Counseling Psychologist, 26*, 827–910.

Rogler, L. H. (1993). Culture in psychiatric diagnosis: An issue of scientific accuracy. *Psychiatry, 56*, 324–327.

Rogler, L. H. (1999). Methodological sources of cultural insensitivity in mental health research. *American Psychologist, 54*, 424–433.

Sartorius, N. (1988). International perspectives of psychiatric classification. *British Journal of Psychiatry, 152*(Supplement 1), 9–14.

Shimoji, A., & Miyakawa, T. (2000). Culture-bound syndrome and a culturally sensitive approach: From a viewpoint of medical anthropology. *Psychiatry and Clinical Neurosciences, 54*, 461–466.

Simons, R. C. (1985). Sorting the culture-bound syndromes. In R. C. Simons & C. C. Hughes (Eds.), *The culture-bound syndromes: Folk illnesses of psychiatric and anthropological interest* (pp. 25–38). Dordrecht: Reidel.

Stengel, E. (1959). Classification of mental disorders. *Bulletin of the World Health Organization, 21,* 601-663.

Tseng, W-S. (1997). Overview: Culture and psychopathology. In W-S. Tseng & J. Streltzer (Eds.), *Culture and psychopathology: A guide to clinical assessment* (pp. 1-27). New York: Brunner/Mazel.

Tseng, W-S., & Streltzer, J. (Eds.). (1997). *Culture and psychopathology: A guide to clinical assessment.* New York: Brunner/Mazel.

Westermeyer, J. (1973). On the epidemicity of amok. *Archives of General Psychiatry, 28,* 873-876.

Westermeyer, J. (1987). Cultural factors in clinical assessment. *Journal of Consulting and Clinical Psychology, 55,* 471-478.

World Health Organization. (1992). *The ICD-10 Classification of Mental and Behaviour Disorders—Clinical Descriptions and Diagnostic Guidelines.* Geneva: WHO.

Yang, K. S., & Bond, M. H. (1990). Exploring implicit personality theories with indigenous or imported constructs: The Chinese case. *Journal of Personality and Social Psychology, 58,* 1087-1089.

Part **IV**

Conclusion

Culturally Responsive
Interventions
Themes and Clinical Implications

Julie R. Ancis

The text chapters describe culturally responsive interventions both within the United States and internationally. Although the chapters differ along a number of dimensions, including client's cultural background, presenting issues, social and cultural context, and so on, similarities also exist. This chapter represents an analysis of the major themes that seem to cut across all chapters, in terms of client factors as well as interventions and approaches. The chapter concludes with a discussion of clinical implications for working with diverse populations, contexts, and presenting issues.

Client Process Themes

The following represent factors that seem to characterize and impact many of the individual clients and families presented in the chapters.

Influence of Culture and Context

The chapters address the influence of culture and social context on client's needs, expectations, presenting issues, and distress narratives, as well as the course and outcome of counseling. Moreover, the chapters demonstrate that culturally influenced beliefs and practices often become more salient for individuals during intimate events in one's life and in personal domains, such as those related to the family. In seems that such personal contexts often bring forth our most primal affective, cognitive, and behavioral reactions, which are often culturally based.

Values, attitudes, and perspectives associated with culture are often passed down from generation to generation in both subtle and obvious ways. These influences often become a fundamental aspect of one's personality, regardless of whether or not one is cognizant of them. The clients presented in the chapters seemed to readily accept the integration of cultural dimensions in the helping process. These dimensions seemed consistent with the clients' world views and styles; most probably contributing to the effectiveness of the approaches described.

Oppression and Discrimination

Several chapters demonstrate the pervasive and often subtle impact of discrimination, marginalization, and oppression on the individual's sense of self and behavior, as well as family dynamics. Social inequities in the form of poverty, corruption, and limited education are often linked to maladaptive and destructive behaviors among those affected.

Acculturative stress is prevalent among individuals whose history is characterized by multigenerational oppression. Reactions associated with such experiences may include anger, passivity, depression, anxiety, and shame. Rage, embarrassment, and feelings of alienation are common among those who have been marginalized from different forms of power and rejected from mainstream society. In some cases, individuals may wholly and uncritically adopt negative messages and beliefs about their own group, thereby fueling maladaptive behaviors and affect.

Family conflicts may be magnified by experiences of discrimination and powerlessness. For example, members who feel marginalized by the dominant society may try to exert power within the family in destructive ways. Alternatively, family members such as parents and primary caregivers may feel powerless in helping their children cope with racist incidents. Differences in experiences and perceptions among family members may create disruptions and conflicts. The impact of multigenerational oppression on families is evident in the types of difficulties often experienced by children and adolescents.

Family and Community

For many cultural groups, the immediate and extended family and community serve as primary sources of socialization and support. The chapters demonstrate how family-based experiences shape the form and expression of behaviors. Individuals' perspectives and world views are absorbed from the family, which is located in a cultural context (Parham, White, & Ajamu, 1999; McGill, 1992). Moreover, the family and community often play a role in the generation of symptoms, explanatory models of distress, behavior-labeling practices, and one's attitudes toward the helping professions (Alarcón et al., 2002). Thus, the client may consist of one individual or a group comprised of immediate and/or extended kin.

Although psychological distress is often related to stressors within the family, kinship systems also assume a significant role in the resolution of psychological problems (Lee, Oh, & Mountcastle, 1992). Both family and community members may provide support to individuals experiencing psychological distress. Lee et al. (1992) discuss the important role of kinship influences in mental health. This includes immediate and extended family and community networks. Research has demonstrated that given equal numbers of stressful life events, as social support systems increase, the likelihood of experiencing psychological distress and subsequently seeking counseling decreases (Goodman, Sewell, & Jampol, 1984). Social support serves as a protective factor against psychological distress (Kirmayer et al., 2000).

Strategic Themes

The following represent issues that seem to characterize many of the interventions and approaches described in the chapters. These themes are consistent with the process themes described in the preceding section.

Problematic Aspects of Western Psychotherapeutic Systems and Cultural Adaptations

Many of the approaches described were developed from a recognition that traditional Western approaches to mental health treatment based predominantly on European values are limited or even harmful when applied to many racial and ethnic minorities. That is, the tacit assumptions and values of dominant mainstream psychotherapy are either oppressive or inconsistent with different cultural dynamics. Assessment, diagnosis, and treatment may require cultural adaptations.

The approaches described have been developed from direct clinical experience with the particular population targeted. As such, cultural salient aspects have been incorporated into each approach. For example, NTU psychotherapy, developed from direct clinical experience with predominantly urban, African American families, incorporates aspects of spirituality, an important dimension for many African Americans. Kameguchi's approach with Japanese families of school refusal children employs mostly nonverbal programs rather than verbal because of many Japanese clients' hesitancy to self-disclose in interviews. Structural Ecosystems Therapy, which integrates both familial and ecological factors, is consistent with the extended family and support networks of many Hispanic families. Culture-Sensitive Strategic Therapy with Ultra-Orthodox Jews in Israel was developed with attention to the influence of religious beliefs and practices, as well as the local culture, on constructions of distress.

In many cases, culturally relevant concepts are integrated with traditional approaches or traditional therapeutic approaches are rearranged and modified in order to make them more responsive to the values and needs of the client.

That is, ideas and concepts that have instrumental benefit are retained, regardless of the therapeutic system from which they are derived. For example, Kameguchi's approach has been adapted from a model developed for American families for use with Japanese families. In some cases, anthropological, sociological, and psychological methods are integrated into a therapeutic approach in a complementary fashion.

Strength-Based

The approaches described reject the deficit model of many psychological theories. For example, the American Indian Constructionalist Family Therapy Model emphasizes clients' strengths and possibilities and relatedly the discarding of disempowering and damaging beliefs internalized from dominant power structures. The approach is described as radically collaborative whereby clients have the power in deciding the direction of therapy. The NTU approach also works with each client from a strength-based perspective in encouraging client competence and resiliency.

Relatedly, many of the interventions involve reframing, providing an opportunity to perceive interactions or situations from a different perspective. Often, this involves reframing a seemingly negative situation in a more positive light. These interventions help to foster stronger relationships between disconnected members or help clients negotiate institutional systems.

Attention to Social Context

The approaches described emphasize the influence of one's social and cultural context on the expression of distress, course of distress, and approach to treatment. Recognition of the impact of social and cultural forces on one's life is incorporated into interventions. The impact of discriminatory, oppressive, or challenging aspects of one's environment on emotional, spiritual, and behavioral problems are explicitly acknowledged. This may include difficulties related to immigration and the process of acculturation. Interventions often aim at helping clients effectively interact with their environment. For example, Structural Ecosystems Therapy (SET) attends to both the adolescent's and family's social ecology. SET's systemic focus aims to reduce the deleterious impact of cultural/contextual factors related to the youth's behavior problems. Kameguchi's approach explicitly acknowledges that children's school refusal is emblematic of the large gap between school systems and family systems and between teachers and students. The South African Community Rebuilding and Reconciliation Model facilitates community self-reflection and agreement within the context of social upheaval related to apartheid, poverty, and the destruction of the family unit.

Family/Community Interventions

Most of the interventions described in the text focus on the family or community as significant to both the advent of difficulties as well as its resolution. Paralikar and coworkers describe the interdependence of family and community in India and its impact on the therapeutic relationship and process. The needs of the family and community are often recognized in the interventions described. Relatedly, the approaches mobilize relatives, friends, peers, and communities into an interdependent group of support. As such, interventions incorporate culturally consistent helping networks that often include relatives and communities. An exclusive focus on the individual is often viewed as culturally inappropriate, limited, or ineffective. Therapists utilizing Culture-Sensitive Strategic Therapy with Ultra-Orthodox Jews may enlist the assistance of religious leaders, family, and community resources in the healing process. The Community Building and Reconciliation Model applied to South Africans recognizes that the process of reconciliation is dependent on a change in mindset and agreement by the community rather than just the individual. Both SET and Kameguchi's approach work to enhance or support the adaptive connections among family members and between the family and other systems.

Clinical Implications

Clinician awareness, knowledge, and behavioral flexibility are essential elements of competence with diverse clientele and presenting concerns. First, the clinician must have an understanding of the impact of culture and social context on world view, expression and manifestation of distress, outcome, and help seeking behavior. There exists a dynamic interplay between individuals and their environments. Theoretical conceptions and interventions that do not acknowledge this interplay are likely to ignore or dismiss significant factors in one's life (Ancis & Ladany, 2001; Ancis & Sanchez-Hucles, 2000). Misdiagnosis and the application of inappropriate interventions are the likely result. Culturally centered practitioners consider the psychological and contextual factors of race, ethnicity, language, gender, sexual orientation, socioeconomic status, and other social dimensions of personal experience in conceptualizing and working with individuals and groups (Fouad & Brown, 2000). Effective clinicians are sensitive to sociocultural influences in people's lives and are cognizant of sociohistorical factors that may have impacted the dynamics of a population.

The broader social context includes power differentials in society that may particularly impact racial, ethnic, and religious minorities. It is essential that therapists are aware of these power dynamics and the stigmatizing experience of being a member of a culturally devalued group (Crocker, Major, & Steele, 1998).

Clinicians may need to work with individuals to help them differentiate those factors that they are personally responsible for from those that relate to discrimination. The demarcation is not always clear. Feelings and behaviors associated with limited access to power and opportunities may manifest in passivity, resistance, or anger, both in family relationships, with others, and in therapy (Franklin, 1993). Clinicians can assist clients in intervening in their environment by challenging themselves or other family members to actively confront discrimination. Thus, clinicians must learn to intervene at multiple levels as clients encounter prejudicial attitudes, language difficulties, unemployment, limited funds, and insufficient childcare. Clinicians who focus solely on emotional issues at the exclusion of these pragmatic issues, may be viewed as unresponsive (Gong-Guy, Cravens, & Patterson, 1991).

Culturally skilled clinicians are able to engage in a variety of verbal and nonverbal helping responses (Sue, Arredondo, & McDavis, 1992). As such, clinicians must possess knowledge of culturally sanctioned healing practices within specific communities and recognize that helping styles and approaches may be culturally based. Indigenous healing practices and helping networks have been utilized effectively for centuries throughout the world. Clients who seek mental health treatment may continue to practice traditional folk healing at home or seek advice from healers in the community (Gong-Guy, Cravens, & Patterson, 1991). In addition, spirituality and religion may influence attributions and expressions of distress as well as perceptions of appropriate treatment. Both spirituality and religion are often primary components of one's self-identity and coping (Lukoff, Lu, & Turner, 1995). It is important that these practices are respected and not prohibited or denigrated.

As many cultural groups are collectivistic, clinicians would benefit from understanding and respecting family influences and participation in decision making (Arredondo et al., 1996). Such influences could include concern about the impact of one's behavior on members of one's in-group (Hui & Triandis, 1986) or concern about bringing shame upon one's family by seeking counseling (Leong, Wagner, & Tata, 1995). The family and community often serve as a natural support system and are viewed as essential to healing. The clinician may need to consult with and enlist the assistance of change agents within the family and community, including community and religious and spiritual leaders and practitioners (APA, 2002; Arredondo et al., 1996; Lewis, Lewis, Daniels, &D'Andrea, 1998). Relatedly, clinicians must be familiar with and use organizations that provide support and services in different cultural communities.

Although similarities exist between marital and family therapy as traditionally practiced and the therapies outlined here, the field of marital and family therapy has been critiqued for its treatment of gender, race, ethnicity, and sexual orientation, and other sociocontextual variables. Specifically, critics argue that marital and family therapy as traditionally practiced: (a) does not attend to the broader social context when examining family dynamics, (b) ignores power differences both within the family and in the larger society, and (c) assumes a mono-lithic family form (Leslie, 1995). The approaches delineated in the text proactively attend to these concerns.

Although knowledge of culturally responsive interventions is important to effective counseling, an exclusive focus on techniques or treatment specifics is limited. In fact, specific techniques may be secondary to other factors in terms of healing. Factors such as therapeutic alliance are significant to establishing trust and engaging in an effective helping relationship (Wampold, 2001). Several au-thors have described the personality and skill of the clinician as important as-pects of successful treatment, particularly for those clients who have been severely traumatized (Kinzie, 2001). Critical events in therapy may include the clinician's ability to listen to the client's story and remain present with the client.

Culture and context impact the clinician as well as the client. Clinician self-awareness of his or her own world view and cultural background is impera-tive to informed and accurate assessment, diagnosis, and interventions. There is a demonstrated relationship between the clinician's own cultural background and related values and expectations, and clinical assessment (Ancis & Ladany, 2001; Tseng et al., 1982). Awareness of the impact of one's social and cultural background on one's own world view allows for an understanding of the rela-tionship between multiple perspectives and contextual forces (Ibrahim, 1991). Such awareness helps to minimize client stereotyping and oppressive counseling approaches that are not consistent with the client's world view. Clinician self-awareness also includes an understanding of attitudes and beliefs that can ad-versely influence perceptions of and interactions with culturally diverse clientele (APA, 2002).

Clinicians, particularly those trained in Western models, often need to expand their perception of what characterizes mental health practices (Sue & Sue, 1999). Counselors may be required to assume the roles of advisor, advo-cate, facilitator of indigenous support or healing systems, consultant, change agent, counselor, or psychotherapist depending on the needs of the client (Atkinson, Thompson, & Grant, 1993). This requires an ability and willingness to reframe the traditional counseling paradigm.

It is important to realize that effective clinicians must be cognizant of cul-ture-bound assumptions located in the major theories of human development and helping, but should not necessarily discard concepts and principles that are effective and useful with particular clients and contexts. In some cases, cultur-ally responsive adaptations to conceptualization and intervention approaches are needed (APA, 2002). Such adaptations require openness to world views and perspectives that may be vastly different from those in which the clinician has been socialized. Fundamentally, this requires flexibility on the part of the clini-cian. Many of the approaches described in the text involve adjustments in the nature and boundaries of the therapeutic relationship. Thus, as Witztum and Goodman relate, knowledge of specific cultural meanings of distress is not sufficient. Successful clinicians are able to navigate a complex web composed of the client's explanatory formulations and clues and clinician's understanding. Such skill involves an appreciation of diversity within cultural groups related to such factors as personality style, socioeconomic status, socioidentity, and level of acculturation and an understanding of how these dimensions interface with one's presenting problem and therapeutic context.

Multicultural training is essential to facilitating clinicians' competence with a diverse clientele in terms of promoting self-awareness, cultural understanding, behavioral skills, and flexibility. Most important, clinicians could benefit from training that challenges our fundamental assumptions about health, illness, and helping. In other words, meeting the needs of a diverse population requires one to transcend limited paradigms that restrict our ability to view persons from a comprehensive perspective and intervene most effectively.

Discussion Questions

1. How may practitioners, already trained in a particular model of counseling, increase their effectiveness with diverse clientele?
2. How can graduate training programs facilitate clinicians' use of culturally responsive approaches?
3. How should clinicians' cultural competency be measured? What types of assessment tools should be used?
4. What are the benefits of integrating traditional therapeutic approaches with culturally relevant concepts? What are the limitations?
5. What are the diagnostic implications of approaches that emphasize clients' strengths and possibilities?

References

Alarcón, R. D., Bell, C. C., Kirmayer, L. J., Lin, K-M., Üstün, B., & Wisner, K. L. (2002). Beyond the funhouse mirrors: Research agenda on culture and psychiatric diagnosis. In D. J. Kupfer, M. B. First, & D. A. Regier (Eds.), *A research agenda for DSM-V* (pp. 219–281). Washington, DC: APA.

American Psychological Association. (2002). *Guidelines on multicultural education, training, research, practice, and organizational change for psychologists*. Washington, DC: APA.

Ancis, J. R., & Ladany, N. (2001). A multicultural framework for counselor supervision. In L. J. Bradley & N. Ladany (Eds.), *Counselor supervision: Principles, process, and practice* (3rd ed., pp. 63–90). Philadelphia: Brunner-Routledge.

Ancis, J. R., & Sanchez-Hucles, J. V. (2000). A preliminary analysis of counseling students' attitudes toward counseling women and women of color: Implications for cultural competency training. *Journal of Multicultural Counseling and Development, 28*, 16–31.

Arredondo, P., Toporek, R., Brown, S. P., Jones, J., Locke, D. C., Sanchez, J., et al. (1996). Operationalization of the multicultural counseling competencies. *Journal of Multicultural Counseling and Development, 24,* 42–78.

Atkinson, D. R., Thompson, C. E., & Grant, S. (1993). A three-dimensional model for counseling racial/ethnic minorities. *The Counseling Psychologist, 21*(2), 257–277.

Crocker, J., Major, B., & Steele, C. (1998). Social stigma. In D. T. Gilbert & S. T. Fiske (Eds.), *The handbook of social psychology,* Vol. 2 (4th ed., pp. 504–553). New York: McGraw-Hill.

Fouad, N. A., & Brown, M. (2000). Race, ethnicity, culture, class and human development. In S. D. Brown & R. W. Lent (Eds.), *Handbook of counseling psychology* (3rd ed., pp. 379–410). New York: Wiley.

Franklin, A. J. (1993). The invisibility syndrome. *The Family Therapy Networker, 17*(4), 32–40.

Gong-Guy, E., Cravens, R. B., & Patterson, T. E. (1991). Clinical issues of mental health service delivery to refugees. *American Psychologist, 46,* 642–648.

Goodman, S. H., Sewell, D. R., & Jampol, R. C. (1984). On going to the counselor: Contributions of life stress and social support to the decision to seek psychological counseling. *Journal of Counseling Psychology, 31*(3), 306–313.

Hui, C. H., & Triandis, H. C. (1986). Individualism and collectivism: A study of cross-cultural researchers. *Journal of Cross-Cultural Psychology, 17,* 225–248.

Ibrahim, F. A. (1991). Contribution of cultural worldview to generic counseling and development. *Journal of Counseling and Development, 70,* 13–19.

Kirmayer, L. J., Boothroyd, L. J., Tanner, A., Adelson, N., & Robinson, E. (2000). Psychological distress among the Cree of James Bay. *Transcultural Psychiatry, 37,* 35–56.

Kinzie, J. D. (2001). Psychotherapy for massively traumatized refugees: The therapist variable. *American Journal of Psychotherapy, 55,* 475–490.

Lee, C. C., Oh, M. Y., & Mountcastle, A. R. (1992). Indigenous models of healing in nonwestern countries: Implications for multicultural counseling. *Journal of Multicultural Counseling and Development, 20,* 3–10.

Leong, F. T. L., Wagner, N. S., & Tata, S. P. (1995). Racial and ethnic variations in help-seeking attitudes. In J. G. Ponterotto, J. M. Casas, L. A. Suzuki, & C. M. Alexander (Eds.), *Handbook of Multicultural Counseling* (pp. 415–438). Thousand Oaks, CA: Sage.

Leslie, L. A. (1995). The evolving treatment of gender, ethnicity, and sexual orientation in marital and family therapy. *Family Relations, 44,* 359–367.

Lewis, J. A., Lewis, M. D., Daniels, J. A., & D'Andrea, M. J. (1998). *Community counseling: Empowerment strategies for a diverse society.* San Francisco: Brooks/Cole.

Lukoff, D., Lu, F. G., & Turner, R. (1995). Cultural considerations in the assessment and treatment of religious and spiritual problems. *Psychiatric Clinic North America, 18,* 467–485.

McGill, D. W. (1992). The cultural story in multicultural family therapy. *Families in Society: The Journal of Contemporary Human Services, 73*(6), 339–349.

Parham, T. A., White, J. L., & Amaju, A. (1999). *The psychology of Blacks: An African centered perspective.* Upper Saddle River, NJ: Prentice-Hall.

Sue, D. W., Arredondo, P., & McDavis, R. J. (1992). Multicultural counseling competencies and standards: A call to the profession. *Journal of Counseling and Development, 70,* 477–486.

Sue, D. W., & Sue, D. (1999). *Counseling the culturally different: Theory and practice* (3rd ed.). New York: Wiley.

Tseng, W. S., McDermott, J. F. Jr., Ogino, K., & Ebata, K. (1982). Cross-cultural differences in parent-child assessment: U.S.A. and Japan. *International Journal of Social Psychiatry, 28,* 305–317.

Wampold, B. E. (2001). *The great psychotherapy debate: Models, methods, and findings.* Mahwah, NJ: Erlbaum.

About the Editor
and Contributing Authors

Julie R. Ancis, Ph.D., is an associate professor in the Department of Counseling and Psychological Services at Georgia State University. Prior to her affiliation with Georgia State University, she was an assistant professor at Old Dominion University. She received her Ph.D. at the University at Albany, State University of New York in 1995. She has published numerous articles and book chapters in the area of racial and gender attitudes, multicultural and feminist theories, cultural competency training, and the educational experiences of women and students of color. Dr. Ancis coauthored a book published by the ACPA entitled *Promoting Student Learning and Student Development at a Distance: Student Affairs Concepts and Practices for Televised Instruction and Other Forms of Distance Learning.* Her work on counseling students' awareness of White privilege was published as a major contribution in *The Counseling Psychologist.* Additionally, she has frequently presented at national and international conferences. Dr. Ancis has served on the editorial board of the *Journal of Counseling and Development* and chaired the Diversity section of the APA Task Force for the Development of Guidelines for Psychological Practice with Girls and Women. Her clinical experience includes work with community health centers, hospitals, and university counseling centers.

Mohan Agashe, M.D., has a long career in both psychiatry and theater spanning over 30 years. His medical experience began at the B.J. Medical College & Sassoon Hospitals where he is currently Director-Professor of the Maharashtra Institute of Mental Health. He has been involved in numerous projects relating to the care of chronic schizophrenic patients, to trauma management with those affected by earthquakes, chronic fatigue and weakness, as well as the functioning of mental health facilities. In this context, he has held several related posts such as Nodal Officer–Psychosocial Management of Marathwada Earthquake Disaster in 1993, Nodal Officer–Deaddiction Training Programme, Government of Maharashtra since 1993, chairman-Trauma Management Sub-Committee of the National Disaster Management Committee in 2002, and the chief coordinator (Mental Health)–Government of Maharashtra. Many of these projects and positions have led to the publication of related articles and presentations at conferences. Dr. Agashe is also the recipient of two particularly high honors—the Padmashri bestowed by the President of India in January 1990 and the Cross of

Order of Merit (highest civilian honor) bestowed by the president of the Federal Republic of Germany in 2002.

Greg Brack, Ph.D., associate professor in the Department of Counseling and Psychological Services, received his Ph.D. in Counseling Psychology from Indiana University in 1989. He is the author of nearly 50 professional publications and over 100 professional presentations. From 1997 to 2002 he served as the U.S. director of the Project for the Empowerment of South African Counselors. Dr. Brack has been researching the mental health infrastructure in South Africa, and since 1997 has worked with various nongovernmental and governmental agencies to promote mental health development to disadvantaged groups. In 1998, he was invited by the Commission for Gender Equality to be an International Delegate at the First National Conference on Witchcraft Violence. During 2000, he served as a Visiting Professor with the University of Northwest in Mmabatho, South Africa.

Yuehong Chen, MBA, is a Counseling Ph.D. student at Georgia State University. She had been a bilingual (English and Chinese) teacher and translator in China for 10 years before she received her MBA degree in Educational Management from the University of Leicester, England in 2001. Over 30 of her writings and translations on education, family relationships, hydroelectric technology, and movie stars were published in China. Her research interests include multicultural school counseling, play therapy, counseling for Chinese, and reading fluency.

Maisha G. Davis, MSW, is currently employed at the Baltimore Office of the Progressive Life Center, Inc., as a Parent Trainer. She holds a Bachelor of Science Degree in Psychology from Morgan State University in Baltimore, Maryland and earned her Masters in Social Work from the University of Maryland. Mrs. Davis has worked in the human services field for the past 7 years. She focuses her expertise in program development, African-centered clinical interventions, and group facilitation on emotionally, behaviorally, and socially challenged youth and their families.

Yehuda Goodman, Ph.D., is a lecturer at the Department of Sociology and Anthropology, Tel Aviv University, Israel. He graduated in Clinical Psychology from the Hebrew University of Jerusalem and wrote his doctoral thesis on madness, therapy, and culture in the Ultra-Orthodox community in Israel. Besides interest in questions of therapy in cross-cultural settings, Yehuda is interested in questions of power, identity, and cultural criticism and has published his work in various journals, including *Ethos, Transcultural Psychiatry, Culture, Medicine and Psychiatry,* and *Social Science and Medicine.*

Henry Gregory, Ph.D., is a clinician and trainer with over 25 years' experience servicing underresourced populations and their helping community. Dr. Gregory is a Family Systems Specialist who has provided direct services, supervised, directed, and trained clinicians in a variety of program formats, including: substance abuse; juvenile justice; therapeutic and traditional foster care; family preservation; community-based family counseling; male involvement, school-based prevention and outpatient private practice. Dr. Gregory holds a doctoral degree in Clinical Psychology, Masters degrees in both Community Mental Health and Psychology and a bachelors. Dr. Gregory has served as the clinical director for the Progressive Life Center (Washington, DC, Prince Georges County, MD, Baltimore, MD, Wilmington, DE, and Zambia, W. Africa) for the last 15 years. Dr. Gregory is also a partner with his wife in his own firm, the Rafiki Consortium, through which he provides consultation and training to public and private organizations nationally. Dr. Gregory presents regularly at regional and national conferences and is frequently interviewed in the media in reference to contemporary issues.

Steve Harrist, Ph.D., earned his doctorate in clinical psychology at the University of Tennessee and completed his internship and postdoctoral training in psychotherapy outcome research at Vanderbilt University. He is an assistant professor in the School of Applied Health and Educational Psychology at Oklahoma State University where he teaches graduate courses in human development and supervises counseling psychology practicum students. His research interests include ameliorating the negative effects of power relations through life history dialog; psychological and health benefits of expressive writing and engagement/disengagement with life goals; philosophical and theoretical psychology, especially philosophical hermeneutics.

Michele B. Hill, Ph.D., Assistant clinical professor in the Counseling Center at Georgia State University, received her Ph.D. in Counseling Psychology from Georgia State University. From 1997 to 2002 she served as U.S. coordinator for the Project for the Empowerment of South African Counselors. Dr. Hill was selected by the Commission on Gender Equality of South Africa to be an International Delegate to the First National Conference on Witchcraft Violence and the subsequent researcher for trauma and reconciliation counseling in rural villages plagued by such conflict. Dr. Hill is a certified mediator and serves on the Association of Conflict Resolution Committee for Public Conflict. In 2000, she served as Visiting Professor for the University of Northwest and director for the Bethlehem Shelter for street children in Mmabatho, South Africa.

Laurence E. Jackson, Ph.D., is a licensed clinical psychologist and presently serves as Executive Director for AIMSE (Assimilating Into Mainstream Society Economically), a nonprofit organization dedicated to helping socioeconomically disadvantaged youth change their lives through educational and vocational services. He formerly served as vice president of Maryland Operations at Progressive Life Center Inc., a private, nonprofit human services firm headquartered in Washington, D.C., with offices in Maryland and Zambia, Africa. PLC is a pioneer in cultural and spiritually based approaches to healing. As vice president, his primary responsibilities involved administrative and budgetary management of an array of community-based child welfare programs and services, including family preservation, foster care, youth diversion, healthy families, therapeutic retreats, prevention and early intervention, and wraparound support services. Dr. Jackson has conducted numerous seminars, workshops, and retreats for private and public agencies and organizations. His expertise is in the areas of team building, stress management, cultural competence, spirituality and healing, conflict resolution, and Africentric psychotherapy.

Kenji Kameguchi, Ph.D., is a professor in the Graduate School of Education, the University of Tokyo. He received a doctoral degree in psychology from Kyushu University, Fukuoka, Japan, in family therapy research. His major interest has been family–school collaboration programs, membrane theory of family systems, family therapy for school refusal students, and family image in Japanese families. His most recent work on family therapy in Japan was published in the *American Psychologist* (2001).

Vasudeo Paralikar, M.D., has been practicing general psychiatry for the last 20 years in Pune, India since obtaining his medical degree in 1983. In spite of not being formally trained in psychotherapy, he has maintained his culturally sensitive clinical orientation with a dynamic humanistic bias. He adopts a holistic approach in treatment by integrating psychotherapy and psychopharmacology. He has been active in research and training activities in the fields of psychiatry and psychotherapy at Maharashtra Institute of Mental Health, a state-level training institute. He has been studying cultural epidemiology of fatigue and weakness since 1993. Other ongoing research interests of his include deliberate self-harm, stigma, stress and related disorders, and culturally appropriate psychotherapies.

Michael S. Robbins, Ph.D., received his clinical psychology doctorate from the University of Utah in 1995. He completed his internship at the University of Miami School of Medicine/Jackson Memorial Hospital and has been on faculty in the University of Miami School of Medicine's Center for Family Studies since June 1995. Dr. Robbins' primary research interest is in examining process and outcome in family-based interventions with drug using, behavior problem adolescents. He has directly led several federal- and private-funded clinical research projects, including clinical trials, efficacy studies, and investigations of change processes in prevention and therapy. For example, over the past 6 years, Dr. Robbins has led two of the most unique studies in the family therapy field. The first is a clinical trial study comparing an ecological approach to traditional family therapy services. This study represents the first attempt to determine if multisystemic interventions outperform traditional family therapy. The second study is a process study that is examining in-session therapist interventions and family processes that predict dropout from family therapy. Using data from three empirically validated family approaches, this study seeks to identify core processes that cut across clinical models and ethnic groups. Dr. Robbins has published numerous articles and chapters in the area of family therapy process and outcome research. He has also published articles on family process with HIV+ African-American women and family therapy processes with Hispanic youth. Dr. Robbins is currently serving as coeditor on the next *Handbook of Family Therapy*.

Rockey Robbins, Ph.D., received his degree in Counseling Psychology from the University of Oklahoma. He is Cherokee/Choctaw and has worked in Indian Education and Indian Behavioral Health programs for over 20 years. As a university professor his major research areas have been in testing the validity of psychological assessment instruments for Indians, looking at psychosocial development issues among Indians in boarding schools, and exploring unique aspects of Indian grandparenting. He has also developed several therapeutic models and approaches for Indian clients, including the American Indian Constructionalist Family Therapy Model, which attempts to undermine the authority of colonialist narratives by offering space for American Indian individuals to explore the social dimension of their individuality.

Doreen Schultz, MA, is a doctoral student at Georgia State University in Counseling Psychology. She has a masters degree in Counseling from the College of New Jersey in Trenton. Her research interests include suicide prevention and aftercare, trauma and health psychology, and professional issues. Doreen also serves on the board of directors for the American Association of Suicidology and participates in many professional activities related to suicide prevention, including serving as the associate director of the Link's National Resource Center for Suicide Prevention and Aftercare. She also currently participates in a research team at Georgia State with Dr. Julie Ancis researching multicultural issues.

Seth Schwartz, Ph.D., is research assistant professor at the Center for Family Studies, Department of Psychiatry and Behavioral Sciences, University of Miami School of Medicine. Dr. Schwartz has a masters degree in family and child sciences from Florida State University and a Ph.D. in developmental psychology from Florida International University. His primary research interests are in adolescent and young adult identity formation, interrelationships between family and individual functioning, and family-level interventions designed to impact adolescent problems.

José Szapocznik, Ph.D., is professor of Psychiatry and Behavioral Sciences, Psychology and Counseling Psychology at the University of Miami. Dr. Szapocznik is director of the Center for Family Studies at the University of Miami School of Medicine, which is considered the nation's flagship program on Hispanic family therapy research. Dr. Szapocznik serves on the National Institute on Drug Abuse National Advisory Council, and has served on the National Institute of Mental Health Extramural Science Advisory Board, the National Institutes of Health Office of AIDS Research Advisory Council and the U.S. Center for Substance Abuse Prevention National Advisory Council. For his groundbreaking contributions in the development and testing of Hispanic family interventions, Dr. Szapocznik has received national recognition awards from the American Psychological Association, the American Family Therapy Academy, the American Association for Marriage and Family Therapy, the Association of Hispanic Mental Health Professionals, the U.S. Center for Substance Abuse Prevention, the Florida Association for Marriage and Family Therapy, the Latino Behavioral Health Institute, the National Coalition of Hispanic Health and Human Services Organizations, the National Institute of Mental Health, the International Society for Prevention Research, and the U.S. Center for Substance Abuse Prevention. Internationally, his work led to the designation of the Spanish Family Guidance Center as a World Health Organization Collaborating Center. Dr. Szapocznik has over 135 professional publications, almost all in the family area, including a seminal book, *Breakthroughs in Family Therapy with Drug-Abusing and Problem Youth,* and the updated version of this work, *Brief Strategic Family Therapy,* published under NIDA'S *Treatment Manual Series.*

Mitchell G. Weiss, M.D., heads the Department of Public Health and Epidemiology at the Swiss Tropical Institute in Basel, where he leads a research group in cultural epidemiology. Trained in psychiatry and a professor at the University of Basel, he teaches courses on cultural dimensions of international health in low- and middle-income countries, focusing on mental health and tropical infectious diseases. His research collaborations in India guide community mental health activities and clinical practice and study local concepts of illness among people with depression, schizophrenia, chronic fatigue syndrome, and other mental health problems in Pune, West Bengal, Mumbai, and Bangalore.

Eliezer Witztum, M.D., is full professor in the Division of Psychiatry, Faculty of Health Sciences, Ben Gurion University of the Negev and Director of Psychotherapy Supervision, Mental Health Center, Beer Sheva. He also serves as Senior Psychiatrist, Jerusalem Mental Health Center, and established a Cultural and Religion Consultation Unit providing culturally sensitive psychiatry service for religious patients. He is well known for his work in the field of medical psychology, forensic and cultural psychiatry, dissociation, and history of PTSD and Arab-Israeli wars. His recent book, *Sanity and Sanctity: Mental Health Care of the Ultra-Orthodox Community in Jerusalem* was published by Yale University Press, and his coedited book *Traumatic and non Traumatic Loss and Bereavement: Clinical Theory and Practice* was published in 2000 by the Psychosocial Press.

Name Index

Subject Index

acculturation, 220
  defined, 8
  and help-seeking, 9
  and Hispanics, 9
  intergenerational differences in, 9,
    89-90, 72, 97
  and language difficulties, 8-9
  process of, 21, 72, 216
acculturative stress, 8, 21, 24, 42, 72
Acquired Immunodeficiency Syndrome
  (AIDS), 189-90
African Americans, 4, 10, 12, 49-70,
  215
  adolescents, 58-68
  African philosophy, therapeutic
    application of, 50, 53-59
  differential diagnosis, 12
  gender roles, 59
  interventions, 60-68
    Libation, 60
    NTU Psychotherapy, 49-69
    Rites of Passage, 58-61
  role of family in therapy, 51, 53-59,
    63-65
  role of therapist, 56-58
  spirituality, 49, 50-51, 53-58, 63, 69,
    215
  strength and resilience, 52, 57, 216
  women, 10
age, 4, 13, 201
  age appropriate behavior, 91, 92-93,
    130
alcohol and drug abuse, 9-10, 27, 73, 96
American Indians, 12, 23-47
  acculturative stress, 24, 42
  alcohol and drug abuse, 9, 27

communalism, 25
cultural values, 24-27
depression, 9
discrimination experienced, 24, 27
interventions, 29-35
  Constructionalist Family Therapy
    Model, 23-47, 216
  Talking Feather Technique, 29-30
storytelling, 26-27
tribal language, 30
tribe, 25-28, 36
unemployment, 9, 27
American Psychiatric Association (APA),
  198-99
American Psychological Association
  (APA), 3
  APA Guidelines on Multicultural
    Education, Training, Research,
    Practice, and Organizational
    Change, 4
  APA Guidelines for Providers of
    Psychological services to Ethnic,
    Linguistic, and Culturally Diverse
    Populations, 3
  APA Guidelines for Psychological
    Practice with Girls and Women, 4
anxiety, 11, 66, 110, 117, 130, 149,
  160
  and acculturative stress, 8, 214
  comorbid with ataques de nervios,
    200
  medication for, 150
  and psychosexual problems, 6
Asians, 10, 13
  Cambodians, 12
  Southeast Asian, 9, 202